# The Ministry of a Wife

# The Ministry of a Wife

June Boisselier

Revival Publications
P.O. Box 364
Plymouth, IN 46563

Library of Congress Catalog Card Number: 89-92037

ISBN—Soft: 0-9625705-4-0 $11.95

Revival Publications
P.O. Box 364
Plymouth, IN 46563

To Trenton, who makes my ministry a joy.

## A Note to Men Who Read This Book

Men would do well to read this book so they can encourage their wives in the ministry God gives them, but please don't beat your wife over the head with what you read here. I'm exhorting women to join me in striving for the high standards for wives set forth in God's Word, but please be patient, God is not finished with us yet. Instead, praise your dear wife for everything she does to minister to you, wash her daily with God's Word, and focus your attention on the responsibilities of ministry that God has given to men for their wives. Please keep your words sweet; you may have to eat them. My husband and I are presently planning a colaboration on *The Ministry of a Husband*. May God richly bless your marriage as you minister to each other.

# ACKNOWLEDGEMENTS

The beautiful art work on the cover was done by Fred Carter, for which I am very grateful.

My sincere gratitude is extended to all the wonderful people who have assisted me with corrections, suggestions, and encouragement, but especially to Tom, John, Rachael, Pastor Worley, Dwayla, and Virginia who offered many valuable hours out of their busy schedules to painstakingly proofread the manuscript. Their sharp eye for catching errors (a talent I sadly lack) and common-sense recommendations have been invaluable. I'm thankful to Jean whose enthusiasm reassured me when I was weary in well-doing.

All scripture references made use of or quoted in this book are from the King James Version of the Bible unless otherwise indicated in the text.

I would also like to express my appreciation to the following authors and/or their publishers who graciously granted permission to quote from their material: *A Song for Lovers* by S. Craig Glickman. Copyright 1976 by InterVarsity Christian Fellowship of the USA and used by permission of InterVarsity Press, P.O. Box 1400, Downers Grove, IL 60515; *Transference of Spirits*, by Alex Ness. Copyright 1978 by Agapre Publications Inc., P.O Box 89 Pefferlaw, Ontario LOE 1NO; "Winning an Unsaved Husband," by Dorothy H. Pentecost. Copyright 1970 by the Good News Broadcasting Association, Inc. All rights reserved. Used by permission; *The Wycliffe Bible Encyclopedia* by Charles F. Pfeiffer, Howard F. Vos, and John Rea, Copyright 1975 by Moody Bible Institute of Chicago. Moody Press. Used by permission; *Peace Prosperity and the Coming Holocaust* copyright 1983 by Dave Hunt and published by Harvest House Publishers, Eugene, OR; "To Manipulate a Woman," a booklet by Beverly LaHaye. Concerned Women For America. 370 L'Enfant Promenade, S.W., Suite 800 Washington, D.C.20024; *Vine's Expository Dictionary of New Testament Words* by W.E. Vine. Riverside Book and Bible House, Iowa Falls, Iowa; *Spiritual Depression: Its Causes and Cure* by D. Martyn Lloyd Jones. Copyright 1965 by Wm. B. Eerdmans Publishing Co., Grand Rapids, MI; *Philippians Through Revelation* by Kenneth S. Wuest. Copyright 1959 by Wm. B. Eerdmans Publishing Co., Grand Rapids, MI; *How to Win Over Depression* by Tim LaHaye. Copyright 1974 by the Zondervan Corporation. Used by permission. *Anger Is a Choice* by

Tim LaHaye and Bob Phillips. Copyright 1982 by the Zondervan Corporation. Used by permission; *The Amplified New Testament.* Copyright 1958, 1987, by the Lockman Foundation. Used by permission.

This book is far richer because these authors and/or their publishers have generously shared the insights God has given to them. These, and other valuable books, are listed in the Bibliography and Footnotes. The reader will be blessed by reading them.

This book contains the opinions of the author, and nothing herein is intended to be either medical or legal advise.

# FOREWORD

I have read with great interest this book authored by a wife and mother from a family who have been members of the Hegewisch Baptist Church for fifteen years. As pastor, it has been my joy and privilege to observe the parents and three sons growing up over the years, physically and spiritually.

So much that is written today for and about Christian women is based almost entirely on emotion and opinion. Often, solutions offered are empty psychological jargon and psychiatric solutions for problems.

These accounts typically run the gamut from the female martyr to Wonder Woman. The latter dominates and controls husband, family, and everything around her, gloriously rescuing them from her mate's inept bumbling and lack of spirituality.

Although there are undoubtedly examples of these two extremes in existence, I am persuaded that the vast number of Christian wives do not fit in either category. June has used a storylike vehicle to anchor her material to scripture and Biblical principles.

I believe that this book will meet a real need, for it focuses on real, everyday problems wives face. Solutions offered are both Biblical and practical.

The thesis of the book is that the ministry of a wife is first and foremost to her own husband. By achieving this she will find her greatest ministry and fulfillment.

If young ladies would read and seriously consider the grave issues involved in the scriptural marriage relationship, it would stop the pell mell rush into unwise marriages with heathens or uncommitted Christians. Certainly it should be a matter of heart-searching prayer, not headlong romantic plunging. Too many have married in haste only to repent at leisure. As a wise man once remarked, "It is better to be single than to wish you were!"

Running the gamut from salvation to deliverance, the book faces up squarely to issues not even alluded to in other works. Although readers might differ with some portions of the book, I still believe that both men and women will find it profitable. Therefore I heartily recommend it.

Pastor Win Worley

## CONTENTS

For even the Son of man came not to be ministered unto, but to minister, and to give his life a ransom for many.

Mark 10:45

# INTRODUCTION

I'm going to take you to meet my Aunt Emily, who has always had an exemplary marriage. She and Uncle Harold have been married for forty-five years now. I've always felt such a peace and harmony in their home over all the years that I've known them, that I want her to share with you the reasons for their happy union and how she has ministered to her husband all these beautiful years they've been together as one.

Emily is a good example of the woman described in Titus 2:3-5:

> The aged women likewise, that they be in behaviour as becometh holiness, not false accusers, not given to much wine, teachers of good things;
>
> That they may teach the young women to be sober, to love their husbands, to love their children,
>
> To be discreet, chaste, keepers at home, good, obedient to their own husbands, that the word of God be not blasphemed.

I can hear you saying, "Is Emily for real?" Sorry about that, but Aunt Emily is a fictional "wrap up". She wraps up all the insights God has been teaching me the hard way through my twenty-eight years of married life. God has spoken to me through His Word, through books, excellent preaching, many dear saints who have shared their insights over the years, my patient husband, and my three sons who are now young men. I've even learned a good bit through my own failures and the failures of others. As some optimist noted, "Nobody is worthless, they can always be used for a bad example." I guess that's why I need Emily, because I haven't yet built into my life all that's exemplified by her in the following pages. My prayer is that, in presenting these insights, I might gather with me others who will ". . . press toward the mark for the prize of the high calling of God in Christ Jesus." (Phil. 3:14).

When I first felt the Lord wanted me to write this book, I started to argue like Moses at the burning bush, "There are so many books about women already on the bookshelves. Everyone has already heard these truths the same as I have. The book isn't needed." But

God's Word spoke an answer to my heart that He had sent more than one prophet to say almost the same message over and over to His people Israel. Some of them listened and some didn't. Some needed to hear more than once, but none could say they never heard, or that they didn't know any better. God let me know that He wants His daughters to hear and heed this message today.

When the Lord continued His urging, I prayed, "Well, Lord, I don't intend to bargain with you, but I've had this low-grade infection for more than three years now, and I can't even begin to be a good wife myself when I don't feel well. How can I try to share with someone else how to be one? If you'll heal me, I'll know you want me to write this book." So, to make a long story short, He healed me, I began to write, and He has nudged me forward every time the clip board sits for too long. Now then, if you have any "fusses," you'll have to take them up with my Heavenly Father; I'm just obeying His orders.

The people and the experiences in our story are for the most part real, though some are combinations of situations, or the names and circumstances have been changed or switched around enough to cover the identity of the people involved. In fact, some of my own sad, but true, experiences are hidden here and there in the story. Please don't say, "Oh, that must be John and Susie!" The Devil is working so hard these days to destroy the home, especially among Christian leaders, that there are thousands of Johns and Susies all over the world.

Where there are strong, united, and righteous homes, there are strong, united, and righteous churches, and a strong, united, and righteous nation. Where there are weak, divided, and unrighteous homes, there are weak, divided, and unrighteous churches, and a weak, divided, and unrighteous nation. Those latter nations have, throughout history, been conquered and destroyed. Is it any wonder that Satan begins his attack in the home.

This can work the other way also. The nation by its laws and policies can strengthen the home or weaken it. The Church is responsible for teaching couples what the Scripture says about how to build their marriages and raise their children. When the Church fails in this ministry, many homes fail. Often Satan begins his attack on the home from the top down.

The man is the head of the home. The woman is the heart of the home. When a killer seeks to slay a victim, he aims either for the head or the heart, or both. "Be sober, be vigilant; because your adversary the devil, as a roaring lion, walketh about, seeking whom he may devour": (I Pet. 5:8). The Adversary wants to destroy every home, and he's working on the woman just as he did in the garden of Eden. Hopefully our trip to Aunt Emily's will help you to better watch and pray so the Destroyer can't fulfill his plans for your family, your church, and your nation.

If you have never fully submitted yourself to Jesus Christ, then please stop right here and take that first step because you can never effectively minister to your husband, or anyone else, until Jesus Christ can pour out His life through you. Count the cost and pray something like this: Lord Jesus Christ, I ask you to forgive me for all my sins. Make me clean and come into my heart. I ask you to govern my life and rule over me as my King. I offer myself to be one of your subjects. I accept your written Word, the Bible, as the instruction book for my life. Help me to obey it and to claim all its promises as well. In Jesus' Name, Amen.

And say to Archippus, Take heed to the ministry which thou hast received in the Lord, that thou fulfil it.

Colossians 4:17

# 1. THE MEANING OF OUR MINISTRY

Trent had gone for a two-week camping trip with the boys down the Tippecanoe River. Since five in a canoe is more than snug, I had suggested I'd go visit Aunt Emily and Uncle Harold, whom I hadn't seen for almost two years.

As I headed down the interstate, I began flicking through memories of the big white farm house nestled among the oak trees, the picturesque barn, the chicken house, and all the little necessary farm sheds, including Snappy's Shack. If one didn't know better, one would think Snappy was a very old rat terrier. However, when the first Snappy died, Uncle Harold just found another terrier that looked the image of the first Snappy, and the second Snappy, etc.. It was like Harold's Bibles; he underlined them, wrote in them, and literally wore them out. Then he started another Bible just like the first one and wore that one out too. Emily probably did the same, because they gave each other new Bibles every other year for birthday gifts.

As I turned off the exit ramp from I-65, I could almost smell the fresh mown hay and hear the crow of a banty rooster. Reminiscing, I could sense the loving warmth and peace that I had always felt, even as a child, when our car would pull into their drive and the family would pour out the door to greet us.

As I turned off the highway, I was hoping Aunt Emily would be making bread for dinner. Sure enough, when I pulled into their lane, the aroma of baking bread wafted through the car window.

A cardinal greeted me with "Good cheer! Good cheer!" I turned off the car and caught sight of Uncle Harold ambling toward my car from the garden. Snappy the third (or fourth) danced circles around my feet as I pulled my suitcase from the trunk. Emily, drying her hands on her apron, came to hug me.

"June must have smelled the bread," teased Harold, taking my suitcase.

"It's just like it always was, Aunt Emily and Uncle Harold, peace and quiet and love."

"Isn't it supposed to be that way?" she said, her eyes twinkling.

"Yes, but you folks have an extra good measure—more than most of us."

Harold took my suitcase up to Ruth's old room. Harold and Emily have four children. The two oldest boys, Mark and Paul, and their wives and children are in South America doing translation work. Pete is pastoring a tiny church about a hundred miles from his folks and working in a factory to support himself. He hasn't found a good prospect of a ministering wife yet. Ruth is married to a school teacher. They live in the next town.

Emily and I chattered our way up the steps past the roses. I stooped to inhale their heady fragrance.

"Here, we'll put a yellow one on the table for suppertime," said Emily, gingerly breaking off one in full bloom.

"So you're playing hooky for two weeks, are you?" asked Emily.

"Well, with nobody to mess up the house and dirty the dishes, they let me have some time off—for good behavior," I replied.

"Well now, I can't let you get lazy. Here's a paring knife. If you want apple pie tonight, you'll have to give me a hand with the apples, while I make the crust."

"No argument, Aunt Emily. When is that bread done? I'm about to drool."

"In time," teased Emily.

"Well, June," Harold said, sniffing his way into the kitchen, "I thought you forgot how to find your way back here."

Harold's smile was always contagious. His arm went around my shoulder and he gave me a quick hug and snatched an apple slice.

We were soon sitting down to give thanks for one of Aunt Emily's unforgettable meals. While we ate, Harold and Emily filled me in on their family. They were proud of their children and, as most good parents, rejoiced to tell of their accomplishments and the lively antics of the grandchildren.

"Aunt Emily, while I'm here, I want you to teach me everything you know about how to be a good wife. You and Uncle Harold have had such a long and happy marriage; I'm sure you can give me some insights that I can pass on to my ladies' Bible class. I told them I was coming back with baskets of food for thought."

Aunt Emily looked thoughtful, and even though she began to clear the table, I could tell her mind was turning over my request.

"That's a pretty tall order," she began. "Have you ever realized, June, that being a wife is a ministry?"

"Well, I guess I hadn't thought about it quite like that," I responded, as I carried a stack of plates to the sink.

Uncle Harold, tapping the half empty pie plate, asked, "Like Emily's ministry of apple pie, eh?"

Emily smiled her appreciation at Harold and proceeded, "You came just at the right time; the women of our church asked me about three months ago if I would lead a Bible study with the women's prayer group on the role of the wife. So I'm all 'studied up' for you. We started our first lesson four weeks ago, so I'll have to catch you up. We will finish the last two lessons while you're still here, so you'll get to meet some of our dear ladies this Friday."

Harold pushed his chair back. "Here, let me wash the chicken off my fingers and I'll get my concordance. I like to get in on these things too."

"Harold always goes to the bottom of everything in Scripture," said Emily, wiping the table clean. "He's been a big help in this project."

Emily ran the dish water and I grabbed a dish towel.

Harold slipped his glasses on. "Let's see what Strong's Concordance says about the meaning of 'minister.' It says here: 'to be an attendant, i.e. wait upon (menially or as a host, friend or fig. teacher . . . )' "[1]

Harold closed the big book and opened his Bible. "Look here in Mark 10:45:

> For even the Son of man came not to be ministered unto, but to minister, and to give his life a ransom for many.

"June," continued Harold, "ministering is synonymous with serving, and Jesus was our example. He didn't consider Himself above serving his disciples. Jesus washed the disciples' feet as a symbolic act of service and told them to do the same thing. He taught that the greatest among his disciples was he who was the servant of all. The servant is not greater than his master."

"Then, Uncle Harold," I teased, "since the one who is the greatest is the one who serves the most, we ladies must be the greatest after all, right?"

"Only if you serve the most."

"Well," Emily added, "God gave women a head start in the garden when He made us help meets. We were created for the purpose of being helpers or servants."

"OK," said Harold, "let me put in another two cents from Strong's. The Hebrew word translated into help meet means to 'surround, i.e. protect or aid:—help, succour.' "[1]

"Just a word of caution," Emily interjected. "This definition has to be understood in the light of the whole of Scripture. The woman is also the weaker vessel—physically and emotionally. Too many times a wife is eager to save her husband from the pressures which come against the family and she gets out in front to blunt the blows. But God didn't create her with the physical or emotional makings to handle it. Some poor gals become nervous wrecks or develop ulcers trying to handle all these pressures. Or they become encased in a wall of hardness in order to protect their tender, emotional structure from being battered, which keeps them from being the true heart in the home. When that happens, they can't respond to love easily, nor give it easily."

I began questioning, "You're talking about shielding him from the unpleasant neighbor who jangles the doorbell when little Tommy has put a baseball through his window?"

"Yes!"

"Or when there are more bills than money?"

"Exactly!"

"Or when his work load gets so large, you're sure he'll crack if you don't do half of it for him?"

"Now she's jumped from asking questions and gone to meddling," mumbled Harold.

"Well," I asked, "where does a woman draw the line? I need to know and so do a lot of other women."

Emily responded, "I'd best say let God draw the line in each woman's particular case. A few principles should be followed: One, the wife is not to be in the position of leadership. Her role, which is supportive, is just as important, but she's not the one who makes the decisions. If she protects him from having to make decisions, the roles in the family will begin to shift, leaving her to handle most of the decision-making business. That puts the family out of Scriptural order.

"The pressures of life make us mature in the Lord. If a woman keeps shielding her husband from everything God allows to come his way, the husband is missing out on the maturing process which God intends for him. God has to keep the trials coming so he'll mature. When we interfere, we delay his progress and suffer needlessly ourselves."

"Let me read Romans 5:3," said Harold:

> And not only so, but we glory in tribulations also: knowing that tribulation worketh patience;

"And in James 1:3 and 4:

> Knowing this, that the trying of your faith worketh patience.
>
> But let patience have her perfect work, that ye may be perfect and entire, wanting nothing.

"See, that's why Harold's perfect, June; I let him take the brunt of all the tribulation."

"Not exactly," said Harold, "but a good modern-day word for *tribulation* is *pressure*, and God allows only as much pressure as a man can take. He wants women to have their own pressures so they mature too, but they're not the leadership-type pressures. That's why so many women are breaking down emotionally or getting divorced; they're taking upon themselves pressures that don't belong to them."

"A second principle," Emily continued, "is that women are physically weaker than men. There are a few strong women who can toss bales of hay or big boxes around like a man, but they're not the general rule, and some of those same dear souls find themselves with strained internal muscles and sagging organs—or worse. As I said before, it's sometimes hard to draw a line that applies to every woman. Each woman needs to ask God if she's doing what He intends for her to do. If the physical help she's giving is straining her, she may be doing her husband's part and she shouldn't."

Emily waited for me to dry the last few dishes so she could put the large glass baking dish in the drain rack.

"Aunt Emily, I've dried all the dishes but I can't figure out where to put the rest of them. If you don't mind, while you put these away, I'll run up and get my notebook so I can write down an outline of what we've discussed this evening and get all these Scriptures down. I want them for my ladies when I get back home."

Harold pulled his chair back. "Let's all go in the living room; it's cooler in there."

I was back in a minute mumbling over a brief outline in my notebook. Harold filled me in on Scripture references while Emily put the finishing touches on her kitchen.

Emily sighed as she eased into her chair: "Feels good to rest. Where were we? Oh yes, we were talking about principles that help us determine what kind of help we give our husbands and what work we leave to them."

"A third principle is for the woman to 'tend to her own knitting.' See that the household runs smoothly, the meals are there on time, the clothes laundered and mended, the children properly cared for and the house clean and tidy. Then see about the work with which she could help him. There are exceptions, of course. A farmer's wife sometimes drives a tractor or truck for a week or more while the housework slides because her help is needed right then. The wife of a businessman may need to mail out 2000 advertising flyers for a special sale. The whole idea is that we're not trying to take over their jobs or run their business. If our own work is done and there's order in our home, they will be able to accomplish their own tasks far more easily. If we just do what they ask us to do, this is a big help to them."

"I'll say," Harold piped up. "I know several men who have complained to me that their wives won't do the little things they ask them to, like mailing a letter or mending their trousers.

"But let's get back to the concept of ministry," Harold said. "In Philippians 2:5-8 it says:

> Let this mind be in you, which was also in Christ Jesus:
>
> Who, being in the form of God, thought it not robbery to be equal with God:
>
> But made himself of no reputation, and took upon him the form of a servant, and was made in the likeness of men:
>
> And being found in fashion as a man, he humbled himself, and became obedient unto death, even the death of the cross.

Emily took it from there: "We women need the mind of Christ, not the mind of the world. The god of this world is launching one of the biggest propaganda programs he can. With the news media screaming about women's rights and women's liberation, it's high time we counter their philosophy with God's viewpoint on this issue. God's viewpoint is submission and obedience just as the example Christ gave us. I'm not opposed to women obtaining their rights, but a good many of these women don't have any real issues at all; they only want to be free from the mature responsibility of a wife and mother. To be 'loose,' in my opinion, is not a noble kind of freedom."

"But Jesus does set us free, Aunt Emily."

"Yes, but free from what? God-given responsibility? No! Free from sin! We must not allow the world to mold or twist our thinking. As Christians, we have the mind of Christ. Liberty is the freedom to do what we know is right, because Jesus Christ has set us free from sin. The world's system has it all backwards—the freedom to do what you want to do even if you know it's wrong. That's not freedom; that's bondage to sin."

"I can tell Harold's got some Scripture there," Emily acknowledged with a nod.

Harold proceeded, "This is Galatians 5:13:

> For, brethren, ye have been called unto liberty; only use not liberty for an occasion to the flesh, but by love serve one another.

"See, there's that word *love* used together with *liberty*," said Emily. "Let's be realistic; we're all going to be servants to something or someone. Read us that verse in Romans 6 about yielding yourselves servants, Harold."

Harold zeroed right in on it: "That's 6:16, and I'd better read a few more verses too:

> Know ye not, that to whom ye yield yourselves servants to obey, his servants ye are to whom ye obey; whether of sin unto death, or of obedience unto righteousness?
>
> But God be thanked, that ye were the servants of sin, but ye have obeyed from the heart that form of doctrine which was delivered you.
>
> Being then made free from sin, ye became the servants of righteousness.
>
> I speak after the manner of men because of the infirmity of your flesh: for as ye have yielded your members servants to uncleanness and to iniquity unto iniquity; even so now yield your members servants to righteousness unto holiness.
>
> For when ye were the servants of sin, ye were free from righteousness.
>
> What fruit had ye then in those things whereof ye are now ashamed? for the end of those things is death.
>
> But now being made free from sin, and become servants to God, ye have your fruit unto holiness, and the end everlasting life.

"My!" I exclaimed. "That puts it under the right light, doesn't it? If women could just see that they are free when they become the servants of Christ. Then when they marry, they serve their husbands in that same freedom. Sure, housework can be a drudgery, and I think we all feel like slaves sometimes; but I'd rather work for people whom I love, as unto the Lord, than out there in the business world doing my thing, so I can 'find myself.' "

Emily nodded, "What could be more enjoyable and liberating than spending your life making the one you love happy? The role of the ministering wife is a high calling of God. The Devil and his henchmen are working overtime to disparage that divinely ordained occupation."

"I know some women, Aunt Emily, who feel ashamed to say 'housewife' when asked to describe their occupation."

"I always answer 'homemaker,' " beamed Emily.

"Why," exclaimed Harold with mock indignation, "Emily is a horticulturist, a farmer, a baker, a barber, a chef, a nutritionist, a practical nurse, an interior designer, a teacher, a secretary, a tailor—why, I could go on and on. She's even a draftsman—she opens and closes the windows."

"Uncle Harold, you're a character. But I know what you're saying; homemaking is a multitude of skills and talents. However, today's women are hit with such a barrage of ungodly ideas, they feel abnormal to be only a homemaker. They're made to feel intellectually inferior if they stay home and take care of their house and family and love their husbands. It's like a continual brainwashing everywhere we turn. I warn the ladies in my Bible class about this deceptive philosophy, but the media definitely does affect their thinking. I left them last week with Colossians 2:8:

> Beware lest any man spoil you through philosophy and vain deceit, after the tradition of men, after the rudiments of the world, and not after Christ.

"Look at the results of their evil philosophy," said Harold.

" 'By their fruits ye shall know them,' " I added.

"Right." agreed Emily. "It's bitter fruit, too. We have a huge increase in broken marriages, homosexuality, incest, juvenile crime, epidemic venereal disease, neurotic fathers, mothers, and kids. Why? The home is out of order, that's why.

"Many families today have what I call 'Hotel Homes.' Each member has a key, comes in and goes out at his or her own decision and schedule, to be involved in life outside the home where they can relate meaningfully to other people. They come home at night to sleep, unless they work the night shift or stay at a friend's house.

Before the Women's Liberation philosophy came along, the woman was the glue that held the family together. She made the house a home. Now she's out finding her identity."

Harold was shaking his head, "Home, sweet home. Not like the good old days when Mom was always there baking goodies, applying band aids to scratches, drying tears, and hugging the tired Daddy when he dragged in from a hard day's work."

Emily continued, "Most women in our culture have grown up with a literary background that sets the man up as a knight in shining armor, the servant of woman, waiting on her and pleasing her in every way. This is not the picture God sets forth in His Word. God made Adam and then to meet his creature's needs fully, he created a woman as a help meet. Woman was created to be her husband's helper. She fulfills him. Her joy is in his fulfillment. The fulfillment of the wife is in seeing her husband accomplish what he was created to do.

"Before sin entered the world, man's job was to tend the creation. Now man has many difficulties to overcome to meet his physical needs, but he also has a ministry of reconciliation. The ministry of the wife is to provide an environment in which her husband can serve God and his fellow man to the greatest extent of his ability. His fulfillment is hers, and his reward is hers.

"A woman's ministry to her husband isn't an incidental—something that fits into her life's work; it *is* her life's work. The role here is different. The woman fits into her husband's life work as a helper, but it is not intended to work the other way around. This doesn't mean husbands are not to help their wives; nor does it mean that a wife doesn't minister to others. Many wives are a tremendous complement to the ministry of their husbands because they have a ministry of their own alongside of his.

"I might add here that above everything else and above everyone else, a woman is called to fellowship with Jesus Christ, as it says in I Corinthians l:9. Read that for us please, Harold."

> God is faithful, by whom ye were called unto the fellowship of his Son Jesus Christ our Lord.

"Our first loyalty," continued Emily, "is to the Lord. Then, if a woman is married, she is a minister to her husband. Her role is a supportive one. As I said before, it's no less important; it's just not the up-front position. We're made very aware of how important that ministry is when we see a home where the wife does not minister.

"But let's get back to a wife's ministry outside her home. That ministry must be kept in its proper position of priority. Her first ministry is to her husband. Too many women allow their ministry to their children to cool their first love for their husbands. Others dive into church work and leave their lonely husbands to fend for themselves. They're pulling apart, not together. Women are to assist their husbands in their ministry. When that's done, if they have time, they can stretch their tent stakes a little further. If the wife will just coordinate her efforts with his melody and timing, they'll harmonize well together."

Harold opened his Bible. "Let's look at Colossians again—chapter 2, verses 9 and 10. It reads:

> For in him dwelleth all the fulness of the Godhead bodily.
>
> And ye are complete in him, which is the head of all principality and power:

"Who is that talking about, June?" asked Harold.

"It's talking about Jesus Christ and His Church. The Church is complete or filled up when it has Christ as its head. A body without a head is not complete, nor is a head without a body. Am I right, Uncle Harold?"

"I'd say so. The relationship of the wife and the husband are a picture of the relationship between the Church and Christ. We call that a type don't we? It's like the pattern of the tabernacle and the sacrifices are a type of the plan of salvation. The ram caught in the thicket and then offered as a sacrifice instead of Isaac is a type of Christ taking our place at Calvary. Types are very important object lessons in the Word of God. The wife is a type of the Church and its submission to Christ. Let's see . . . that's right here in Ephesians 5. We'll start with verse 21:

> Submitting yourselves one to another in the fear of God.
>
> Wives, submit yourselves unto your own husbands, as unto the Lord.
>
> For the husband is the head of the wife, even as Christ is the head of the church: and he is the saviour of the body.
>
> Therefore as the church is subject unto Christ, so let the wives be to their own husbands in every thing.

I was absorbing the whole concept. Finally I responded, "This is not a completely new thought to me, Uncle Harold, but it's sobering to think of what an immense responsibility it is to be a living type of what the Church should be. That ought to challenge my ladies, too."

"It should," said Emily. "Since we're compassed about with so great a cloud of witnesses, we should walk in submission to our husbands so the whole world, the angels, demons, our children, and our Lord can see how much Jesus means to the Church, so they can have an object lesson of how the Church should serve the Lord. God will get glory from this obedience."

"Let's put these pictures together here, if we can," said Harold. "In Ephesians 1:22 and 23 it says:

> And hath put all things under his feet, and gave him to be the head over all things to the church,
>
> Which is his body, the fullness of him that filleth all in all.

"Now between the passage I read to you in Colossians 2 a few minutes ago and this one in Ephesians, it appears that Jesus Christ completes the Church as the head and we complete Him as the body. I believe, in just such a way, the wife completes her husband. He's a complete individual without her and he could stay single, but there's a certain special quality of fullness that's there when the two become one. In the same way, the wife is a total personality by herself, but there's a quality of fulfillment when a woman puts herself under the headship of the husband. This oneness is a picture of the oneness the Church has with Jesus Christ. In John 17, verse 21 it says:

> That they all may be one; as thou, Father, art in me, and I in thee, that they also may be one in us: that the world may believe that thou hast sent me.

"See what a powerful spiritual effect this has? When the members of the Church are one with each other, and the Church, as a whole, is one with Jesus Christ and the Father, people on the outside become believers. Since the wife is a type or picture of this whole thing, as she relates to her husband, don't you suppose the same spiritual principle would be at work here—that people would find salvation because of the picture they see of the oneness of the Church with Christ?"

"Oh me!" I exclaimed. "That makes our responsibility as wives even more important. How can women say they have nothing important to do for the Lord?"

"Just being what God wants us to be," said Emily, "is incredibly important from His viewpoint. I'm not minimizing the aspect of doing things in cooperation with God, but our attitudes of submission and obedience to our husbands underlie what we do, and it's all very important in the spiritual realm."

"Well," replied Harold, "we moved from Philippians 2 where Jesus is described as an obedient servant, to Ephesians 5, where it speaks of the wife's submission to her husband as a picture of the Church's submission to Christ. Let's go back to Philippians for a few minutes. Jesus is equal with the Father, isn't He? He said, 'I and my Father are one' (John 10:30), and here in Philippians 2 it says He thought it not robbery to be equal with God. As we mentioned at the beginning of this lesson, Jesus made himself a servant. He put himself in a position where He was in submission to His heavenly Father, His earthly parents, and civil authorities too. Why should we find it so difficult to be subject to those whom God put in authority over us? Are we greater than Jesus? In John 5:30 Jesus said, 'I seek not mine own will, but the will of the Father which sent me.' "

"Ouch!"

"Shall we go on?"

"Yes, but when you compare Jesus' submission with ours, it gets painful."

"I Corinthians 15:28 says, ' . . . then shall the Son also himself be subject unto him that put all things under him, that God may be all in all.' "

"Well," said Emily, "that's pretty heavy for one evening."

"I'll say! Let me see if I missed anything:

1. Being a wife is a ministry.
2. Jesus was an example of a servant.
   a. He was obedient.
   b. He was subject to authority.
   c. He washed the disciples' feet as an example.
3. The wife was created for the purpose of being a helper.
4. We always serve something or someone—sin or righteousness, so it's best to serve the Lord and minister unto our husbands as God's servants.

5. As Jesus Christ completes the Church and the Church completes Christ, so the husband completes the wife and she completes him.
6. The relationship of the Church to Christ is pictured in type by the relationship of the wife to the husband.
7. As the wife walks in oneness with her husband, she portrays a picture of the Church's oneness with the Lord, and those outside the Church may become believers because of the object lesson."

"That will do for tonight," said Emily, handing me a piece of paper. "That's all the further I got in the first lesson. We had a lot of class discussion. I asked them to pray the prayer that's on that piece of paper, if they could or would. Maybe you want to pray it too. I gave each of them a copy."

I gave Emily and Harold a thankful hug good night, climbed the stairs, and sat down on the bed to read through the prayer. "Hmmm," I thought, "what would happen to America if every woman in this country prayed this prayer and meant it?" Maybe you'd like to pray this prayer too—and mean it:

Lord Jesus Christ, I submit myself to You, as Your servant, because You made Yourself a servant for my sake and were obedient unto death so You could save me from sin. Now because You left me an example of a servant and because You said, 'as the church is subject unto Christ so let the wives be to their own husbands in every thing,' I'm asking You to live Your life through me as a servant to my husband. Help me to help him in a manner that pleases You. I'll obey him and reverence him as long as he doesn't tell me to disobey You. Love him through me and make my ministry to him a glory to Your name. Make my life a picture of the Church's submission to Jesus Christ. In the Name of our Lord Jesus Christ. Amen.

## RESTING

My Spirit ached within me
As I sought the Lord each day,
As I searched and begged for victory.
Then I heard Him say,
"Enter into my rest."

But resting would not come,
For I clung to self and pride.
Then I saw the cross one day
And something in me cried,
"Cease from thine own works."

And so the victory came at last
As I denied my gain and pride
And crucified myself with Him.
Then Christ at last to me replied
"Now Rest."

## 2. THE POSITION OF OUR MINISTRY

"Up, up, or we'll send Snappy to fetch you," called Emily cheerfully.

"No, no, I'm coming," I called from the top of the stairs. I hurried down and into the kitchen. "I was just admiring your soloist. There was a cardinal on my windowsill this morning, helping me in the Psalms. I looked out to see if I could spot a nest when you called me."

"Isn't he nice? I call him Barnabas; he lifts me up when I feel discouraged."

"Come on, Aunt Emily, I've never seen you discouraged."

"That's because he lifts me up. He sings, 'Good Cheer,' which is from John 16:33:

> These things I have spoken unto you, that in me ye might have peace. In the world ye shall have tribulation: but be of good cheer; I have overcome the world.

"I put that one on a 3x5 and memorized it years ago. See my file is growing." Emily pointed to a couple of pretty file boxes on the shelf with her recipe books. "I do need to review them better than I do, though. When you get my age, you tend to forget more than you learn."

"May I look?"

"Certainly."

"Have you memorized all these verses, Aunt Emily?"

"Yes, but as I said, my reviewing is slipping. There are many more verses now than when I first started. Not all the verses are there. When I memorize a whole book, I don't always put it on cards."

"How many books have you memorized?"

"Only a few in the New Testament. 1st, 2nd and 3rd John, James, Romans, John, Philippians, and Ephesians. Right now I'm working on Colossians. I helped a lady teach Bible school every summer when I was just a young Christian. She had memorized the entire New Testament and was working on Psalms. She really knew her Bible. That's what got me excited about memorizing; but I'm not as steadfast as she was."

"You put me to shame. I thought I knew a lot of verses."

"Do you review often?"

"Not very often."

"That's where you lose it. That's why I started the card file. Almost every day, I sit down and review several verses, then put them at the back. By the time I come to them again, they need reviewing. The newer verses get reviewed more than the ones I've known for many years because they need it more. That's why I've got two boxes. When I have very little trouble remembering them, they get moved to the other box. For the review of whole books, I use those little Scripture portion booklets. That way I don't fray my Bible so badly. I carry them in the car and prop them up over the sink while I do the dishes. Harold listens to my verses and I listen to his."

"I'm writing that down in my notebook. When I get home, I'll make a renewed effort. Aunt Emily what are you baking that smells so good?"

"Granola. I'm going to be canning all day today and a good bit this week. This is a nourishing breakfast that doesn't take much time to fix each morning—just add milk, eat, and wash a couple of bowls. Most of the cold cereals you buy in the store are full of sugar and other devitalized and chemicalized ingredients that we don't care to eat. Want the recipe?"

"Sure do, if it tastes as good as it smells."

Emily handed me an attractive mimeographed recipe booklet. "I put this together several years ago and sold them through an ad in the paper for a little 'egg' money. It was fun.

"Well, here's the first batch. I'll call Harold. He should be done with his chores now and we'll eat."

Emily pulled the dinner bell just outside the back door.

"Yum. I'll probably gain ten pounds while I'm here."

"I doubt it. When you eat food with real nourishment in it, you don't crave food in between meals as much. That's especially true with B vitamins. I understand that refined sugar needs B vitamins in order to metabolize it for the body. Since it doesn't have any B vitamins in it, it draws on what B vitamins the body does have. Then, queer as it may seem, the body craves sweet things. Then you eat more sugar and the vicious cycle continues until you get off the merry-go-round."

"So how do you get off?"

"Eat natural sweets like honey, molasses, and maple syrup and keep those low. Fruit gives you plenty of sugar as do many of your vegetables. We often have fruit for dessert or no dessert at all."

"Good morning, Sleepy Head," teased Harold with his usual bright smile.

"Good morning, Uncle Harold." I was glad he sat down and offered thanks so I could taste this wonderful smelling cereal. "This stuff is great, Aunt Emily. How did you learn all this information about nutrition? Did you study it in school?"

"No, I just started collecting books and subscribing to magazines about nutrition. Harold and I both had a number of physical problems, and I figured at forty we weren't quite old enough to fall apart. As the cook, I felt responsible, so I began investigating nutritional material to find the cause of our problems. Everyone liked my cooking, but what I was cooking wasn't building up our bodies, it was tearing them down. Oh, we were building *big* bodies; all of us were overweight. But we weren't building strength, energy, and endurance—just fat. Not only did I read a lot of secular and Christian books on nutrition, but as Harold and I read through the Bible together, I kept a little notebook with my Bible for the purpose of writing down everything the Bible said about eating—what did Abraham feed the three men that came to see him? What did Jesus eat? What did God tell His people not to eat? It's very interesting and informative." Emily reached into her desk and handed me a small notebook. "Here, take a look at my notes."

"Manufacturer's directions for the type of fuel to use in the machinery, right?" mused Harold.

He waited a few minutes while I absorbed the contents of Emily's research, then he spoke again. "Let me say this, June, you have to be cautious about nutritional reading because a good bit of it is saturated with occult propaganda. A good portion of the holistic health movement is an integral part of the New Age Movement and the foundation of the New Age Movement is occult. So watch and pray and be careful what you recommend to other people."

Harold stood up. "Well, I guess I'll leave you ladies to your canning. I've got to run some steers to the market today."

Emily gave Harold a kiss and handed him a lunch pail. She followed him to the door and quoted a Scripture verse to him as he was leaving:

> Now the God of hope fill you with all joy and peace in believing, that ye may abound in hope, through the power of the Holy Ghost (Rom. 15:13).

Emily turned and smiled. "I try to remember to bless Harold as he goes off somewhere. If you make a list of benedictions in your notebook and use them each day to bless your husband and children, I'm sure you'll find a delight in it. Blessings do have spiritual power too; it's not just nice words. And if the last thing they hear when they leave the house is something pleasant, it makes them eager to come back home again too."

Emily began clearing the table. "After I got into all that reading about nutrition, I felt a real responsibility to change our eating habits. I make an attempt to serve a large percentage of raw fruits and vegetables, seeds, and nuts."

"I noticed you had a large mixed salad last night and no cooked vegetables."

"But there were raw peas, raw corn, and raw green beans in the salad as well as the lettuce and other greens and tomatoes."

"It was delicious. I also noticed that you used whole wheat flour for your pie crust. It was excellent too. Oh yes, and honey to sweeten the apples. Did your family mind the switch to more natural foods?"

"Well, we survived the adjustment pretty well. There were a few recipes that I tried that were awful. They still tease me about protein burgers. They were so unpalatable, even the dog wouldn't eat them."

Emily ran fresh dish water and began washing canning bottles. "Just let these drain, June. They have to be sterilized anyway before we fill them. O.K., let's go pick beans; here's a bowl for you."

It was such a beautiful day, I was glad to get outside.

"Aunt Emily, your garden is delightful. Do you do all this work by yourself?"

"No, Harold helps me with the heavier work like digging and weeding (if the weeds get ahead of me). He lets me fine tune it. Now our neighbor down the road is eighty-two. She does her whole garden by herself, but it's a lot smaller. Then there's Mary Lou who is closer to town. She's much younger and used to work to help meet the family's needs. Now she and the kids do a big garden and she cans, freezes, dries, and puts a lot of fresh things in a fruit cellar. They even sell some of it at a little stand next to the road. They did such a booming business last year, that Mark, her oldest son, is going around buying from other gardeners and selling their produce too. Best part of it is Mary Lou can be home all day with the children. The whole family is much healthier and the kids are much better behaved."

"Busy hands improve behavior, right?"

"You bet it does. So does having Mom instead of a baby-sitter."

"I assume you're against working wives."

"Why no; all wives should work. God wouldn't want women to be lazy just because they were married." Emily's eyes were twinkling.

"You know what I mean, Aunt Emily; I mean career women."

"What's wrong with making homemaking a career?"

"Nothing, but do you believe a married woman should take a job outside the home?"

"Generally speaking, no. But each case should be considered individually. There are several considerations involved. First, does her husband want her to work? If so, why? Is it really necessary for them to have two paychecks in order to exist? Is she putting him through school? Are they starting a business and they're working together all day long? Are the children grown and she's assisting him at his office so they can be together and save the money it would cost to hire someone else? Do they have children? Who will baby-sit? Is that person able to provide the spiritual and disciplinary foundation as well as the mother could? Could the mother just as easily economize at home by canning, cooking things from scratch, sewing, and perhaps selling something she made?

"If you consider the money spent for transportation, the extra money spent on ready-made and convenience foods, as well as her lunch, the additions to her wardrobe to be dressed well for the job, and babysitting costs, the working wife may find it more expensive to work than to stay at home.

"Is she foolishly spending money on things that are taxing the budget unnecessarily? Does she waste food? Willful waste makes woeful want. Some women are really lazy when it comes to the kitchen—they buy instant potatoes, instant tea, instant supper. Most of that food is loaded with harmful chemicals, and the refining process often depletes it of natural minerals and vitamins. Besides, it's frightfully more expensive than cooking from scratch."

"But cooking from scratch takes more time."

"That's true. Take a can of chicken, for example. It costs almost as much as a whole chicken, but you get far more from the whole chicken by cooking it yourself and you avoid the chemicals and the blah taste. Doing your own baking can save scads of money as well."

"And it sure beats the store-bought bread in taste."

"Yes, and try to find real whole wheat or whole grain rye in the super market. Most of it is just colored with carmel coloring to look like brown bread. Women need to start reading the ingredient labels on packaged food. These labels read like a chemistry book. The lettering on the bag is misleading, too. For example 'wheat' bread, unless it says 100% whole wheat, usually means wheat that has had most of the nutrients, bran, and wheat germ taken out of it. All this good stuff is made into hog and dog food and then what remains is bleached with a poison chemical, has synthetic vitamins added to it along with preservatives and artificial colors to make it look like whole wheat bread. Don't get me started; we'll be talking about nutrition in our lesson on the body.

"By the way, Mary Lou sells a few loaves of bread at their vegetable stand each week. She could go into business doing just that. People are always asking for more. She also sews clothes for the whole family and does a beautiful job. Sometimes I run into Mary Lou at a garage sale. Often we can find things cheaper at a garage sale than if we bought material and made it. Harold says I pinch the old nickel so hard, I make the Indian ride the buffalo. Frugality complements generosity."

"That doesn't make sense to me, Aunt Emily. Those seem like opposite terms."

"No, they're not, really. When people work hard and are careful with what God provides for them, they have more than other folks. Then they have an overabundance to share with those in need. It's very rewarding to me to take a box of fresh goodies from my garden or a jar of my canned meat, fruit, or vegetables into town to Mrs. Sanders. She's a widow on a little pension and she's all stiff with arthritis. I tell her the Lord wants me to bring it to her because He's blessed me with so much and He loves her. Then I chat with her about the Lord.

"When we invited her to come with us to church, she was delighted. She doesn't always feel good enough to come, but she has come enough to feed her soul. Last winter she finally realized she needed a Saviour, and gave her heart to the Lord. She was always a good, moral person and thought her good life would gain her an entrance into heaven. When she heard a sermon on Jesus' words from the cross—'It is finished'—the Holy Spirit opened her eyes and she realized it was His finished work on the cross that could save her, and not her own righteousness."

"A lot of church people believe that way, Aunt Emily, but Ephesians 2:8 and 9 says:

> For by grace are ye saved through faith; and that not of yourselves: it is the gift of God:
>
> Not of works, lest any man should boast.

"See, I know some verses."

"Good. There's another one in Titus 3:5:

> Not by works of righteousness which we have done, but according to his mercy he saved us, by the washing of regeneration, and renewing of the Holy Ghost;

"That's the verse that convinced my heart years ago. I could really relate to Mrs. Sanders because I also came up in a church that didn't preach the need for a personal salvation experience with Jesus Christ. It was all head knowledge. It wasn't until I started going to another church that I realized I needed to appropriate the salvation that Jesus Christ provided for me.

"I think we have enough beans now, June; let's go in. We'll steam some for lunch, too."

We settled down to snapping beans. I prodded Emily, "Do you think it's right for women without children to work outside of the home?"

"That depends on how much her job demands of her and how much her home demands of her. It would also depend on the kind of place in which she was working. I can relate to you some sad cases of women who went to work, met men at work who seduced them, and completely devastated their marriages.

"Unfortunately, these women had children who suffered tragically from the upheaval. In one case it threw the husband for a loop. He backslid too and went back to drinking. The kids were left alone much of the time. Thankfully, the oldest girl was able to hold things together as best she could until God turned them around. Some of the damage done in these situations is irreparable. These women were Christians; I knew them well. I don't believe women should be thrown in with men in close job situations. There are too many temptations for most women to handle, and the ones who think they can handle it are most often the ones who fall."

"Trent tells me the same thing about factories where he has worked. He says the machinists watch the women more than they watch their machines."

"Let's go back to what I was saying about the demands of a job. If the wife teaches school six hours a day and plans carefully enough to have her papers graded during school, so she's not bringing her job home with her; and the kids don't wear her out being naughty all day, so she can clean the house and prepare a good home-cooked meal and be a companion to her husband, it would probably be O.K. Many women don't have that much energy. There's this to consider, too:

some men work the night shift, or a swing shift. They would never see each other for days at a time."

"Or maybe she works nights and they wave to one another as they pass on the highway," I interjected.

"There are several principles to be considered in deciding whether the wife works outside the home:

"One, the husband should agree to it, not just acquiesce.

"Secondly, it should be in a working situation where women are held in high respect and not expected to do a man's heavy work.

"Thirdly, if she does not have the energy to meet her husband's needs and the needs of the house, she should stay home if she possibly can. The only reason I leave a loop-hole is because there are a few circumstances such as an invalid or sick husband, where the wife finds it necessary to work."

The speed of Emily's nimble fingers, as she filled her bowl with snapped beans, kept pace with her nimble mind. I had to hurry to keep up with her.

Emily continued, "That brings us to the fourth principle—not the least consideration, by any means. If, after considerable prayer, there is no peace about working outside the home, perhaps God desires to provide for the family in some other way, and we're standing in His way. God may be leading the husband to a better-paying job, but as long as two salaries are making it, he'll never launch out to find something else. Perhaps he would do well in business for himself, but as long as the wife is working, he does not feel any necessity to do so. The woman and her husband should really know God's will in this area.

"The fifth area relates to those with children. Children are best cared for by their own parents, especially during their formative years. If the children are in school and she can work part time or on a schedule which allows her to be there when the kids get home from school, there may not be any difficulty."

"I read an article about latch-key children, Aunt Emily. It's a growing problem. More and more women are working, and kids are home alone for hours with no proper supervision. It's dangerous and psychologically damaging. The authors weren't even discussing it from a spiritual standpoint. Think of the hours a working mother misses to train up her children in the nurture and admonition of the Lord. I've only worked a few months in all the time we've been married. I can count on the fingers of one hand the times we've been away from the kids when they were little. Even though I've been home and really spent quality and quantity time with them, I feel they've grown up so fast, I haven't had time enough to prepare them spiritually for all they're going to face in these last days."

Emily nodded her agreement and went on: "When kids are teens, they need a lot of attention. Some women feel their kids are grown, and go to work leaving teenagers alone when they really need adult supervision, direction, counsel, and companionship in order to develop into responsible adults. They desperately need a good example walking around near them who is coping with life as it is—someone whom they can observe under the everyday pressures such as company coming and the pie falling upside down on the fresh waxed floor or the dog eating the Thanksgiving turkey. We teach far more to our children by how we respond to a situation than by telling them how to do what's right.

"Even though they may seem to give us about as much attention as a kitchen chair, our just being there gives them a tremendous stability and security. We make the house a home. That's also true for our husbands; they need us to just *be* there. Loneliness is a very painful malady. We minister companionship to our families.

"A sixth principle would be that the wife's motive for working should be worthwhile. She should honestly examine her heart and mind. Is it really necessary to make ends meet? Is it a spiritual ministry such as a church secretary, a singer on a Christian radio station, a Christian school teacher, or even a public school teacher? Is it to buy luxuries that aren't really necessary? Is it to escape housework? the children? Is she competing with her husband or someone else? Has she been brainwashed into thinking she has to find fulfillment in a career? Is she trying to be a 'free' woman? If the motive is not right, she'd best stay home and be a career homemaker."

"Actually, Aunt Emily," I said, snapping two beans at once, "the wife at home is more free than the working wife. For the most part, she can organize her own day; she's free from a lot of pressures that a working woman has, like worrying about being late to work or if she'll be laid off or fired.

"She can arrange her schedule to get her work all done and go off for the day to the museum with the kids if she feels like it. She has endless freedom to do creative things like writing poetry, painting a picture, making up songs.

"I have occasionally made homemade birthday cards and Mother's Day cards. They indicate we care enough to invest time and effort in our card. Once I even catered a wedding with all the little decorated sandwiches. I had a great time! And I made a little money too. I could do it as a full-time business, but I felt the Lord was saying no to that idea."

"I'm glad I don't have to sign out on a time clock to go out and talk to my bird friend Barnabas.

"Here, let's get these beans in the canner now. You get your notebook and your Bible, and we'll get into the second lesson on the position of our ministry while these are processing."

I scurried after my things.

"O.K., I'm ready to go. I've already learned a lot this morning."

"Those were sidelines, but not unimportant. We discussed working in class too, but it wasn't in my outline. I guess this is a question troubling a lot of women. We could probably debate the subject for countless hours, either justifying or condemning the wife working outside the home, but each married woman needs to seek the face of the Lord with her husband and ask His guidance on the subject. In the Bible class, we ended our discussion of this subject with a look at Titus 2:3-5:

> The aged women likewise, that they be in behaviour as becometh holiness, not false accusers, not given to much wine, teachers of good things;
>
> That they may teach the young women to be sober, to love their husbands, to love their children,
>
> To be discreet, chaste, keepers at home, good, obedient to their own husbands, that the word of God be not blasphemed.

"Now the phrase 'keepers at home,' according to *Strong's Concordance*, is from two Greek words. The first meaning 'a dwelling, a family, a home, or house (hold) or a temple.' The second, meaning a 'guard.' Together they mean: 'a stayer at home, i.e., domestically inclined (a "good housekeeper"); —keeper at home.'[1]

"*The Analytical Greek Lexicon of the New Testament* by Wigram says, '(a watcher) pr. a keeper or guard of a house; a home keeper, stay-at-home, domestic.' "[2]

Emily handed me *Wuest's Expanded Translation of the Greek New Testament.* "Here, June, read Titus 2:3-5 to us out of Wuest's."

> ...aged women likewise, that they be worthy of reverence in their demeanor, not slanderers, not enslaved to much wine, teachers of that which is good, in order that they may train the young women to be fond of their

> husbands, to be fond of their children, to be discreet, chaste, workers at home, kind, in subjection to their own husbands with implicit obedience, in order that the word of God may not be reproachfully spoken of.[3]

"*The Amplified New Testament* uses the word 'homemakers' and concludes by saying: '. . . that the word of God may not be exposed to reproach-blasphemed or discredited.' "[4]

"Aunt Emily, you didn't leave anyone with any doubt about what a keeper at home meant."

"No. Nor did I leave anyone in any doubt about the consequences of what happens when we aren't keepers at home. I think Paul is referring to the whole exhortation when he says, 'that the word of God be not blasphemed.' "

"And we're always grumbling about not having spiritual responsibilities. Aunt Emily, the home is the most important institution in the world and we have the responsibility to guard it, to keep it, and maintain it. That should keep anybody out of mischief, if they see the fullness of it."

"After I taught this lesson, Maureen loaned me a book by Mary Pride called *The Way Home*. I'm strongly admonishing the ladies in the class to read it. She expounds this Titus 2 passage and some others with so much common sense that you'd have to have a screw loose to reject it.

"Here's one last thought," said Emily. "I believe that if all the married women who now work stayed home, our unemployment problems in America would be almost eliminated, the economy would greatly improve, juvenile delinquency would decrease, homosexuality would decrease, crime in general would go down, less marriages would end in divorce, and probably the insane asylums would be less crowded. It's my opinion that many of our social, economic, and spiritual ills have developed, in a good measure, because the keeper of the home is no longer there. 'Nuff said. Let's go on to the second lesson.

"We'll start in Genesis 1 and 2 with the creation of Eve. Notice, God brought all the beasts and fowls which he had made unto Adam for him to name, but none of these creatures were suitable for a partner for Adam; so he put Adam to sleep, and from one of Adam's ribs God made woman and brought her to Adam. Adam recognized in chapter 2 verse 23, that she was:

> . . . bone of my bones, and flesh of my flesh: she shall be called Woman, because she was taken out of Man.
>
> Therefore shall a man leave his father and his mother, and shall cleave unto his wife: and they shall be one flesh.

"Aunt Emily, I understand Martin Luther used to call his wife 'Katie, my rib.' "

"That's where we belong, June—near our husband's heart and under his protective and embracing arm.

"I should put in a little parenthesis here about verse 24; women need to realize when they marry, that they leave Mom and Dad. When a woman marries, she puts herself under a new headship. Her first loyalty is to her husband. If a woman is wrongfully tied to her parents, this can cause conflicts between the woman's parents and her husband that would never occur if she were in her rightful position. If the wife's parents have plans or desires that aren't in agreement with what her husband wants to do, his plans come first. She should sweetly, but firmly, tell her folks that she and her husband have formed a new household over which he is the head and she must follow his leadership.

"I'd like to add another caution here. When things aren't working out real well, especially in a new marriage where the newlyweds are just beginning to see each other's faults and failures, the woman should not go running home to tell her parents that her husband is an unbearable cad. He'll probably mature and change his ways. (We all grow up.) But Mom and Dad may not forget what this terrible fellow did or said to their dear daughter. Years after the cause of the complaint has disappeared, her folks may have a dislike for their son-in-law.

"Incidentally, the same holds true for the girlfriends on whom we unload our problems. When women have complaints about their husbands, they should tell God about it, because He's the only One Who can effect a change anyway. He won't offer us sympathy we shouldn't be getting, nor will He encourage self-pity as our friends and relatives tend to do. Sometimes God never does change the husband; He changes the wife so she can cheerfully accept her husband's faults and failures.

"Let's go on to Genesis 3. This is where Eve got out of her proper position."

"I'm glad Uncle Harold's not here; he'd have too many wise-cracks on this one."

"He wouldn't say much. Eve was deceived. However, when it came to Adam eating of the forbidden fruit, it was not a situation where he was deceived. He knew full well what he was doing. Read verses l-3 for us please."

> Now the serpent was more subtle than any beast of the field which the Lord God had made. And he said unto the woman, Yea, hath God said, Ye shall not eat of every tree of the garden?
>
> And the woman said unto the serpent, We may eat of the fruit of the trees of the garden:
>
> But of the fruit of the tree which is in the midst of the garden, God hath said, Ye shall not eat of it, neither shall ye touch it, lest ye die.

"Was she right in what she answered, June?"

"Not exactly, Aunt Emily; she added something else. God hadn't said anything about touching the tree. But she had to know what God said because she had most of it right."

"God gave the commandment to Adam before Eve was created. In chapter 2 verse l6 and 17 it says:

> And the Lord God commanded the man, saying, Of every tree of the garden thou mayest freely eat:
>
> But of the tree of the knowledge of good and evil, thou shalt not eat of it: for in the day that thou eatest thereof thou shalt surely die.

"You'll notice, June, that God gave the commandment to the man. He was the one responsible for his own actions and those of his wife. God made Eve's husband her authority. God was over Adam. That put her under the authority of both of them. She disobeyed both when she disobeyed the commandment. You noticed that she was not careful with the word of God. She added something to it: some people subtract. Both are very dangerous. When we tamper with the Scripture, or disregard it, we place ourselves on slippery ground. Go ahead and read 3:4 and 5, please."

> And the serpent said unto the woman, Ye shall not surely die:

> For God doth know that in the day ye eat thereof, then your eyes shall be opened, and ye shall be as gods, knowing good and evil.

"He was a liar from the beginning, wasn't he, Aunt Emily?"

"He's still telling the same two lies; he just gives them a little different twist. Today's humanists are teaching reincarnation, and that all men can eventually develop their human potential until they become gods.

"Now then, back to Genesis 3:6. We see that Eve was deceived.

> And when the woman saw that the tree was good for food, and that it was pleasant to the eyes, and a tree to be desired to make one wise, she took of the fruit thereof, and did eat, and gave also unto her husband with her; and he did eat.

"See, there's the lust of the eyes, the lust of the flesh, and the pride of life which is described in I John 2. She doubted God's word, she lusted, and she disobeyed her husband and God. Not only that, but she gave some of the fruit to Adam too. I Timothy 2:14 tells us:

> And Adam was not deceived, but the woman being deceived was in the transgression.

"And in II Corinthians ll:3, it says:

> But I fear, lest by any means, as the serpent beguiled Eve through his subtilty, so your minds should be corrupted from the simplicity that is in Christ.

"Aunt Emily, I think women tend to be more easily deceived than men. God seems to have made females to be naturally more trusting, dependent, and obedient. The male is generally more aggressive and independent. When I took personal evangelism in college, the teacher pointed out that most of the false cults were started by women or their writings. It's interesting, too, that many of those women were divorced a time or two. Obviously, they weren't under the protection of authority."

"You're right, June. The occult groups have an overwhelming female percentage in their leadership, too. It stems, I believe, from the Babylon Mystery Religion. Nimrod, a priest of devil-worship, established a kingdom in the land of Shinar. When he died, his wife, Queen Semiramis, carried on the Babylonian religion and claimed that Nimrod was now the Sun-god.

"When she gave birth to an illegitimate son, Tammuz, she proclaimed that he was Nimrod reborn, and that he was the promised saviour. She claimed that he was supernaturally conceived. You can read the whole story in *Babylon Mystery Religion* by Ralph Woodrow. This Babylonian religion was the foundation for all the pagan religions that followed later throughout the world, both ancient and modern.

"In Judges 2:13 we're told the Israelites 'forsook the Lord, and served Baal and Ashtaroth.' Ashtaroth is the mother goddess; Baal was her son. Jezebel and Athaliah were wicked queens in Israel who encouraged the people to worship Baal.

"O.K., let's see what happened to Adam and Eve. Their eyes were opened, all right; and when God came to speak with them, they hid themselves. When God questioned them, Adam blamed Eve and Eve blamed the serpent. Let's read it—verses 12 and 13 of Genesis 3:

> And the man said, The woman whom thou gavest to be with me, she gave me of the tree, and I did eat.
>
> And the Lord God said unto the woman, What is this that thou hast done? And the woman said, The serpent beguiled me, and I did eat.

"In verses 14 and 15, God cursed the serpent. Now let's read what he said to Eve in verse 16. You read that for us, please."

> Unto the woman he said, I will greatly multiply thy sorrow and thy conception; in sorrow thou shalt bring forth children; and thy desire shall be to thy husband, and he shall rule over thee.

"Let's see now what God says to Adam. I'll read 17:

> And unto Adam he said, Because thou hast harkened unto the voice of thy wife, and hast eaten of the tree, of which I commanded thee, saying, Thou shalt not eat of it: cursed is the ground for thy sake; in sorrow shalt thou eat of it all the days of thy life;

"Then God continues with Adam's curse and puts them out of the garden of Eden. Adam was cursed because he obeyed the voice of his wife instead of God's voice. Satan still tries to get to men through women. God's handmaidens must be careful to keep themselves in a proper position under authority so they can't be used of the Devil to destroy their husbands. Many times people will look at a broken marriage and surmise that because the husband drinks or has run off with another woman, the blame rests on his shoulders, and sometimes it should, but often that seemingly sweet little woman drove him to it by constant criticism or bedroom blackmail."

"Aunt Emily, are you saying that a woman is never to be in a position of authority?"

"No, every believer is under authority before he can be in a position of authority over someone else. The order begins with God."

Emily reached for my notebook and began drawing a diagram.

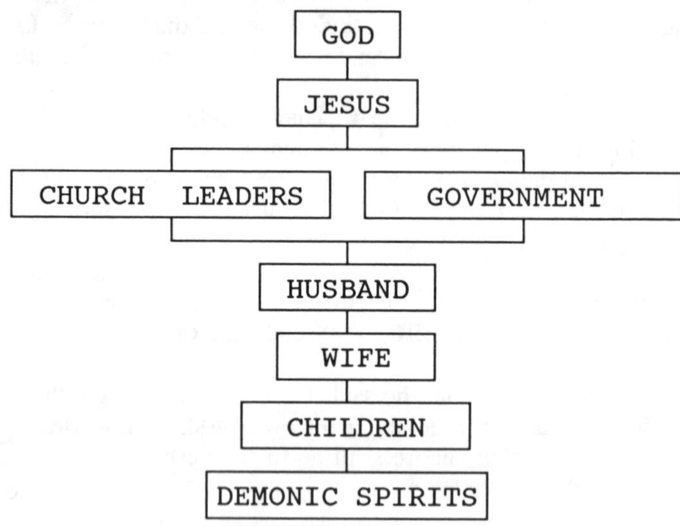


"Now please don't misunderstand my diagram here. Demonic spirits are under the authority of the Father and the Son, but when the Lord gave His disciples power and authority over all devils in Luke 9:1, I believe that includes today's believers too. We come in His name and authority (like a policeman uses his badge). And we come in the power of the Holy Spirit. Even children who are Christians, and appropriate this authority, can bind up evil spirits and cast them out.

"However, when we're out from under the authority God places over us, we no longer have the same strength of authority to wield against demonic powers either. God puts every person under authority. Even Jesus was under authority. The only time we disobey God's appointed authority is when the person in authority definitely tells us to disobey God.

"In Acts the disciples were told plainly by the Lord to preach the Gospel. The religious rulers commanded them to stop. Peter and John answered them, 'Whether it be right in the sight of God to hearken unto you more than to God judge ye.' So they preached. When the religious leaders confronted them again, they replied, 'We ought to obey God rather than men.' "

Emily continued, "Some women just blindly obey everything their husbands tell them to do regardless of what the word of God says—abortion, lying for him, perversion, all sorts of sin."

"What should she do, Aunt Emily?"

"First, figure out why he's asking her to do the wrong thing. For example, oral sex. This is part of sodomy—abnormal sex—which is being pushed upon society by the humanistic crowd. And, I might add, is opening up many marriages to the entrance of evil spirits. I believe God has cursed this practice with Herpes II and A.I.D.S.

"Perhaps the husband senses that his wife doesn't enjoy sex, so he's trying to find some way to interest and excite her. He's heard the fellows at work talk or he's read something that makes him think oral sex will give their relationship new zip. She needs to communicate to him her love and discuss it frankly and openly, letting him know that she feels it is wrong, and it takes away from the expression of their love rather than adding to it."

"It chills her rather than thrills her."

"Exactly. However, she must not approach him in anger or criticism, but with a sincere desire to improve their relationship, never letting him doubt her love. After all, this may have been his purpose—to improve their relationship. Later, when we talk about the ministry of our bodies, I'll give you a list of books that will help your ladies become better lovers."

"Great! I've looked in the library, but they all seem to be written by dirty old men (or dirty old women). I glance through a book and put it back on the self. Some of the world's people are really sick when it comes to sex. I'd be ashamed to check out most of those books at the desk."

"Back to authority," continued Emily. "If a woman is under the authority of her husband, she is also under his protective covering.

That's one reason we need to pray for those in authority over us. I liked the phrase you used a little bit ago—under the protection of authority. This is why a woman wears a hat when she's praying or prophesying, and a man takes off his hat. Turn to I Corinthians 11:3-16. You read it, please."

> But I would have you know, that the head of every man is Christ; and the head of the woman is the man; and the head of Christ is God.
>
> Every man praying or prophesying, having his head covered, dishonoreth his head.
>
> But every woman that prayeth or prophesieth with her head uncovered dishonoreth her head: for that is even all one as if she were shaven.
>
> For if the woman be not covered, let her also be shorn: but if it be a shame for a woman to be shorn or shaven, let her be covered.
>
> For a man indeed ought not to cover his head, forasmuch as he is the image and glory of God: but the woman is the glory of the man.
>
> For the man is not of the woman; but the woman of the man.
>
> Neither was the man created for the woman; but the woman for the man.
>
> For this cause ought the woman to have power on her head because of the angels.
>
> Nevertheless neither is the man without the woman, neither the woman without the man, in the Lord.
>
> For as the woman is of the man, even so is the man also by the woman; but all things of God.
>
> Judge in yourselves: is it comely that a woman pray unto God uncovered?
>
> Doth not even nature itself teach you, that, if a man have long hair, it is a shame unto him?
>
> But if a woman have long hair, it is a glory to her: for her hair is given her for a covering.
>
> But if any man seem to be contentious, we have no such custom, neither the churches of God.

"Aunt Emily, some churches teach that a woman's hair is her covering."

"Have you ever noticed that some of those same churches have women preaching, women leading the Sunday school, and leading the singing, while the men sit back? If there *are* any men, that is."

"Now that you mention it . . . "

"I believe women should have long hair, June, just as women should wear clothes which distinguish them from men. A woman's hair is her glory. The head covering here, however, I believe, is a hat, or scarf of one variety or another. The word is *veil.* The principle is to cover her head as a symbol that her husband is her protective covering; she's under his authority. It's an outward witness to everyone, including good and evil spirits that she's under his covering. You'll also notice that in all the churches, the men take off their hats when they pray. They don't say, 'My hair is short, so my head is uncovered.' By the same token, I don't think a woman can say, 'my hair is long, so my head is covered.' I think women fight against covering their heads because there's an evil spirit of Jezebel involved."

"A spirit of Jezebel?"

"Yes. Oh, there goes our timer for the beans. Would you please move the canner off the burner? I have a tract on Jezebel. I'll go find it."

Emily was back before I sat down again. "You must have your books in better order than mine; it didn't take you long."

"This tract is from Win Worley's book, *Conquering the Host of Hell.* It's a little long, but I read it to the class as part of this lesson. It's entitled *The Curse of Jezebel.* Let me just read it to you:

> Isaiah 3:12 *"As for my people, children are their oppressors, and women rule over them. O my people, they which lead thee cause thee to err, and destroy the way of thy paths."*
>
> Isaiah wrote these words hundreds of years ago, but it is aptly descriptive of a largely matriarchal society we have had in America for over two generation. Female dominance has heavily influenced, and at times controlled, the social and spiritual sectors of life. The unfortunate results of this are clearly apparent in families, churches and the government.
>
> When children are reared in an atmosphere of fear, insecurity and frustration, families are sapped of strength. These are the by-products of the systematic emasculation of men in the social, spiritual and even the physical realms.

There is a driving force operating through female dominance which has turned the churches into powerless groups filled with discord, slander and corruption. This same force has invaded the fields of finance, business and religion, expressing itself in outright sorcery and witchcraft, affecting every strata of society. Because of the years of Jezebelic leavening, men have become as adept as women in utilizing and developing this power to manipulate and control people.

The Jezebel influence is rooted in witchcraft and causes women to forsake the protection and place given them in God's word. There is also a corresponding or complementary spirit to Jezebel which we call the Ahab spirit. This brings destruction of the family priesthood, laziness and sluggishness in males who allow females to dominate and control, but despise and hate them for it.

The Ahab spirit, rooted in the Destruction of the Family Priesthood, causes a man to forsake his responsibilities as the head of the household. He will not only refuse to take the spiritual headship, but often will not take responsibility for working to make the living for the wife and children. He has overlooked the spiritual admonition that a man who does not work should not eat (II Thessalonians 3:10), and that if a man fails to provide for his own, he has denied the faith and is worse than an infidel (I Timothy 5:8). A man is to provide both spiritual and material security for his family. If he cannot or will not, he is in trouble with God. As the spiritual umbrella of protection for his wife and children, he is charged with the demanding role of **prophet** and **priest** for them.

If girls were more carefully taught about the divine order of the home and how vital it is that a man be a man of God over his family, they would choose much more carefully in the matter of a mate. Bad and hasty choices in this area have left many women with long and bitter experiences that last for years and, except for the intervention of God, they are never changed. Many marry in haste and repent at leisure.

Some men gravitate toward a woman with Jezebellian spirits. The reason for this is because they feel that she is hard and can take any punishment or abuse they want to dish out. If she were soft, feminine and submissive, it would make them feel terrible when they drank, committed adultery or otherwise ignored commitments to her. To ease their conscience they seek a female with these spirits of dominance and they can rationalize (falsely) that she is only getting what she deserves when they choose to mistreat and violate her confidence. Note how many Jezebellian women have attracted this type of male. They live their whole lives in unhappiness, frustration and bitter disappointment.

These spiritual forces do their most deadly and telling damage when they are able to work covertly, undetected. It is a sad fact that those most active in this maneuvering for control are usually oblivious to the fact that they themselves are being controlled and driven.

Hopefully those who read this will be alerted to the danger by seeing the connection between matriarchism and witchcraft. It is not intended as an attack on women, but to expose the workings of the enemy to ensnare, degrade and enslave them.

In the Bible, Queen Jezebel is presented as a prime example of female dominance and witchcraft (I Kings 16:22; II Kings 9). In Revelation 2:18-29, the false prophetess of Thyatira is labelled as Jezebel. Both these women are characterized by their attempts to control those around them through false teachings and the use of occult power. Each paraded her schemes under the cover of religion and "good" motives. Christian men and women today are often deceived and driven by the religious pretensions of these demonic forces. There are also multitudes snared in false religious cult systems. The end result in either case is always evil and disastrous.

Sorcery is a specific type of witchcraft used to gain one's own ends through manipulative spiritual power. It operates through the mind and ego of the sorcerer and is carried out by spirits of witchcraft. Mind control spirits work to subject the mind, the emotions, will and body to the control and whims of the sorcerer.

With her wiles and witchcraft Queen Jezebel of Israel persuaded her husband to allow her to usurp authority in the kingdom. By doing this he sold himself into her spiritual whoredom (I Kings 21:4-10, 20, 25; II Kings 9:22). In Thyatira, Jezebel was judged because her thoughts, feelings and purposes are declared wrong in the sight of God (Revelation 2:20-23 **Amplified New Testament**). Just as Satan sought worship for himself, these women worked to become the center of worship and attention, and demanded obedience to their every command. Knowingly or unknowingly sorcery is always used to bring worship and adoration to the sorcerer.

Just as Satan used questions to challenge the validity of God's Word and create doubts (i.e., in Eden, "Yea and did God say . . . ?"; to Jesus, "If thou be the Son of God . . . ") so those moved by the Jezebelic demons still employ the same tactics. Directly or indirectly, through attitudes, emotions and insinuations, they question those around them. This is calculated to cause doubt about a person's manhood, worth and ability.

A woman may tell her husband that if he were a **real** man he would be able to make more money. Or she might be more subtle and just sigh that it would be nice to have this or that—but, of course, they cannot afford it. The man, already sensitive and feeling inadequate because of the need for more money, will be pressured to secure what his wife wants. Next in the campaign of intimidation and insinuation is the spoken or implied statement that if he really loved her he would provide for her needs. Often she determines to go to work because of dissatisfaction with her husband's provision.

These maneuvers can bring incredible pressure on the man and force him to strike out to prove his own worth and preserve his self-respect. In a woman driven by the Jezebel spirits there is no satiating of her constant "needs" and endless demands. Eventually, disgusted and frustrated, the husband is driven into a life of defeat and hopelessness by his wife's ceaseless demands and complaints. Angrily he may agree to her going to work in order to satisfy her appetite for the things he cannot supply. He hopes this will pacify her. She increasingly assumes control and direction of the finances in the family. As the discouraged husband retreats from responsibility, he makes the most tragic abdication of all, that of spiritual head of the house and family.

The husband's life becomes a series of quiet but furious refusals to become involved. At home he winces under her proud looks, sharp tongue, emotional outbursts, and bedroom blackmail. Increasingly he retreats into newspapers, sleep, alcohol, work, TV, adultery, or some other area outside the home, striving to find appreciation and satisfaction.

To prove his manhood and escape her emasculating blows to his male ego, he may withdraw physically from his wife. If she becomes repulsive to him with her driving, ranting and accusing, he often becomes impotent. The sex drive, strong though it is, can be blunted by such a barrage. No matter what he does, it is not enough, nor is it done right. If he attends church, he seldom does more than sit back, fearful of the sharp and critical tongue of his wife. She speaks out for the family in spiritual matters and he becomes more silent.

Children reared in this kind of atmosphere will grow up with the same desires to manipulate the lives of those around them. Divorced women many times have strong Jezebel spirits. The same spirit is obviously at work in the lives of many who are not divorced but whose marriages are filled with strife and whose children are full of rebellion.

The pattern of rebellion of the mother against the authority of the father in the home strongly influences the children to become rebels. Continuous complaining and pointing out every weakness of the husband undermines the children's respect for him. This in turn becomes a source of deep-rooted conflict and upset to the children.

The Jezebel spirit does not always assume a brash, bossy and aggressive stance, openly overbearing or dominant. There is a more subtle manifestation. The woman is outwardly sweet and unassuming, a picture of demure helplessness and feminine flutterings. Actually, there is a mailed fist of fiercest determination and rebellion under that velvet glove. There is not a helpless bone in her delicate body! She is just as determined to have her own way as the most openly rebellious female, and is an expert in the art of bedroom blackmail. What she actually does is to create disgust in the males of her life for her conniving ways.

Often a woman will complain about her husband with such finesse that it does not seem to be that. For example she may sweetly remark, "Well, I've been wanting this done for months, but your Dad is so busy that he doesn't have time to fix it." This thinly veiled criticism is interpreted by the children to mean that he does not care about the needs of the family, especially longsuffering Mama. Repeated over a period of years, this practice can damage the family structure. The wife adopts a "sweet" martyr attitude in order to draw attention to herself as the injured party.

Another way the spirits drive is to arrange for the husband never to have any rest or relaxation from her demands on his time and attention. She works constantly to cause him to feel guilty and neglectful when he devotes himself to being a hard worker to make a living. If the money is sufficient, there is constant whining about the time spent at work. She comes up with endless projects at home, many of which should be handled by her, to drain him of all spare time and energy. She evidently never read of the woman who "looketh well to the ways of her household, and eateth not the bread of idleness" (Proverbs 31:27).

False sickness is another convenient way of dodging responsibility and gaining sympathy at the same time. If the husband is tired and wishes to relax, he is lazy. If he wants to postpone something because he is weary, then he is deliberately neglecting the needs of his family. Many women have this procedure down to a science and keep their husbands in a constant state of turmoil, guilt and weariness, often to cover the fact that they have neglected their own duties at home.

A man has a strong sense of right and wrong, and has fought with his conscience all his life. By becoming his conscience, she provokes endless battles with him. What she needs is to bring her spirit under control and to become a meek and quiet wife as the Word declares. (I Peter 3:1-6).

Bedroom blackmail and rationing are another form of the Jezebellian strategy. Unfortunate is the man who will give in to this sort of thing. This situation is the source of much marital discord. Many women use sex as a tool to get their own way and bargain with their husbands until the men feel as if they were dealing with a prostitute. If she is displeased, she will communicate her sullen rebellion, even in submission, and her husband certainly finds no satisfaction in such a strained episode. Without a word she can severely wound his male ego, often causing him to become impotent with her and raising serious doubts in his own mind about his virility. This impotence is a cross which has driven many a man to other women, drink and other pursuits to drown out the bitter defeat he feels with the woman he loves.

She is defeating her purpose. In attempting to bind him closer to herself, control and direct him, she forces him to rebel and seek satisfaction elsewhere. The morsel of sex which he receives from her is so degrading to him personally that it becomes repulsive and, far from eager anticipation, he begins to dread and shun such contact. The wife will never win in this sort of contest but always loses far more than any concession she may wring from her husband.

Many times Christian women will **talk** much about submission and obedience to their husbands, but both husbands and children know that it is all just talk. When she asks her husband what she should do and he answers the way she wants, fine and good. If not, then a series of determined maneuvers begin, calculated to force him to change his decision. She has not the slightest inclination to cheerfully submit to his judgment and her campaign to have her own way in the matter will eventually provoke him into anger. She then "meekly" points out that she can never talk to him about anything without his becoming argumentative. Rather than to believe that God will give her husband wisdom to guide the family because of his position of authority and her praying for him, she sets about to accomplish things in her own devious ways. This constant maneuvering and pressuring is sensed and resented by all the males in the household and leads to many problems.

The spirit of Jezebel enters the family situation wherever God's order of authority is either not known or ignored. God's order is basically simple: The authority of man is Christ; the authority of women is man; the authority of Christ is God (I Corinthians 11:3). Friends, death, circumstances, the economy, war, famine, nor anything else can change the fact that the head of every woman is man, no more than they would change the fact that God is the head of Christ. Any tampering with God's structuring of family authority will open the women and children to satanic attack.

When a woman chooses or is seemingly forced into headship of the family, she is put in a position for which God has not fitted her; body, soul or spirit. Because she is the weaker vessel (I Peter 3:7) when she is put into the place of authority she has no choice but to utilize methods and techniques of securing dominance which are not approved of God. Rebellion is as the sin of witchcraft (I Samuel 15:23) and when a woman usurps authority in a man's place, no matter how noble the motivation, she ends up using occult power to achieve her ends.

An earthly and natural reaction is to take authority from necessity. Because a woman is not designed mentally, physically or spiritually to wield authority, her actions soon become sensual. Because of her limitations she is forced to connive and manipulate to control those around her, resorting to tears, anger, pouting and fake sickness to coerce. At this point her actions become demonic, controlled by demons, because she is out of the will of God (James 3:15). The woman in rebellion will produce rebellious children, no matter how sincerely she may rationalize her position. This is one of the chief reasons for this generation of rebels in America, filled with lawlessness and anarchy.

Of course there are cases where women are thrown into the headship of the family because of death or legitimate separation from their husbands. In these instances God's Word provides covering for them through remarriage, the elders and pastors of the churches, and, in some cases, through a male relative.

Discipline of the children is an area where the Jezebel influence is often noticeable. Bible instructions direct parents to take the rod of correction and drive foolishness far from the heart of the child (Proverbs 22:15). Our witchcraft influenced society urges instead that children be bribed, manipulated, and tricked into obedience. "If you loved me, you would not do such and such" is a common approach. Used repeatedly on a child, he is put under constant pressure to prove his love. This victim is never sure if his love is believed and accepted. This kind of badgering can produce spiritual and physical problems and can open the door to a spirit which makes it difficult or impossible to give or receive love.

Strong emotions are another form of Jezebellic discipline. Threatened with storms of weeping, recriminations or great fits of anger, a family can be forced under a control spirit. The demons of Fear, Failure and Rejection plague them and they learn that to obey every whim is better than to suffer constant outbursts.

Another cruel method of control is a silence which is sort of hypnotic control, or charming. The person given this treatment is often left guessing what he has done and must bend every effort to discover how he has offended. Again this makes the one exercising the control spirit the center of attention and the one who must be mollified.

Often businesses are invaded by the Jezebellic control spirits. It was inevitable that this happen in a society so structured and controlled by this evil influence. Routinely many companies utilize handwriting analysis and astrology in conjunction with hiring workers. Preplanned sales presentation often utilize ESP and Mental Telepathy to anticipate and program customer reaction. God's Word says that the Great Whore system of the end times will be run by merchants who will deceive the nations by their **sorceries** (Revelation 18:23). As we move deeper into an intensely computerized society, it is not hard to see that we are moving closer to this period.

Jezebel spirits have done some of their most evil work in the spiritual realm. Whole churches are under the domination and control of a few powerful families and/or personalities. They attempt to control and dictate every move pastors and other spiritual leaders make. This form of pressure leads to resignations by thousands of discouraged pastors each year. Instead of honoring and obeying their shepherds (Hebrews 13:17) the flock becomes a grief to him. The more spiritually minded a church grows, the more dangerous is the operation of the Jezebel spirits.

Often persons with the Jezebellic control spirits will deceive persons seeking God's will by the use of soulish prophecy. These spirits will always seek to beguile people

**to a person** and his own peculiar teachings rather than to center on Jesus Christ. One tactic is to keep seeking souls in spiritual suspense by use of counterfeit spiritual gifts, enchanting people to stay with them and their causes. They promote the idea that they are the "spiritual" ones. God's Word declares that one who speaks from **himself** seeks his own glory and/or worship (John 16:13,14). Unfortunately, much that passes for "word of knowledge" and "word of wisdom" could just as well be called charismatic fortune telling!

The effects of unsuspected practicing of witchcraft are just as disastrous as open contact with the occult. Confusion, suicide, spiritual blindness, loss of children and broken homes are a few by-products. Impotence in husbands, frigidity in wives, doubts and fears, all work together to prevent and destroy any meaningful and satisfying sexual relationship. Remember the enemy comes to steal, to kill, and to destroy.

Persons driven by Jezebellic spirits can be recognized (James 3:13-18). They are motivated and driven by dominance, not meekness and wisdom. Surrounded by bitter envyings in home and churches, the lives of those closest to them will stay in a state of constant confusion. There will be other evil works manifested, including rebellion. Breaking the laws of man, backbiting and slander are often present.

Always we must check for the fruit of the Holy Spirit (Galatians 5:22) in lives and ministries. If the wrong fruit is being produced, then the wisdom by which they are operating began in the natural and became an extension of a desire for power and attention. Entrance of a Jezebellic spirit gives demonic drawing power, a beguiling power, not of the Lord. Charisma given by the Holy Spirit attracts people to Christ and freedom. Satanic powers emphasize a personality and create bondage. Unfortunates snared in such bondage will desire freedom and then suffer guilt for having felt disloyal.

Still another characteristic of persons under a Jezebellic control spirit is an inability to designate authority. Rather than to allow persons under them to work, they will constantly interfere and hinder, often doing the work themselves trying to demonstrate incompetence in others. Driven to control, dominate and arrange the lives of all close to them, these people thrive on keeping all those around them on edge and nervous.

A victim of any one or a combination of these pressures for any length of time will be crippled in some way. They are dulled by confusion, tormented by fears, and often become so indecisive that they have trouble making the simplest decisions. Doubts and apprehension will many times keep them spiritually immature and weak.

God has given inner warning against submitting to this insidious influence. Jehoshaphat had a check in his spirit about an alliance with Ahab (I Kings 22) and called for a word from the Lord. Jezebel's lying prophets brought a false prediction of victory. Unsatisfied, Jehoshaphat asked for a prophet of the Lord and Micaiah came, warning of lying spirits in the false prophets. By believing a lie Ahab paid with his life and Jehoshaphat saw his armies humiliated in defeat. God warns that if we do not love the truth, God will cause belief in a lie (II Thessalonians 2:9-12). If we submit to bondage and unscriptural authorities not ordained of God we are asking to be overcome by a delusion.

Although this spirit has affected men, it still seems to go to the worst extremes in women. In the spirit of every man (saved or unsaved) there is the knowledge that the woman was deceived in the Garden, not the man. Adam was drawn into sin by his wife and because of this, men hesitate and rebel against a woman seeking to lead or usurp authority over them. They may react and attempt to escape through over-indulgence in sports, business or adultery but the voice of the law remains true (I Timothy 2:11-15; Romans 2:14,15).

This is the reason why so many lost husbands refuse to accept Christ and others resist receiving the baptism of Jesus in the Holy Spirit. Militant pushing by their mates turns them off. Wives who bombard with tapes, books, and testimonies seeking to force them to do what is right almost always fail. Certainly their approach is unscriptural. Instinctively the male knows that spiritual leadership is a masculine prerogative. Scripture is clear that an unbelieving husband is to be won by the quiet and obedient submission of his wife, as he sees her godly life and walk. A woman must be and do rather than to talk the way of God if she wants to see in her family the realization of her heart's desire (Psalm 37:4,5: I Peter 3:1,2).

The wicked bondage of Jezebellic spirits can be broken only by an Elijah ministry. These demonic forces hate and fear the ministries of the Elijahs, for these men have successfully resisted both physical and spiritual seduction of Jezebel. Because they cannot be bought by the clever pretensions and wiles of the enemy they are hated and slandered as troublemakers and disturbers—the enemy of those they are sent to rescue (I Kings 18:17,18; 21:20). Only by the demolishing of the strongholds of Jezebel can God's rightful authority be reestablished.

In Malachi 4:5-6, God says the hearts of the **fathers** (not the mothers) will be turned to the children by this Elijah ministry. Preachers of this truth will help men everywhere to realize their responsibility to take their place as prophet and priest in the family unit, sheltering and protecting wives and children. Women will be relieved of the strain and struggle of attempting to pull leadership loads for which God did not design them. As men take their rightful place to love, cherish and protect, wives will find the blessing and fulfillment which God intended for them. In a very real sense it behooves wives to pray for their husbands to come under proper spiritual leadership and authority.

Oftentimes a woman will pray for years for the Lord to bring her husband to Himself and will faithfully request others to pray for him. Seldom does she realize that when God does answer and galvanize the man into action, He will immediately groom him to be the head of the house. Instead of a spiritual cripple and weak dependent, a wife is faced with a strong and rapidly growing rival who will easily outdistance her in spiritual matters **if** he really applies himself. Due to God's authority structure, the man will be given wisdom and knowledge to equip him for leadership. Many a woman caught in this whirlwind of change has wondered if it is fair for God to make such sweeping changes and upset the status quo. Very often traits of dominance and masculine protest, cleverly concealed for years, will rear up in rebellion revealing their presence at this time.

Isaiah 3 and 4 warns sternly of judgment which will fall upon those resisting the establishment of God's order. Rebellious women will be shamed by baldness and have their secret parts uncovered. Could this be a reference to the epidemic proportions of female cancer and chemotherapy which often results in baldness? In Isaiah 3:24 the prophet speaks of a stench and burning where there had been perfume. Again the reference is strikingly similar to some common symptoms of cancer.

Isaiah 4:1,2 speaks of a time when all will repent and seek the path of Scriptural submission. In the church today God is calling for a return to Biblical submission, discipleship and restoration. If you have been practicing unsuspected witchcraft, dominating husband, pastor, children, friends, or prayer group, repent at once and renounce this evil force in Jesus' name. If you realize that you have been under this type of bondage for any length of time, renounce it at once and sever the wicked cords which bind you in unscriptural servitude to the one who dominates you.

Here is a prayer which has been helpful to free many: Father, I come to you in the name of Jesus Christ, the Shepherd of my soul. I confess and renounce as sin everything I have ever done to manipulate, dominate and control other people. I hate and renounce the foul Jezebellic spirits and claim deliverance from them in Jesus' name (Psalm 139).

Because Jesus died on the cross for my sins and became a curse for me, blotting out the handwriting of ordinances which were against me, I declare every curse having to do with the Jezebellic spirits to be broken from whatever source, even back to seven generations on both sides of my family.

I also ask Father, that You sever any ties of bondage which may exist between me and those who have practiced sorcery against me.

Direct me to the undershepherd You have ordained for me, and above all else, help me to come into true submission to You, Father. Jesus said: *"Those who believe in Me, in my name shall they cast out demons."* I am a believer, and in Jesus' name I now command all spirits

> associated with the Jezebellic influence to leave me now and set me completely free in Jesus' name, Amen.
>
> —Based on a tract: "The Jezebel Influence" by Jim Croft.

"Well, that's it," said Emily.

"Wow! Aunt Emily, that could leave someone in shock!"

"It's sort of like a sledge hammer, isn't it? Or more Scripturally, a battle axe."

"I have a question, Aunt Emily. What about Deborah? She led the whole Israelite army."

"Did she? As a prophetess, she told Barak to go, but he refused to go without her. Look what she says. It's in Judges 4:9:

> And she said, I will surely go with thee: notwithstanding the journey that thou takest shall not be for thine honour; for the Lord shall sell Sisera into the hand of a woman . . . .

"This was prophetic. Sisera fled on foot with Barak pursuing, but a woman named Jael killed him in her tent. I don't want to read into the story something that isn't there, but it does seem to indicate that because he insisted on Deborah's accompaniment, he lost the honor of destroying God's enemy. Deborah went with him, but she didn't enter the battle when they got there. She just told him what God said. Look at verse 14:

> And Deborah said unto Barak, Up; for this is the day in which the Lord hath delivered Sisera into thine hand: is not the Lord gone out before thee? So Barak went down from mount Tabor, and ten thousand men after him.

"I guess Deborah gave him moral support, sort of like when Israel would take the ark into battle—some reminder of God's presence with them. You might say she went as a chaplain, because she was a prophetess and knew the voice of God. Remember, she sat and judged the people before Barak is mentioned. Deborah called for him and told him God said to get 10,000 soldiers and go fight Sisera."

"Well, doesn't being a prophetess and a judge mean she was in a place of spiritual leadership?"

"At the surface it may look that way. However, if you take the Scripture as a whole, it's clear that God does not want the women in positions of leadership. He did not design them for that role and from His viewpoint it's a shame when women take the lead, whether it be the nation, the Church, or the home. I really don't see Deborah leading anyone. She is described as the wife of Lapidoth so she seemed to be in submission in her home. As a prophetess, Deborah knew God, He spoke through her, and she was able to tell people what God said. I don't think the Scripture explicitly says a judge was a ruler. A judge, as I see it, told people what was right and wrong from God's viewpoint. And some of them went out and executed God's judgement upon Israel's enemies such as Sampson, Ehud, and Gideon. Judges 17:6 says:

> In those days there was no king in Israel, but every man did that which was right in his own eyes.

"If more of our modern-day judges would ask God what He thought about the cases they decided, as Deborah no doubt did, instead of making their bench a throne, our country would probably experience the blessing of God that Israel saw when Deborah was judge.

Many people have a misconception of prophecy. They think that to prophesy means to preach or teach, but in I Timothy 2:12-14 Paul says:

> I suffer not a woman to teach, nor to usurp authority over the man, but to be in silence.
>
> For Adam was first formed, then Eve.
>
> And Adam was not deceived, but the woman being deceived was in the transgression.

"Women are not to teach, yet they can pray or prophesy (I Cor. 11:5). When men or women prophesy, they tell forth the mind of God, using their tongue and their own language, but not their own thoughts. One who prophesies speaks forth the word of God with God's authority, in the power of the Holy Spirit; but true prophecy does not proceed out of the prophet's own heart or his own spirit. Look at Ezekiel 13:1-4:

> And the word of the Lord came unto me, saying,
>
> Son of man, prophesy against the prophets of Israel that prophesy, and say thou unto them that prophesy out of their own hearts, Hear ye the word of the Lord;

> Thus saith the Lord God; Woe unto the foolish prophets, that follow their own spirit, and have seen nothing!

"Now verse 7:

> Have ye not seen a vain vision, and have ye not spoken a lying divination, whereas ye say, The Lord saith it; albeit I have not spoken?

"Now skip down to verse 17; this pertains to women prophetesses. Please read that for us, June."

> Likewise, thou son of man, set thy face against the daughters of thy people, which prophesy out of their own heart; and prophesy thou against them,

"If you read the rest of this chapter, you'll see that these women were involved in making witchcraft amulets and ensnaring the souls of God's people. The Devil always counterfeits the way God does things. He tries to confuse and turn people aside from the truth. That's why Paul set up guidelines for prophecy in I Corinthians 14. In verse 29 he says, 'Let the prophets speak two or three, and let the other judge.' If the prophecy comes forth and the men discern that it was not from God, but from the person's own heart or spirit, they are to speak up and say so.

"Look in verse 34 of that same chapter. Read verses 34 and 35 for us, please."

> Let your women keep silence in the churches: for it is not permitted unto them to speak; but they are commanded to be under obedience, as also saith the law.
>
> And if they will learn anything, let them ask their husbands at home: for it is a shame for women to speak in the church.

"In chapter 11 Paul tells the women they can pray or prophecy with their heads covered. In chapter 14, he says they are not to speak. It appears like a contradiction, but it's not when you understand the nature of prophecy. Teaching comes forth from your own heart and spirit—a product of your study of the Word and fellowship with the

Lord. Prophecy by-passes the human heart and spirit—if it's true prophecy.

"So you're saying that prophecy comes from the mind of God through the mouth of the prophet by the gift of the Holy Spirit."

"Yes, but the 'spirit of the prophet is subject to the prophet.' He's not just taken over (if he is, it's an unholy spirit), but his own thinking process is set aside. It's as though he's standing to the side listening to what he's saying.

"Here, let me read you a few excerpts from *Vine's Expository Dictionary of New Testament Words* concerning prophecy. He believes that prophecy passed away with the completion of the cannon of Scripture, but he makes clear the distinction between teaching and prophecy:

> ... Prophecy is not necessarily, nor even primarily fore-telling. It is the declaration of that which cannot be known by natural means, Matt. 26:68, it is the forth-telling of the will of God whether with reference to the past, the present, or the future, ...
>
> ..................................................
>
> ... Whereas the message of the prophet was a direct revelation of the mind of God for the occasion, the message of the teacher is gathered from the completed revelation contained in the Scriptures.[5]

"A woman is more easily deceived because of the very nature God gave her; therefore God doesn't want her to teach. Teaching puts her in a position of leadership, which He also doesn't want. Even though the feminists argue that women should be allowed to pastor churches, there is no Scriptural way for a woman to be an overseer. How can a woman be the husband of one wife, which is one of the qualifications of an elder?"

"What about teaching women and children?"

"That's fine. Paul said, as we read just a little while ago, that the older women should teach the younger women. He was also specific about *what* they were to teach them.

"Can you picture what would happen in this country if the women in the Church would stop trying to take over the leadership of the congregation and got behind the men with real powerful prayer and encouragement?

"If the older women would teach the younger women how to be good wives and mothers, the church would attract a lot of troubled families who desperately need this example. And if the older women taught the younger women how to provide the home environment in which both the wives and their husbands could be the ministers of reconciliation that God intended for them to be, we might see revival yet. If the family in America dies, as the humanists are hoping and planning, the older women will have to accept part of the blame because they did not fulfill their God-given mission.

"In the hospitality of the home, the woman, as well as her husband, may be able to share something to win a person to the Lord or to edify a believer. It was both Aquilla and Pricilla who expounded unto Apollos, the preacher, the way of God more perfectly (Acts 19:26).

"However, women are not to teach in the general meeting of the church where men are present and where we would be supplanting them were we to teach. In fact, on the basis of I Corinthians 14:34 and 35, I'm wondering whether we women should also confine our praying and prophesying to situations outside of the general Church meeting. I'm still thinking on that one."

"Aunt Emily, are you purposely avoiding the word *preach*? You keep using the word *teach*."

"*Preach* means to publish or proclaim the good news of the Gospel as a herald. That's my condensation of what *Vine's Expository Dictionary of New Testament Words* says about the word *preach*. The women who discovered the empty tomb ran back to the disciples and proclaimed the good news. If Vine's definitions are correct, we can't say women can't preach. How or where they preach, however, is another issue. They are to keep silent in the Church meeting.

"Teaching, on the other hand, means to instruct or impart knowledge—sometimes to disciple. There is a clear implication that the one doing the teaching is superior in knowledge to the one being taught.

"Let's just examine that from a common sense viewpoint aside from what the Scripture says. Men somehow know, without being told, that the man is to be in a leadership position. If we are perceptive at all, we will observe that most men resent women teaching them anything. They may tend to reject what the woman is teaching simply because it is being taught by a woman. Let's be realistic; if you have women teaching in the Church, you'll have a congregation comprised mostly of women. The men are not readily going to come and be led by women. You've probably heard men say that they feel that church is for the old folks, women, and children. If you have a church where the men do all the teaching, the church is packed with men, but the women come as well. Would a godly woman want to drive men from the church?

"Let the woman exercise her ability to teach by home schooling. If every godly woman would teach her children the three R's and God's truth instead of sending them off to humanistic government schools, we could at least count on a major revival in the next generation. That's what Susanna Wesley did. She was the mother of John and Charles Wesley. She played a major part in the revival that swept England and America. By the way, she had nineteen children."

"I feel inadequate. No, I'll be more positive; I feel challenged!"

"Let's get back to your question about Deborah. She did not lead Israel to battle; Barak did. Hers was a supportive role as a prophetess. She's not even mentioned with Barak in the Hebrews ll 'Hall of Faith,' although Rahab and Sara are included in this list of faithful people. I'm not saying Deborah was not a great woman; she was. And I'm not downplaying her ministry either. It was because she could communicate to God's people the Word of the Lord that Israel had peace for forty years. What I am saying is that the Lord intended for Barak to lead the people to battle; that's why He spoke through Deborah telling him to go. It is very clear in the Scripture that God's will is for men to lead and for the women to support their leadership.

"Why so-called 'Christian feminists' are forever pushing God to acquiesce His already revealed will is beyond my understanding. God *will* speak and do His will. If he can't find an obedient and willing servant through whom He can work, He can send an angel, a donkey, or even cause the rocks to cry out.

"Even if it were shown that Deborah was in a position of leadership," said Emily, "it was not the norm. Women should not be interested in finding a loophole so they can move into leadership positions. We have plenty to do in the areas where God tells us to move freely.

"Let's go on, June. Turn to Colossians 3:18. Oh wait, there's the phone."

Emily picked up the phone in the kitchen, "Hello. Yes, Fran. You are? Why? I was aware that you were upset, but I figured I'd just leave you to work it out with the Holy Spirit's help. I thought you'd call sooner. Sure. Can you come over now? My niece, June, is here. We were just going over the material we covered the second week. June has a ladies' Bible class at home and she asked me to share all these goodies with her, so your questions will help her to be better prepared for what she'll face when she gets back home. You're not alone you know; many women feel the same way. You won't feel uncomfortable with June. O.K., will you have lunch with us? Sure. No, Harold won't be home until about eight tonight. We'll see you in a bit then. Bring your Bible. Bye now.

"That was Fran," said Emily, hanging up the phone. "She's been agitated since we covered this lesson almost three weeks ago. I was surprised she kept coming. She was fuming mad. I've know Fran since she was a little girl. She's a good person and a very fine Christian wife and mother, but obviously I blew a fuse when I plugged into something she has suppressed way down inside of her."

"You've been turning me inside out too, you know."

"That's usually healthy if we respond to the cleansing process. Don't you pull the pockets out on Trent's pants when you wash them?"

"O.K, O.K. . . . "

"Here, I'd better take these beans out of the canner now. Will you rinse those beans we set aside and put them in this steamer, please? I'd like to cover a couple more Scriptures before Fran gets here. She's supposed to drop off the kids at her Mom's and come right over. Lord, give us the wisdom to help her."

"My, those beans look good, Aunt Emily. You judged seven quarts and a lunch pretty close."

"That comes with experience."

We were soon settled back to the table.

"Let's go back to Colossians 3:18. I'll read this one:

> Wives, submit yourselves unto your own husbands, as it is fit in the Lord.

"It's your turn, June. Read I Peter 3:1-6, please."

> Likewise, ye wives, be in subjection to your own husbands; that, if any obey not the word, they also may without the word be won by the conversation of the wives;

"Let me interrupt you here, June. The word *conversation* here means behavior, which includes what we call conversation today, but it's much broader. Today we'd probably say life-style. Continue, please."

> While they behold your chaste conversation coupled with fear.

> Whose adorning let it not be that outward adorning of plaiting the hair, and of wearing of gold, or of putting on of apparel;
>
> But let it be the hidden man of the heart, in that which is not corruptible, even the ornament of a meek and quiet spirit, which is in the sight of God of great price.
>
> For after this manner in the old time the holy women also, who trusted in God, adorned themselves, being in subjection unto their own husbands:
>
> Even as Sarah obeyed Abraham, calling him Lord: whose daughters ye are, as long as ye do well, and are not afraid with any amazement.

"Just a moment," said Emily.

She went into the living room and came back with a magazine.

"I shared this article with the class. This is the January 1970 issue of *The Good News Broadcaster.* The article is entitled, "Winning An Unsaved Husband," by Dorothy H. Pentecost. I'll just read you a paragraph:

> In I Peter 3:6 Sara is mentioned by name. We learn from the story of her life in the Old Testament that her name was originally Sari, which means "contentious," until she came to the place of giving her husband the headship of the home. This she did by calling him lord. Then God changed her name to Sarah, which means "princess," and gave her the son that had been promised many years before this. Isaac, which means "laughter," did not come into that home until Abraham was 100 years old and Sara was 90. This should make us wives wonder if God might be holding back some blessing or something we have earnestly prayed for until we find our rightful place as wives.[6]

"You know, Aunt Emily, disobedience to God's will has very far-reaching consequences. Adam listened to Eve and all of mankind has suffered the consequences of the fall. Abraham listened to Sarah when he took Hagar, Sarah's maid, as a surrogate mother to bear his child. Ishmael was born, and the Arabs, who are his descendants, have been fighting with the Israelites ever since."

Emily pointed, "See the signs on my wall?"

I read them aloud:

> Set a watch, O Lord, before my mouth; keep the door of my lips. Psalm 141:3.

> And that ye study to be quiet, and to do your own business, and to work with your own hands, as we commanded you. I Thessalonians 4:11.

"I need those in my kitchen too, Aunt Emily."

"June, a wife is very influential in her husband's life. An old fellow told Harold and me, when we were engaged, that the husband is the head of the house, but the wife was the neck that turned the head. Sometimes the wife *does* turn the head—the right direction or the wrong direction. We need to walk in the Spirit and let the Lord speak His wisdom through us. When we cover the lesson about the tongue, we'll go into a lot more detail about this."

"Oh me, this is going to be a very painful week; I can tell."

"Take heart, June; it gets better as we go along; or maybe I should say worse. It depends on your perspective. Let's look at this question of authority in a different context. Turn to Ezekiel 28."

"Isn't this the passage about the Devil?"

"Yes, June, verse 12 says he was full of wisdom and perfect in beauty. Verse 13 tells us every precious stone was his covering. He had musical ability created into him. Verse 14 indicates he was the anointed cherub that covereth and God had put him in that position. Verse 15 tells us that he was perfect in his ways from the day he was created, till iniquity was found in him. Verse 17 shows us that Lucifer's heart was lifted up because of his beauty, that he corrupted his wisdom by reason of his brightness. Satan had a very important position in heaven. He was righteous, obedient, and wise. He had tremendous musical talent and responsibility. BUT he was not content with his position in God's scheme of things. He was lifted up with pride and wanted to be God Himself.

"I'm beginning to see where you're going with this, Aunt Emily."

"Good. Turn back to Isaiah 14. Read verses 12-15, please."

> How art thou fallen from heaven, O Lucifer, son of the morning! how art thou cut down to the ground, which didst weaken the nations!
>
> For thou hast said in thine heart, I will ascend into heaven, I will exalt my throne above the stars of God: I will sit also upon the mount of the congregation, in the sides of the north:

> I will ascend above the heights of the clouds; I will be like the most high.
>
> Yet thou shalt be brought down to hell, to the sides of the pit.

"That, June, is the five 'I wills' that caused the fall of Lucifer. The same pride and rebellion that caused Satan to fall, he used to bring about the fall of Adam and Eve—'ye shall be as gods.' He's still on the same track. Lucifer had a very honorable and useful position of ministry in Heaven, but he was not content; he wanted to be the boss. He was lifted up with pride, exalted himself, rebelled, sought others to rebel with him, and lost everything—his position, his honor, his beauty, his ministry, and his home."

"The parallel is discontented wives?"

"It's there isn't it? Each wife has a very honored position of ministry in which God has set her, but some women are not content. They listen to the same hiss of the serpent that Eve heard in the garden. They're lifted up with pride, they exalt themselves, and they want their husbands' positions. In many cases they lose everything just like Satan did."

"Including their beauty, Aunt Emily. Have you ever noticed the faces of some women who have gotten all wound up in the women's lib thing and destroyed their homes? They look hard and miserable—even ugly."

"Yes, and misery loves company."

Emily moved our Bibles to her kitchen desk, and started pulling things from the refrigerator. "That concludes lesson two of our series. I think the Scripture is pretty clear about the position of our ministry, don't you?"

"Yes, all *too* clear."

"How does a fruit dish sound, June?"

"Delicious."

"You cut up the apples and bananas, please, and I'll do the oranges. I think I have some pineapple chunks too. A touch of cinnamon and honey, a few strawberries, and we'll have a feast."

I loved to watch Emily work in the kitchen. She was the picture of efficiency.

"Aunt Emily, I have all this fruit done. If you don't mind, I'd like to run upstairs and pray until Fran gets here."

"Oh, that's fine; go right ahead. There's not much left to do."

I sat down at Ruth's desk and jotted down a condensed version of what we'd gone over that day.

1. Keep Bible verses in card files and review regularly.
2. Principles concerning working wives are subject to praying through for God's will and Titus 2:3-5.

Lesson 2

1. Eve was created from Adam's rib to be a suitable helper for Adam.
2. God gave His commandment to Adam and held him accountable for both himself and his wife.
3. Eve disobeyed her husband and God when she took of the fruit and gave it to her husband.
4. They both suffered because Eve was deceived by Satan.
5. We should disobey those in authority over us only when they clearly tell us to disobey God.
6. Submission puts us under the protective covering of authority.
7. Women wear a head covering when they pray or prophecy, as a symbol of their submission to their husbands (or a single woman to her father or church leadership).
8. Jezebel is an evil spirit that drives women to usurp the leadership of the home, the church, or a business. It causes women to manipulate their husbands and children through witchcraft and destroys the family priesthood vested in the husband.
9. Satan wasn't satisfied with his position of ministering before the Lord and rebelled. Just so, we wives can exalt ourselves over our husbands, in rebellion against God's order, and lose our position, our honor, our ministry, our beauty and our home.

I knelt by Ruth's bed and prayed. Perhaps you'd like to pray something similar.

Dear Lord, thank you for placing me under the protective covering of my husband's authority. Forgive me for all my silent rebellion and my open rebellion too. Help me to be content with the position of my ministry. Enable me to be keeper and guard of my home so the word of God won't be blasphemed. Develop in me a meek and quiet spirit. I submit myself to Your position for me in my family and my church. In Jesus' name. Amen.

# 3. THE POSITION OF OUR MINISTRY (CONTINUED)

I heard Fran's car in the driveway and the Happy Snappy Greeting Committee.

"This should prove interesting," I thought to myself, as I made my way downstairs.

Emily pushed open the screen door. "Hi Fran. Just ignore Snappy; he only bites burglars."

Fran made no comment. I could tell she was in no mood for humor. She reminded me of a big storm cloud all ready to roll out thunder. Emily introduced us and offered Fran a chair at the table. She handed me a stack of plates.

"Here, June, put these on with the silverware, please, and I'll dish up the beans. Get the carrot and celery sticks out of the 'fridge' too, if you will, please?"

"Looks good, Emily," Fran finally managed to say.

"Would you like to give thanks for us, Fran?" asked Emily.

"No, but I will. Father, we thank Thee for this food and ask that You'll bless it and nourish us with it. Lord, I don't want to walk outside of Your will, but I'm not enjoying walking in it either. Something is decidedly wrong somewhere. Please help me to find the answer here today. In Jesus' name. Amen."

"Now then," invited Emily, "what's been eating you?"

"I'm just not coping with what you've been saying, Emily. I know it's God's Word and I know it's truth, but it just doesn't seem fair. Just because I'm a woman, I have no rights. I have to live like a child all my life and ask 'may I do this and may I do that,' and never be able to just order my own circumstances as I see fit. It just seems unreasonable. It makes me hate being a woman. A man gets to make all the decisions. A woman has no choices. She just has to go along with the program whether he's made a good decision or a bad one. It makes me feel like a perfect slave—no will of my own; no rights. Why should God give everything to the man and nothing to the woman? I've got to resolve all this bitterness. I didn't even know it was there. Bill keeps asking me if he's done something to offend me. I just told him I was going through some spiritual cleansing and I'd share it with him when I came out of the wash. At this point everything he asks me to do rankles me. I feel like answering, 'I will not have this man to rule over me.' Do you think I have a Jezebel spirit, Emily?"

"Probably. But you'd best remove the grounds for that spirit to be there before you get rid of it, or it might go off and fetch seven more and come back."

"Ugh! Go ahead, pull the rug out from under it. I've got to get some answers before I become a basket case."

"Did you bring your Bible, Fran?"

"No, I forgot, even when you reminded me."

"Well, let me get one for you; that's where the answers are."

"Emily doesn't leave us any room for argument, does she?" I remarked to Fran.

"No, one does not argue with God. You know He's right. That's why I came here today. I know that what Emily is teaching about a woman's position is right, but there's something wrong in my thinking that I should react to it like this."

"Well, I hope you can get some answers because I have a few questions dancing around in my head too."

Emily smiled understandingly at Fran as she laid a Bible down beside her plate. "Now then, let's back up all the way to the beginning. I think you're looking at this whole thing from the world's viewpoint. We, as Christians, need to get above the crowd and look at life the way God sees it. I Corinthians 2:14-16 says:

> But the natural man receiveth not the things of the Spirit of God: for they are foolishness unto him: neither can he know them, because they are spiritually discerned.
>
> But he that is spiritual judgeth all things, yet he himself is judged of no man.
>
> For who hath known the mind of the Lord, that he may instruct him? But we have the mind of Christ.

"Read I Peter 5:5 for us, Fran. A friend of ours sent us a tape by Malcolm Smith entitled 'The Humble Slave.' I'll share with you some of his thoughts as we go here. Read verses 5 and 6."

> Likewise, ye younger, submit yourselves unto the elder. Yea, all of you be subject one to another, and be clothed with humility: for God resisteth the proud, and giveth grace to the humble.

> Humble yourselves therefore under the mighty hand of God, that he may exalt you in due time:

"Emily, this isn't addressed to women; it's for everyone in the church."

"Exactly. That's my point. Naturally, in a women's class I've been pointing out how the wife is specifically a minister to her husband, but everyone in the church is a minister—or you can actually say bond slave. It's just easier for us women."

"I don't think so."

"You'll see. Malcolm Smith says the meaning of *minister* means the servant of a slave. He points out that in the early church the highest position you could rise to was to be a more perfect slave. Paul addressed his letters referring to himself as the servant—actually bond slave—of Jesus Christ. In the early church, the higher you went, the lower you got. When you got to a position of leadership, you were serving everybody. You became a servant of servants. While you were on your way to being a slave, you were called a deacon or a servant. The whole idea is that everyone was serving everyone else, and the more you led, the more you served. Now, Fran, that's not just for women, that's for the whole body of Christ."

"Yes, but I'm Bill's slave, only he's not my slave."

"Yes he is."

"But if I told him what to do, I'd be out of order. I'm not his boss, he's mine. I don't have any say-so about anything. How can you say he's *my* slave? He's *God's* slave and so am I, but I resent being his slave. I guess, really, I resent not being a man so I can be a chief instead of just an Indian."

"What you're saying, Fran, is that you want your own way, right?"

"Putting it that way makes it sound awfully self-centered, but I guess you're right. I really do want God's will in every area of my life, Emily, or I wouldn't be here right now."

"I know you do; that's why I'm being very frank with you. Does Bill work?"

"You know where he works, Emily. He's an excellent provider. I have no gripe about his care for me and the kids."

"Isn't that a service to you and the children on his part? Don't we tease our husbands about going off to the salt mines, the daily grind, or some other term of slavery?"

"Yes, but he's still my boss."

"That's true. We'll get to that in a minute. First I want to establish in your mind that Bill is your slave just as much as you're his.

Malcolm Smith brought out that if you were a slave, you had no rights of your own. You were totally owned by your master. First of all, Bill is the slave of Jesus Christ, then he serves you because he *is* a slave of Jesus Christ. June, read Colossians 3:22-24, please."

> Servants, obey in all things your masters according to the flesh; not with eyeservice, as men pleasers; but in singleness of heart, fearing God:
>
> And whatsoever ye do, do it heartily, as to the Lord, and not unto men;
>
> Knowing that of the Lord ye shall receive the reward of the inheritance: for ye serve the Lord Christ.

"Who is Paul talking to here, Fran?"

"Those who work for someone else, like Bill works for his factory."

"Now the picture here is that Bill is a slave of Jesus Christ. The apostle Paul told the slaves to obey their masters according to the flesh, as unto the Lord. He says when you work for someone else—an earthly boss—you're really working for Me. Don't do your work to please them; do your work to please Me. Do it heartily as unto the Lord. This applies to everyone in the body of Christ. We all have work to do. The Bible does not approve of laziness. Bill is a slave of Jesus Christ, but when he goes to that factory, he serves his employer as if he were serving the Lord. He serves you and the children as to the Lord, and he serves at the church as to the Lord. All the time he's really doing it for Jesus Christ as an obedient slave. He is under authority and in some cases in authority, but always a slave. At his job, he's under authority and he takes orders and he serves. At home he's in authority, he gives orders, but he still serves."

"But he has the right to make all the decisions."

"Wait now, is that a right or a responsibility? Would you want to answer to God for the responsibility of leading your family in the ways of God? Would you really want to be held accountable before God and men for every decision you made? Put yourself in Bill's shoes. Think of some decision that Bill made that you don't think was the best. If you had made that choice, and your family had to suffer the consequences, how would you have felt?"

"I'd hate myself. I'd hide in a hole somewhere."

"What happens when you have an organization where everyone is vying for leadership?"

"You have confusion and envy and jealousy, and everyone is mad at everyone else. Nothing gets done—nothing. We came out of a church like that; it was awful. Everyone was ambitious for some position of leadership."

"So they could do things *their* way?"

"Yeah. I'm getting the picture. It's just more selfishness, and selfishness is sin. I guess I need to go back to Romans 6, 7, and 8 and reckon myself dead indeed unto sin. I thought I had offered myself as a sacrifice to God before; that's the whole idea of baptism—dying and being raised to a new life in Christ."

"Well, when the Old Testament priest offered a sacrifice, he killed it first; then he cut it in pieces and burned it piece by piece. Sometimes we offer ourselves and then, as God shows us areas in our lives that aren't surrendered, we have to throw another piece on the fire.

"God tells us in James 4:7:

> Submit yourselves therefore to God. Resist the devil, and he will flee from you

"Sanctification means that something or someone has been dedicated unto the Lord. One does not sanctify a person or thing; it must be sanctified *unto* something or someone. When we submit ourselves to the Lord, in a general way, we are sanctifying ourselves to the Lord. When we see an area that is not submitted to the Lord, we must immediately sanctify it to the Lord. The Devil finds ground in the areas which are not sanctified unto the Lord. That which is the Lord's territory is legally off-limits for Satan, and we can then resist him. Many people try to claim the last part of James 4:7 without fulfilling the first part of the verse.

"But before we build a fire, Fran, let me finish a few thoughts here. Your master, according to the flesh, is Bill. When you work for him, you're really working for Jesus. It's like Bill is your foreman. Do you clean your house the way Jesus wants it? Do you train your children the way He wants them trained?"

"Don't say anymore; I left the house looking like burglars had been there."

"Really now, Fran, I would say job importance was determined by the importance of the responsibilities. Just plain old homemaking, as far as I'm concerned, has been all the important responsibility I care to handle."

Emily started turning pages in her Bible. "Do you remember the story of the centurion who came to Jesus asking him to heal his servant?"

"Yes," Fran replied, "he was commended for his faith because he knew Jesus could heal his servant without even coming to see him."

"Look at Luke 7:7 and 8. Read it to us, June."

> Wherefore neither thought I myself worthy to come unto thee: but say in a word, and my servant shall be healed.
>
> For I also am a man set under authority, having under me soldiers, and I say unto one, Go and he goeth; and to another, Come and he cometh; and to my servant, Do this and he doeth it.

Emily continued, "Those who are under authority and who respond in obedience and submission to that authority are also able to wield authority over those who are *under* their authority. If they are in rebellion to authority, even a silent rebellion, then those over whom they have authority will often be in rebellion to them."

"Is that why my kids are so hard to manage?"

"Could be. It's worth examining. God was a perfect Father and Israel was still rebellious, but if we who aren't perfect give some cause for our children to be rebellious . . . well, we'd just better eliminate all the causes.

"In this passage of Scripture it's clear that the centurion understood authority. The centurion represented the man in authority over him who represented the Roman government. When the centurion spoke, the men under him knew he was speaking on behalf of the man over him. He believed that Jesus was a man with spiritual authority who could speak and His will would be carried out. He no doubt knew that Jesus was speaking on the behalf of God."

I could tell Fran's cloud was dissipating as the anger drained out of her.

"Let's sum up a few things here," said Emily. "One, all believers should be slaves of Jesus Christ—both men and women. We should all be under his authority. Two, we can't all be in a position of leadership or there would be disorder, so God puts those that serve the most in the positions of leadership in the church, and they're always men. In the family it's always the husband. But everyone serves everyone else, so no one, really, is any more a slave to someone else, as far as position goes. This service is based on love—love for

Christ and love for his body, love for husband, love for wife. If we're grateful that our Lord loved us unto death, we serve Him.

"We don't really have anything to offer Him to express our thanks, except to offer ourselves. When we do, He tells us, 'This is my commandment that ye love one another.' He says, in effect: 'show me how much you love me by loving and serving one another.' Then He says, 'By this shall all men know that ye are my disciples, if ye have love one for another.' " Emily looked at both of us, "And how do we show that love?"

We answered in unison, "By serving."

Emily continued, " '. . . Inasmuch as ye have done it unto one of the least of these my brethren, ye have done it unto me.' So then, by position we're all slaves. In actual practice the ones who love the Lord the most are the ones that serve everyone else the most.

"Thirdly, our position as women under authority in the church and in the home, (if we're in sincere submission that is) enables us to show forth to all the world the submission of the Church to Christ."

"Fourth, we as wives do not have the terrific burden and responsibility of planning, decision making, leadership, and accountability that the men do. I'm afraid the women who have desired that position and gotten it have found it to be like the Israelites when they complained for meat. Remember the story? God gave them what they wanted, but they all got sick. It says they buried the people that lusted. We can lust for power too, you know, but it's of the world just like the lust of the flesh and the lust of the eyes.

"The philosophy of the world is ambition. Climb over the heads of everyone until you're on the top. Envy and hate everyone in your way. When you get to the top, where have you gotten? To the top. Many just jump off—literally. Some women play this 'king of the hill' game with their husbands. The husband, in order to maintain his rightful position as the head of the house, will sometimes seem overbearing or harsh; but if the woman is seeking to usurp that position, subtly or openly, she's the one who is out of order. When the little woman is content to assume her supportive role, and hubby no longer feels his position as head is challenged, he usually becomes very easy to get along with. I think I could safely say that 80% of the arguments couples get into are over the challenge to his position as head in one form or another."

Fran sighed, "I guess that's where I've been in my thinking. I'll just have to be content with my own spot. I haven't been outwardly rebellious, but it's there on the inside, and now and then it leaks out through the holes."

"Speaking of contentment, look what Paul wrote to Timothy about slaves. It's in I Timothy 6:1. June, you read that for us, please. Read through verse 6. I don't want you to feel left out of this conversation because I'm answering Fran's questions."

"Oh I'm not. You're dealing with *my* silent rebellion too.

> Let as many servants as are under the yoke count their masters worthy of all honour, that the name of God and his doctrine be not blasphemed.
>
> And they that have believing masters, let them not despise them, because they are brethren; but rather do them service, because they are faithful and beloved, partakers of the benefit. These things teach and exhort.
>
> If any man teach otherwise, and consent not to wholesome words, even the words of our Lord Jesus Christ, and to the doctrine which is according to godliness;
>
> He is proud, knowing nothing, but doting about questions and strifes of words, whereof cometh envy, strife, railings, evil surmisings,
>
> Perverse disputings of men of corrupt minds, and destitute of the truth, supposing that gain is godliness: from such withdraw thyself.
>
> But godliness with contentment is great gain.

"That word *contentment*," said Emily, "means a 'satisfaction with what one has' according to *Vine's Expository Dictionary of New Testament Words*.[5] We need to be satisfied with the position of ministry God has given us as well as with the material things he has given us. To covet someone else's position is the same sin of covetousness as when we covet someone else's things. It does something destructive inside of us."

"Sure does," moaned Fran. "My whole digestive system has been on the fritz for months—actually years, I guess. It's bad news."

"Ah ha," chided Emily. "The world's philosophy *is* bad news, but the Gospel means good news. However, it is contrary to what we would do in the natural, just as reckoning ourselves dead unto sin, as Paul tells us to do in Romans 6:11, is the unnatural thing to do."

"Well, I'm ready to hold up the white flag."

"Wait, I'm not done yet."

"Oh, me, she's got me dead and now she's going to bury me too."

"At least you've got a good picture of it theologically."

Emily was enjoying this: She could see the enemy being routed out of Fran's mind. "What a ministry," I thought, "To help handmaidens of the Lord to cast down 'imaginations and every high thing that exalteth itself against the knowledge of God' and teach them to bring 'into captivity every thought to the obedience of Christ.'."

Emily picked it up again, "I want to get back to the area of who gives the orders, since that's what seems to bother you the most."

"When I see the rest of it in proper perspective, it doesn't bother me that much anymore. I can die to that too."

"Good, but let's go over it anyway."

We nodded our consent.

"Bill is under authority, right? So he gets his orders from those in authority over him. Emily snatched a tablet off her desk and drew her diagram again:

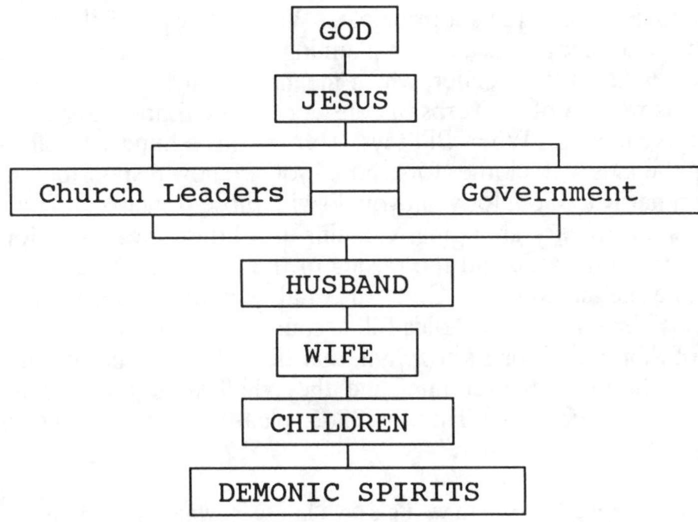


"Bill reads the Word of God; and as he grows in grace, he knows more fully what is God's will and what isn't. New Christians have more to learn than old ones. I know Harold's will because I've been close to him for many years. I don't have to ask him if he wants his eggs sunny-side-up, because I know.

"Bill learns, in general, a set of principles about what is pleasing to God and what isn't. Every decision that comes up he tests by those principles. Should the kids go to Ginny's house for a slumber party? Should we buy a new car? Fix up the old one? Whose parents will we visit at Thanksgiving? Bill sizes up all these problems with the general principles from Scripture, then he issues orders of action.

"Now in certain areas he delegates some of his authority to you. I think the Devil exaggerates this whole decision making thing out of perspective in women's minds these days. '. . . Hath God said ye shall not eat . . . ?' Do you recognize the lines from the scene in the garden of Eden? It's the same song Lucifer crooned to Eve. In essence he said what he's saying today. 'Poor thing, can't you do what you want to do?' In fact, maybe he's actually saying, 'Can't you do what I told you you want to do?' "

We nodded with new understanding.

"Now when Bill delegates his authority to you, you in turn are responsible to operate under the same principles of God's Word, so you have to know these principles too. Here's an example: Bill is responsible to provide for his own house or he's worse than an infidel (an unbeliever). That's a principle. Within that principle are many others concerning finances like planning ahead like the ant does, not being servant to the lender, which means not buying on credit. The virtuous woman of Proverbs 31 considered a field and bought it—no impulsive buying. When Bill says, 'Here's three hundred dollars; go fit up the kids with clothes for school,' you are now responsible to Bill, but primarily to God, for what you do with those principles. The same applies to grocery shopping, cleaning the house, your relationship with your neighbors, and the raising of the children. You answer to Bill and he answers to God for what you do. God holds you responsible; but He also holds Bill accountable for what you do. God said of Abraham 'For I know him, that he will command his children and his household after him, and they shall keep the way of the Lord . . .' June, read I Timothy 3:4-5, please. This is in the list of requirements for an elder."

> One that ruleth well his own house, having his children in subjection with all gravity;
>
> (For if a man know not how to rule his own house, how shall he take care of the church of God?)

"See," said Emily. "God holds the man accountable. Would you really want all that responsibility, Fran?—or as you call it, the right?"

"I see what you mean, Emily; no, I guess I wouldn't."

"Who did God come to first when Eve gave Adam some of the forbidden fruit?"

"Adam," we both replied.

"The Devil would like to make light of the responsibilities our husbands delegate to us, but they are no light thing." Emily put her hand inside of her apron, Napoleon style, and waved a pointed finger overhead in a circle. "Some women are out there trying to conquer the world when they haven't conquered the kitchen sink."

"Ooooh, Emily," whined Fran, grimacing. "Now you're shoveling dirt in on my dead body."

"You only feel it because you're not quite dead yet."

"I guess . . ." she sighed.

"Here's another picture," said Emily, drawing again:

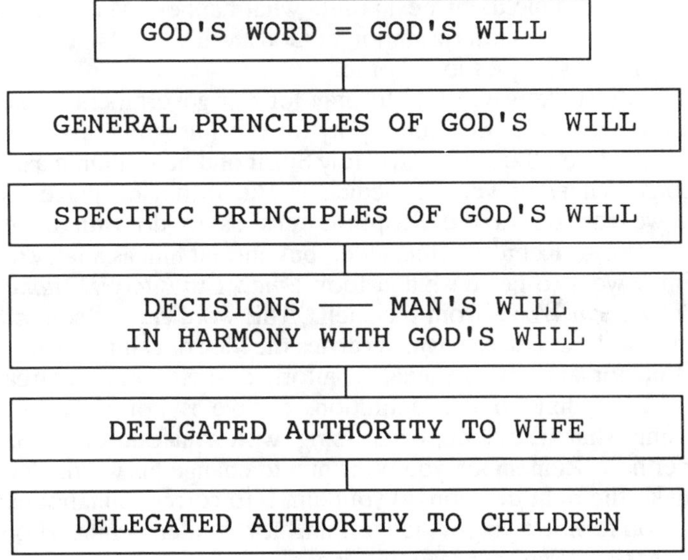


Emily explained, "God transmits His will to Bill, Bill to you, and you to the children. The Devil would like to make very light of our delegated responsibility over the children, too, as though children don't count; but they are the future leaders of the next generation. If the Deceiver can get the home all out of order and get the woman feeling as though giving delegated orders to children is an unimportant task, he's got the next generation all wrapped up. That's how he whipped Israel; the parents didn't explain to their children what God had done for them and what God required of them. The children forgot God and went into idolatry and sin. That's what has happened in America today.

"But let me emphasize, it's not the husband's 'say so' and it's not the wife's 'say so'; it's God's 'say so.' (At least it better be).

"I also want to emphasize that we as women need to know the mind of God as well as our husbands in order to confirm what God is telling them and also to carry out what has been delegated to our realm of managing the household. This also is not an unimportant task. Many a marriage has been strained or damaged beyond repair because the wife has overspent or managed the household so poorly they could not make ends meet. When our husbands delegate authority to us, we cannot point the finger at them when we make an error in judgment.

"That brings me to my next point: what happens when Bill makes a blatant error in his interpretation of God's will?"

"Don't obey?" questioned Fran.

"First, just like we're told to pray for our government so we can live a peaceable life, we should pray for our husbands that God will guide them into all truth by His Holy Spirit and help them make wise decisions. That's preventive medicine. But if they do make a gross error, we can do as the Scripture tells us to do with an elder; I Tim. 5:1 says, 'Rebuke not an elder, but entreat him as a father.' "

Emily went to her desk and took *Vine's Expository Dictionary of New Testament Words* from the shelf. This word *entreat* comes from the same word as *beseech*, which carries the idea of calling someone to your side for aid. It can mean comfort, desire, exhort, entreat, or pray.[5] According to this definition, rebuke is not in order, and discussing what he's done, or is doing, with someone else is not in order either. Remember, you want him to change his wrong decision and make the right decision, so your aim is to correct him, not expose him. You're not trying to judge him, nor condemn him. Look at Galatians 6:1. Fran, you read this one, please."

> Brethren, if a man be overtaken in a fault, ye which are spiritual, restore such an one in the spirit of meekness; considering thyself, lest thou also be tempted.

"I'm going to hopscotch in Vine's and read a few things he has to say about meekness:

> . . . it [meekness] is an inwrought grace of the soul; and the exercises of it are first and chiefly towards God. It is

> that temper of spirit in which we accept His dealings with us as good, and therefore without disputing or resisting; it is closely linked with the word *tapeinophrosune* [humility], and follows directly upon it. . . . it is only the humble heart which is also the meek, and which, as such, does not fight against God and more or less struggle and contend with Him. This meekness, however, being first of all a meekness before God, is also such in the face of men, even of evil men, out of a sense that these, with the insults and injuries which they may inflict, are permitted and employed by Him for the chastening and purifying of His elect." (Trench, Syn.xlii.)
>
> . . . . . . . . . . . . . . . . . . . . . . . . . . . . . . . . . . . . . . . . . . . . .
>
> The meaning of *prautes* "is not readily expressed in English, for the terms meekness, mildness, commonly used, suggest weakness and pusillanimity to a greater or lesser extent, whereas *prautes* does nothing of the kind. Nevertheless, it is difficult to find a rendering less open to objection than 'meekness;' 'gentleness' has been suggested, but as *prautes* describes a condition of mind and heart, and as 'gentleness' is appropriate rather to actions, this word is no better than that used in both English versions. It must be clearly understood, therefore, that the meekness manifested by the Lord and commended to the believer is the fruit of power. The common assumption is that when a man is meek it is because he cannot help himself; but the Lord was 'meek' because he had the infinite resources of God at his command. Described negatively, meekness is the opposite to self-assertiveness and self-interest; it is equanimity of spirit that is neither elated nor cast down, simply because it is not occupied with self at all.[5]

"Part of what Vine is saying here is from *Notes on Galatians* by Hogg and Vine. I'd like to order that one and do an in-depth study on Galatians."

Emily went after another book. "This is *Wycliffe Bible Encyclopedia.* They have some good things to say about meekness, too. I'm taking the extra time to define this word because we're told in I Peter 3:4 to be adorned with the ornament of a meek and quiet spirit, which is in the sight of God of great price. I'm going to just read bits and snatches in Wycliffe too:

> It [meekness] carries the basic idea of the inward attitude of submission to God and His Word [Jas. 1:21). While the noun also conveys the idea of gentleness expressed in outward action, it does not include timidity. Meekness does not mean weakness; rather it suggests controlled and bridled strength. Other adjectives describing this quality are "considerate," "unassuming," "courteous," and "humble." It has the idea of submission without struggle, a holy gentleness in the face of wrath or in situations where one is experiencing mistreatment or injustice.[7]

"Notice the total unselfishness, described here. If we are meek, we will not come across with any attitudes of pride when we correct our husbands. Our interest is God's glory, not having our own way. Our attitude says, 'I'm concerned that you're making a mistake and God's glory is at stake.' No ranting, no raving, no sarcastic digs, no reviling, no rebukes; just a meek, gentle humble exhortation. Then let the Holy Spirit take it from there. Back off and pray."

"What if he continues his folly?" I asked.

"Ask the Lord to set a watch over your mouth so you don't say 'I told you so' when the Lord chastens him, and pray that he'll learn from his mistake the first time around. It's also possible that he is right and you're wrong. Have the grace to admit it."

Emily proceeded, "There's another area of communication, too, which I feel is a woman's 'right.' In the same spirit of meekness, we need to let our husbands know if they have offended us, hurt us, or disappointed us. We are, after all, one flesh and we don't want their prayers to be hindered because of us. Read I Peter 3:7 to us, Fran, will you please?"

> Likewise ye husbands, dwell with them according to knowledge, giving honour unto the wife, as unto the weaker vessel, and as being heirs together of the grace of life; that your prayers be not hindered.

"If our husbands are told to dwell with us according to knowledge, they have to have some idea of what we're thinking. Now I'm not talking about the self-centered whining and complaining that some women do, but so many times a woman will bury all sorts of offenses down inside and a root of bitterness springs up. If you let him know how you feel, he can ask forgiveness."

"What if he doesn't?" Fran asked.

"Forgive him anyway, and ask God to forgive him. It will only make you a sick person to enjoy feeling sorry for yourself. Forgive him for his pride or stubbornness too, which is probably what prevents him from asking forgiveness. He'll probably try making it up to you some other way like buying you a gift or taking you out, even making love, which is actually the highest form of expressing his love. Never demand that he offer you an apology or ask your forgiveness. By the way, never correct your husband in front of others, especially the children.

"I believe we also have a right to counsel. Notice the word is not spelled N.A.G., nor is it spelled T.E.A.C.H. Sometimes our husbands can use a little insight on an issue which we have.

"For example, one of our sons was dating a girl whom Harold didn't object to at all. I did. I pointed out to him several areas where she was leading Mark astray. Harold wasn't around much when they were here together, so I had more opportunity to observe the situation. But also as a woman, I understood much better what she was up to. Harold took Mark aside and warned him about the ways of a strange woman, which opened Mark's eyes too. The girl wasn't even a Christian, though she came to church with Mark. Nor did she want to become a Christian when Mark spoke with her about the issue. Needless to say, they parted company and a few months later she married another fellow because she was pregnant. We had tried to help the girl, but she didn't want to change her ways.

"Another time an encyclopedia salesman came to the door with an innocent young woman as his assistant. His line was that the company was looking for a family where they could place a free set of encyclopedias as a means of advertisement in the area. He went on for awhile about how expensive advertising was and that it was cheaper to place one set in a home where it would really be used and appreciated and the owners would advertise by word of mouth how good it was. We were candid about wanting to know what the catch was, but he assured us there was no catch.

"By this time, we were trying to convince him why we liked the books as he pointed out their fine points. Then he decided we were the right family in our area. He went to his car and got all his papers, filled out a contract for Harold to sign, and asked us a few last incidental questions. The company would want the set kept up to date, of course, so the contract included our guarantee that we would keep up the year books for the next several years at so many dollars a volume. We could pay it all at once—$400.00 I think it was—or pay it by the month.

"Harold thought that was fair and signed. But I saw it all in a flash. I merely said, 'Harold, you realize what we're doing is buying a set of encyclopedias for $400.00.' (That's what most sets were going for at that time and $400.00 was a lot of money.) I was just pulling the wool off Harold's eyes."

"Or the wool off that wolf," Fran noted.

"Right. Harold saw through the whole scheme too. Without much more being said, the slick salesman tore up the contract and made a grumpy exit with his assistant. We were saved some monthly payments for something we really didn't need. Harold often refers to that situation with real gratefulness.

"Another time Harold was buying a pair of shoes and I went along. He buys dress shoes about once every ten years or so. In front of the salesman, I admonished him to try on both shoes and walk around in them to be sure they fit. I could feel him resisting me and he became very stubborn. Just then the salesman went into the stock room. 'But if they don't fit . . . ,' I started to say.

" 'Please,' Harold said, 'you're embarrassing me; I'm not a little boy and you're not my mother.'

"I realized that I was the one that was out of order and backed off quickly. I think if I had said the same thing to him when the salesman was not around, he would never have noticed it. Also if I had put it in a question rather than an admonition, he would have been able to receive what I said. We need to be sensitive to when, where, how, and how much we offer our counsel."

"What if you feel you really need to talk to him about something and you know you'll get a negative reaction? "Fran asked.

"Ask the Lord for wisdom in presenting it. Let's say Bill chews his fingernails and spits them on the carpet—nasty habit. So one day, when he's in a good mood, and you're alone, you tell him you have something to tell him but you don't want to hurt him or make him feel that you love him any less because of this. You don't want people to think ill of him. He'll be readied for the blow. Then simply tell him that chomping his fingernails and littering somebody's rug is obnoxious to you and would be to anyone else too. Then volunteer to help him break the habit—if he wants your help. However, if he tells you that snapping your gum is just as obnoxious, then you'll thank him for his counsel and ask him to help you quit your habit."

Fran whined, "Emily, you'll have me completely buried before I'm even dead "

"If we are gracious when our husbands correct or counsel us and don't react with pride, they will probably respond to us in the same manner, though not always. I think men do have a little more trouble with pride and stubbornness than women.

"I want to add something here before we finish: when our husbands make mistakes, they need our support".

"Support!" Fran exclaimed. "You mean help them do the wrong thing?"

"No. Help them *because* they did the wrong thing. God made Eve out of Adam's rib. That rib protected his heart. We can still cover his heart by staying close to him, making him feel how much we need his protective arm around us, forgiving him, loving him, understanding him, just standing with him and encouraging him."

"Lift up the hands that hang down?" I asked.

"Right. This is where many women have missed it. Men go through life anticipating certain goals in their minds. We should know those goals and understand why they're discouraged when they don't arrive at those goals. We should share their goals. If the goals are wrong, we should prayerfully try to help him get his goals in line with God's will. Just be sure you're not working to get his goals in line with *your* will.

"Most men around forty or fifty begin to feel like failures in life because they haven't accomplished anything by their own evaluation. The greater a man's accomplishments are, the more goals he may have set for himself which he has not fulfilled and which he realizes he may never accomplish in his lifetime.

"Also the more successful a man is, the less likely his wife will be able to understand that he feels like a failure. This is a crucial time in their lives. If they don't have an encouraging ear at home, the Devil will easily find them one somewhere else. And if you do have an encouraging ear, the Adversary stirs up strife so you aren't able to comfort or encourage him. The groundwork for a man feeling comfortable with his wife is laid in the early years of their marriage. Men don't like to talk about their failures, especially with someone who has been critical of them all their married life. They're thinking, 'If I tell her how I feel, she'll only say, 'I told you so!' 'I warned you about that.' 'My Dad would have done that long ago.' They really need a sympathetic ear—just someone to listen."

"That sounds like my aunt in New York," said Fran. "She picked at everything Uncle Frank did. He would go down in the basement and pout like a little boy. He was a very prosperous businessman, but he made a very poor decision on one of his businesses, and he lost it.

(He owned five.) She never let him forget it. She yapped at him like the dog at the mailman. He finally went off with another woman and left her with the whole works."

"The businesses too?" I asked.

"Yep. She's only got one left, though. She wasn't as smart as he was. She's not so harsh anymore, though. She probably realizes now how devastating it is to fail."

"And how she let him down when he needed lifting up," Emily added shaking her head. "I could tell you many more sad stories and from Christian homes too. See what an important position we have in the home? See what damage is done to the Church when we step out of our proper role?"

"All right, Emily," said Fran. "I think you're trying to torture me to death. Let's pray before you think of something else. It's hard enough to surrender my self-life."

"Don't you want to know one more of your so-called rights?"

"Oh sure," replied Fran with resignation."

"We also have a right to go over our husband's head—straight to the throne of God. In the army they call this chain of command, only they have to go through all the ranks. We can come boldly to the throne of grace. If our protective covering has holes, we can ask the Father to do a patch job or a total repair, whichever He feels is necessary. But watch out; it will often get worse before it gets better. When God works a man over, he tends to take out some of that pressure on you and the kids. It's sort of like when you decorate the house; it's a terrible mess while you're going through the process, but when you're done, you're happy with the results."

Emily sat back in her chair. "So then women do have some rights, if you want to call them that: a right to correct, a right to communicate, a right to counsel, and a right to chain of command. I'm sure you could list others, but I just wanted to point out that wives do have rights and they do have some 'say so' as long as they aren't trying to usurp the leadership God put in the hands of the husband."

Emily opened her Bible again. "Let me remind you of a story in Scripture about a couple of folks who didn't think their brother should have all the leadership to himself. Things had gone kind of rough and they figured if they had a hand on the steering wheel, they might be able to smooth things out a bit. They didn't like his wife either."

"Moses?" I asked.

"Yes, June. Turn to Numbers 12. Start at the second verse, and read it to us, please."

> And they said, Hath the Lord indeed spoken only by Moses? Hath he not spoken also by us? And the Lord heard it.

"Now," said Emily, "this didn't set too well with God. He told them He spoke to ordinary prophets by visions and dreams, but to Moses He spoke mouth to mouth. Look at the last sentence in verse 8. 'Wherefore then were ye not afraid to speak against my servant Moses?' God was angry with them. Miriam became leprous. Aaron entreated Moses on her behalf and Moses had to beseech God to heal her. You see, God placed Moses in that position of leadership and Moses didn't need to defend it; God did.

"Here's another one in Numbers l6."

"One's enough," pleaded Fran.

I put my hand on Fran's arm, "This is called overkill."

Emily continued undaunted. "It's Numbers 16:3. Read it for us, please, Fran. It's about Korah and his crowd."

> And they gathered themselves together against Moses and against Aaron, and said unto them, Ye take too much upon you, see all the congregation are holy, every one of them, and the Lord is among them; wherefore then lift ye up yourselves above the congregation of the Lord?

"Now look in verse 9," said Emily. "They were Levites and they served in the temple, but that position was not high enough for them obviously. Let's read verses 10 and 11:

> And he hath brought thee near to him, and all thy brethren the sons of Levi with thee; and seek ye the priesthood also? For which cause both thou and thy company are gathered together against the Lord: and what is Aaron, that thou murmur against him?

"God was the one who placed Aaron in the position of high priest, so Moses considered them to be coming against God and it angered him. God puts the elders in position in the church and he puts the husband in position as the head of the home. Who are we coming against when we dispute that leadership? "You know the rest of the story. God opened up the ground and Korah, Dathan, and Abiram and their families disappeared into the hole and it closed up again. Then fire fell from heaven on 250 men who had agreed with them and had joined them in offering incense which was not part of their ministry.

"Then a big bunch from the congregation came complaining to Moses and Aaron the next day, verse 4l: 'Ye have killed the people of the Lord.' So God sent a plague on all of them. When all was said and done, 14,700 people died beside Korah and his friends. God is sovereign and He will sovereignly put in leadership positions the people He desires to place there. We challenge Him when we challenge their leadership, including the leadership of the family which is vested in the husband."

"Now you're trying to scare me to death," said Fran seriously. "Let's pray before you think of something else."

Emily knelt beside her chair and we followed suit. The tears began to flow as Fran sobbed out a prayer of surrender. In my heart I joined her. I wasn't aware all that resentment was buried down inside of me. Fran's storm cloud had dropped its burden, but it was a cleansing rain. Tears do that. Emily handed her a Kleenex and Fran hugged her.

"I feel like a big burden has been lifted, Emily. There's a freedom I didn't have when I came in here."

Emily looked at me and shrugged her shoulders. "She just surrenders herself as a slave and now she feels free. Isn't that strange?" Her eyes twinkled with delight.

Fran glanced at her watch and bid us both a thankful and hasty good-bye. Emily called after her from the screen door: "If you experience any further torment about your position as a wife, you'll probably need to get rid of a Jezebel spirit. If you need some help, we'll be available."

"Aunt Emily," I said, clearing the last of the plates off the table, "if you don't mind, I'm going up and get some of this stuff down in my notebook and spend some more time on my knees."

"Fine. I'll be out along the fence line picking berries."

I went up to Ruth's room, spread my notes out on her bed and jotted down an outline.

1. We're all slaves of Jesus Christ regardless of our position of authority. We serve one another as though we were serving the Lord.
2. The right to make decisions carries a tremendous responsibility. God holds the husband responsible.

3. When we're under authority, those who are under our authority will more readily respond to us, such as our children. The centurion understood the power of being under authority.
4. The authority our husbands delegate to us is no light responsibility. The future of our children and our country depends on what we do.
5. We have a 'right' to correct, to communicate, to counsel, to chain of command.
6. Miriam, Aaron, and Korah questioned and coveted Moses' leadership position and were severely punished by God.

I wrote down Fran's prayer as well as I could remember it, adding some of my own thoughts. I prayed it again as I wrote. Perhaps you'd like to pray it with me and add something too.

Dear Lord, forgive me for rebelling in my heart against You and the leadership You've ordained in the home. I've been selfish in wanting my own way. I surrender myself completely to You. Thank You, Lord, for making me a woman. Forgive me for saying to the Potter, 'What have You made?' I humble myself under Your mighty hand, thankful that You've made me the vessel You want to use. Do use me, Lord; I offer myself as Your vessel. I want to serve my husband as though I'm serving You. Help me to submit to my husband's leadership on a daily, practical basis, not just in theory. I accept my position of ministry under Your hand. Take away any resentment I have for being a woman. Show me the tremendous responsibilities I have and the opportunities to bring glory to Your name as a wife. I reckon myself dead indeed unto sin but alive through Christ to walk in newness of life—a life of ministering as a wife.

In Jesus' name. Amen.

# HIS DESIRE

A mystery no heart can fathom,
Rich truth each soul finds hard to see
Just as the bridegroom craves his bride
So Jesus Christ desires me.

To Him my love is sweetly fragrant
My garments white since Calvary,
I am His garden sealed forever
My blessed Bridegroom seeketh me.

And yet ofttimes my heart does spurn Him,
So tangled with this world's care.
He seeks an entrance to His garden,
But I have failed to meet Him there.

What more could draw me to my lover?
His love acknowledged on the tree.
He draws me, ever draws me to Him
For love's communion at His knee.

# 4. THE MINISTRY OF OUR MINDS

The burden of resentment and resistance was gone now, and a sense of peace and joy enveloped me. I gazed out of the window and saw Emily picking berries. "I should be helping," I scolded myself as I raced down the stairway. There's a time to be a Mary, but there's also a time to be a Martha. I snatched a large plastic bowl from the cupboard and hurried out to the fence row.

"Well," said Aunt Emily with a bright smile, "think you can catch up?"

"Never! But at least I can earn my supper. Are you making a pie with some of these?"

"Not tonight—cheesecake tonight. It's Harold's favorite. Real quick too. I demonstrated it at the Ladies' Fellowship Day last month and they were crazy about it."

"What do you do on a Fellowship Day?" I mumbled, poking berries in my mouth.

"The ladies in the church meet at someone's house once a month for fellowship and learning practical homemaking skills from one another. We also invite neighbors and friends in so we can share our faith with them and make them feel welcome with us. Many have come to the church because they felt the love and warmth in our relationships toward one another and towards them. It's not a preaching service or even a Bible study. We have a Bible study every Friday afternoon. There's no gossip either. That turns off a lot of unsaved women when they go to a woman's meeting at a church and watch little huddles of vultures clawing apart their victims.

"Each of us demonstrates how to make something that's a specialty with us. Margie crochets beautifully and now almost all of the women can at least make pot holders. I've taught them to knit. Mrs. Watsen is 86; she's quite good at tatting. Two of the ladies do beautiful embroidery. We've all got a special delicious recipe. Marlene's husband is a long-distance truck driver so she has lots of time on her hands. She organizes the day and sees that we have a balanced meal with our demonstrations. She also copies the recipes on the church copier. She makes an artistically attractive booklet complete with Scriptures and an invitation to the next Fellowship Day. We give them to neighbors when we invite them to come.

"Fellowship Day gives the older women the opportunity to teach the younger women as Titus 2:3-5 instructs us to do. Of course we learn a lot from the younger women, too. This month Nancy showed us ten ways to dress up our flower pots so our house plants would look nicer. Sheri showed us how to make cute little picture frames by covering cardboard with foam and brightly colored cotton prints. These girls are just teenagers, but they're made to feel welcome and they're learning valuable skills as well as developing the skill of teaching what they know."

"I noticed your flower pots; they *are* nice. And these raspberries are nice too."

"Sometimes we make things together," continued Emily. "Once we all knitted a good size square; then we crocheted them into a big blanket and sent it to our missionary couple in Canada. They were very appreciative. Another time we all brought scraps, and Fern taught us how to make a quilt. We worked on that for several Fellowship Days—about an hour each time and then sent it off to some missionaries in the Andes. It gets cold up in the mountains.

"We also have a room in the church where we store good used clothes, shoes, blankets, and non-perishable food items such as canned goods. If someone is laid off or fired or their house burns down, there's plenty there to share. We all bring some item each Fellowship Day, and Beth sorts it all out by sizes and arranges it neatly in the storeroom at the church."

"Did you say you meet at a different house each month?" I asked, carefully freeing my sleeve from a stubborn bramble.

"Yes, that way we all get to know where everyone lives, so there's a lot more visiting and real friendships formed. No one is asked to host the Fellowship Day. Some ladies can't for one reason or another. One woman has an alcoholic husband who gets very obnoxious when she has anyone over. Some of the newlyweds are renting apartments that are really too small. If the attendance continues to grow, we may need to hold all the Fellowships in the church basement. I hate to see that; the younger women especially need to learn hospitality. Since television came into the home, hospitality has diminished. People don't invite others over for an evening of food and fellowship as much as they did when I was young. Many women have missed this as they were growing up, so they've never learned how to be a good hostess.

"Hospitality is mentioned along with other ministries in Romans 12. Verse 13 says, 'Distributing to the necessity of saints; given to hospitality.' If a woman's husband is desirous of being hospitable, she needs to know how to support him in every way possible. I Peter 4:9 says, 'Use hospitality one to another without grudging.' And in I Timothy and Titus where it talks about the qualifications for elders, it lists hospitality. Widows who were to be considered for financial aid were to have exhibited hospitality during their married life—in other words, they would now reap what they sowed. I Timothy 5:10 tells us:

> Well reported of for good works; if she have brought up children, if she have lodged strangers, if she have washed the saints' feet, if she have relieved the afflicted, if she have diligently followed every good work.

"I taught about hospitality one day for the ladies' Bible class. It's a ministry that definitely needs reviving in the Church. I think we'd see more people saved and a lot more love flowing if there were more people stirring up their ministry of hospitality. Many times a husband wants to have people come to the house, but the wife is not willing. This is another reason why women should be keepers at home; so they can support their husbands in being hospitable. It's hard to come home after work and fix a lovely dinner."

"What do the ladies do with their children on Fellowship Day, Aunt Emily? Does someone babysit?"

"Oh, no, they bring the children. You might say we *all* babysit. I often have a toddler asleep on my lap after lunch. That's an important part of our program. Each lady brings an idea about child care, discipline, or things to entertain kids indoors and out, even toys you can make. Each mother brings a toy or two, and the kids have a grand time playing. They're actually pretty quiet. The older ones are encouraged to 'mother' the tiny ones.

"Sheila takes notes on the child-care lessons and makes up another little booklet like the recipe booklet. She does some really cute little stick-men illustrations, too. At this point we have a kitty to which we donate, so we can reimburse the church for paper and copy fluid. Everyone donates generously because it's used as a church outreach. The booklets are practical and they're loaded with scripture so they make excellent gifts to saved and unsaved alike. If the kitty grows, we'll probably consolidate them into a book.

"Sheila is a real go-getter. She considers this her ministry. She's a registered nurse, but she hasn't worked in a hospital for many years because she has eight children. She invites all the pregnant mothers she sees to the Fellowship Day, handing them one of the booklets.

"Each meeting she demonstrates, with her own baby, practical things like washing the baby, curing diaper rash, vitamins, dressing the navel, feeding, burping, breast feeding, how to check the baby for physical problems, what to do in case of colic, fever, hives—she really covers the ground. She has a meek and gentle spirit that comes through everything she says too. She has a question and answer period at the end of her talk. She never makes anyone feel stupid no matter how dumb their questions may be."

"Am I going to get in on one of these Fellowship Days?"

"No, you just missed it. We had it last Saturday. I give the ladies about ten or fifteen minutes of instruction on nutrition each month too. I write it out in condensed form and Marlene adds it to the recipe book. This month I covered the proper nutrition for menopause and aging."

"Oh, good. Do you mean something for hot flashes and insomnia?"

"Yes, there's no reason for a healthy woman to suffer all that discomfort during the years of her 'change.' Take a good quality mineral supplement, vitamin A, vitamin E (work up to 200 International Units.) Take Golden Seal tea or capsules—you can get too much so don't overdo it. Avoid estrogen if you can; it can have dangerous side effects. That's it in a nutshell. I got most of those suggestions from *Women and the Crisis in Sex Hormones* by Barbara Seaman, and Gideon Seaman, M.D. It helped me and has helped several others, too."

"Remind me to put that in my notebook, Aunt Emily."

"Another thing we encourage the single young women to do is build a hope chest. Several of the girls have been given beautiful cedar chests for eighth grade or high school graduation. It sets a positive mental stage of expectation for being a homemaker, rather than a career worker outside the home. Most girls look forward to getting married, but not all of them look forward to the housekeeping aspect of that relationship. The blame for that lies with us older women. We've failed to perform our Titus 2 obligations.

"Well, let's leave the rest of these berries to the mosquitoes and we'll go up to the house and get the cheesecake made. Harold won't be home until around eight. We'll get dinner on its way; then we can sit down and cover lesson three before he comes home."

"Sounds good."

"Cheesecake or Bible study?"

"Both."

"Here, June, carry in my bowl, please, so I can get some carrots and a few greens from the garden."

I stepped over a sleeping Snappy, who was enjoying a cool spot on the back steps, then began rinsing berries while I waited for Aunt Emily.

"Now then," pronounced Emily, setting her garden goodies in the sink, "you're about to have a cheesecake demonstration!"

In about 15 minutes, I watched Emily create 'Harold's favorite' and tuck it away to chill in the refrigerator.

"Do I get that recipe too?"

"Certainly, it's in the booklet I gave you. Here, will you rinse these greens and the carrots, please? I'll boil some eggs and get the steamer ready for the carrots."

"Sure."

We soon had things lined up for supper and the table was set, so I fetched my notebook and Bible, and Emily and I went into the living room.

"We launched off lesson three," began Emily, "with Luke 10:27:

> . . . Thou shalt love the Lord thy God with all thy heart, and with all thy soul, and with all thy strength and with all thy mind; and thy neighbor as thyself.

"If we submit ourselves to our husbands as unto the Lord and we hold that our marriage relationship is a testimony to others of the Biblical type of the Church's relation to Christ, then it holds that we should love our husbands with all our heart, soul, strength, and mind."

"Aunt Emily, we both have good, godly husbands, which should make it a whole lot easier to do that, but I feel that I don't really show Trent the extent of love God is talking about in that verse. How would a woman manage this kind of expression if she had a husband who was unsaved or a carnal Christian? Some of the husbands of the ladies in my Bible class are really 'ugh'—I mean awful things like never paying the bills, having affairs with other women, drinking, beating their wives. How could you love someone like that?"

"With difficulty," Emily smiled with understanding. "Actually you and I can't really love our lovable husbands in our own strength. Christ has to love them through us by the power of the Holy Spirit. Our love for our husbands originates in God's heart and flows from Him through us as obedient vessels. We submit ourselves to God and obey Him. Our own love falls apart too easily when we hit the rough places.

"If God can love sinners enough to send His Son to die for them, He can pour sufficient love through us to nice husbands and even the not-so-nice husbands of those unfortunate ladies. It's just harder to keep our own critical attitudes and self-pity out of the way so He can flow His love through us unhindered when a husband is 'ugh.' It can be done; I've seen it produce exciting results.

"Back to Luke 10:27, June. Each one is a whole person and whatever we do is done as a whole person; but even the Scripture divides us up when it talks about the heart, soul, mind, will, spirit, body, etc. For example: 'the heart is deceitful' in one place and 'we have the mind of Christ' in another.

"For the sake of examining how we can minister to our husbands in different areas of our lives, I've divided the next three lessons on the basis of Luke 10:27, though not in the same order. This lesson is 'The Ministry of our Mind,' lesson four is 'The Ministry of Our Emotions.' Frankly, I'm not sure whether the emotions correspond to the heart or the soul. For all the research I did looking up both of these words, I am still unsure of how the heart differs from the soul. These two words seem to be different in some passages and the same in others. Suffice it to say, we should minister with our whole inner self and that should cover it pretty well. The fifth is 'The Ministry of Our Bodies,' which corresponds to strength in Luke 10:27.

"When we give ourselves to Christ, June, we want to know Him and understand Him as a person. We desire to know His will in every area. Our mind is open before Him. We're not telling Him what to do, rather we're continually trying to discover what He wants *us* to do. We seek to know what His plans are and then we obey them. This is having the mind of Christ.

"As wives, we should also relate to our husbands with this same attitude. In the marriage relationship we should be serving God together as one. Have you ever studied soul ties in the Scripture?"

"I'm not sure I know what you mean."

"Soul tie isn't exactly Scriptural terminology, but then neither is the 'rapture.' It tells us in I Samuel 18:1:

> ... The soul of Jonathan was knit with the soul of David, and Jonathan loved him as his own soul.

"They had a godly soul tie." Emily went over to her book case and handed me a book entitled *Transference of Spirits* by Alex Ness.

"This book is really good on this subject. Maybe you can read it while you're here. Ness discusses our human spirit in relation to

God's Spirit and in relation to the human spirits in other people. For example, concerning Moses in Numbers 11:16,17:

> . . . And I will take of the spirit which is upon thee, and put it upon them; and they shall bear the burden with thee, that thou bear it not thyself alone.

Emily took Ness's book from me again and began to read from it:

> This great anointing that was upon Moses was placed upon the seventy and they prophesied. The Spirit came from the Lord upon Moses. From Moses the Lord took the spirit that was upon Moses and gave it to the seventy elders. If they were to be of one mind, of one accord, then they had to be of one spirit. The men who would work with Moses must have of his spirit. Where this does not happen, there you will find discord, division and separation. This becomes very evident where assistant pastors, youth leaders or elders have contrary spirits.[8]

"Win Worley's books are also good on this subject. You can read some of his books while you're here too. Every wife should be of the same spirit as her husband. She should also be sure that she has no ungodly soul ties to other people."

"Like old boyfriends or former husbands?"

"Especially. But sometimes a woman has ungodly soul ties with her parents or girlfriends and even brothers or sisters. It is not wrong to have soul ties with friends or relatives. That's healthy. However, some women maintain a relationship which pulls them away from their husband and children and eventually destroys their marriage. These are unhealthy relationships and I would consider them ungodly soul ties, though she may have godly soul ties with the same people.

"A woman's husband often has evil spirits apart from his own spirit. The wife will tend to pick up these spirits. She needs to break any ungodly soul ties or ungodly transference of spirits between her husband and herself. For example in Proverbs 22:24, and 25 it says:

> Make no friendship with an angry man; and with a furious man thou shalt not go.
>
> Lest thou learn his ways, and get a snare to thy soul.

"Wrong spirits can transfer from her to him also. Although a man or woman each has his or her own spirit, each should have the Holy Spirit (which we receive when we are born again), and then there are evil spirits from Satan and ministering spirits from God. The woman should learn to bind the evil spirits in herself and her husband and ask the Heavenly Father to send His ministering spirits to help them. Read Matthew 18:18 for us, June."

> Verily I say unto you, Whatsoever ye shall bind on earth shall be bound in heaven: and whatsoever ye shall loose on earth shall be loosed in heaven.

"I'll be discussing this in more detail in our last lesson. Suffice it to say here that the wife should want to be one spirit with her husband. If the woman is knit together with her husband, she knows his will, she communicates with him at a very close level, she has his mind, and she's in agreement with him."

"Always?"

"Well, if she's not, they'd better discuss it until they come to an agreement. Remember he's got the final word. He's responsible to God for the decisions, but if he appears to be making a poor choice, there's nothing wrong with entreating him with a meek and gentle spirit to reconsider. Even Moses asked God to reconsider a few things—like wiping out Israel and making a new nation from Moses' descendants.

"There are many things that a couple may disagree about that are unimportant—just differences of taste. They can just agree to disagree. We're not all alike in our likes and dislikes; we each have a different personality, and a woman isn't supposed to be brainless just because she's of the female gender. It's how you work through these differences that make the difference. Here are the rules that I gave the class. We added the last four during our class discussion:

"1. Have a clear understanding between you that he makes the final decision. He will not feel his authority threatened if you make that clear. You might say something like, 'I know you're responsible for making the final decision, but I want to share with you how I feel about this. I'd like you to hear me out before you finalize your decision.'

"2. Never raise your voice. Assure him that you're not opposing him, you're opposing the idea or the action or whatever . Use an easy, calm tone of voice.

"3. Be reasonable, logical, and use common sense. Explain clearly why you feel the way you do. List the pros and cons. Project what the end result of the action will be as you see it.

"4. If you merely have a negative inner feeling about a certain thing, tell him you don't have any reason, you just have an inner check about this particular thing or person and wanted him to know because if the Lord is telling him something through you, you don't want to hold back. Some folks have called it woman's intuition. Some would call it discernment. Whatever it is, it often warns a woman to avoid bad deals and bad people. Just never use it deceptively to manipulate your husband so you get your own way.

"5. Never attack him personally. Remember you're discussing a subject of disagreement. Never name call—stupid, fool, jerk, etc. When you attack him, you cause inner wounds that may never be forgotten. Personal attacks are seeds of bitterness and you'll later reap what you've sown.

"6. Don't drag out all the dumb decisions he's made since you've been married.

"7. Don't get sarcastic or sharp with your tongue. Be loving and kind, meek, and quiet. Don't get pushy like a high-pressure salesman.

"8. If you feel a strong resistance, drop the subject immediately. Nothing is worth damaging your relationship one with another. You may try bringing up the subject when he's in a more amiable mood. He may be tired or hungry or worried about something else, and his irritation and negativism is attaching itself to what you're presently discussing. Tomorrow or next week he may totally agree with you. Don't force him to reject your ideas now, and then be reluctant to backtrack. A man can get very contrary when he feels he's being pushed.

"9. Don't try to get him to agree with you because you bring up something when his mother or your mother or some other 'outsider' is present. He may just be saving face—yours or his—but you don't really have his mind in the matter and it might backfire tomorrow.

"10. Don't say anything you'll regret tomorrow or ten years from now. Don't say anything in anger. Never make your words bitter, you may have to eat them. Don't say anything that might wound him; this is one of the things that causes a bitter spirit in a husband. If he gets angry and loud, return with a soft answer. 'A soft answer turneth away wrath.' If either of you is becoming angry, drop the discussion by tabling it. Say something like, 'Let's table this and we'll both pray about it and continue the discussion another time.' If he says the discussion is terminated, it *is*. If you feel he's making some disastrous mistake, ask God to tell him what His will is, or to send someone else to speak to him. Sometimes a friend of your husband will tell him the same thing you've tried to tell him and he'll accept it without batting an eye.

"11. Never give him cause to think that you don't trust his judgment or that you think he's stupid. When a wife treats a man with disdain, she kills his love for her. He must feel her respect and admiration or something dies inside of him. If she has a prideful attitude of disrespect, it will slip out during a heated discussion, and it may never be forgotten by the husband.

"12. Realize that in matters of likes and dislikes he should not always be expected to acquiesce his choice to yours. Let's say he wants a bright yellow bedroom with lots of light. You'd prefer a soft rose with heavy drapes. He may say, 'O.K., let's do it your way!' but if he doesn't, enjoy the bright yellow without pouting. 'Godliness with contentment is great gain.'

"13. Try to figure out why he feels the way he does about the subject you're discussing. Ask questions so you understand where he's coming from, but not so he thinks you're questioning his judgment. Don't assume you know what's on his mind.

"14. Keep in mind that you want God to be glorified in all that you do. That must be the basis for all your discussions.

"15. Don't start a controversial discussion at the wrong time. Never try to settle your disagreements just as you're getting ready for bed. He has to go to work in the morning and it may quash any desired love-making too. This could make him irritable toward you and the subject you're discussing, resulting in a negative reaction. Don't discuss unpleasant things at the dinner table either; it can cause digestive problems. Don't push him into making hasty decisions while he's heading out the door for work. Think ahead. Keep a list of things to discuss with your husband in your notebook—a special section. If the kids want an answer about an activity, make them responsible to ask Dad. That takes you out of the middle. We had a rule; no answer meant no. They soon learned to find out for themselves whether they could go somewhere and obtained that permission in time. If Harold was out in the back forty when the school bus came in the morning, it was too late to ask for permission, and the answer was no.

"16. Don't assume you're always right.

"17. Do not refuse to discuss disagreeable things with your husband. If you cannot talk things through, you will never be able to come to any agreement about anything. Two different people must bring things out in the open and diplomatically talk them out so they can be of one mind. The only difficulty in this is if the wife refuses to submit to her husband. It is immature for a woman to go pout in a corner and refuse to tell her husband what is bothering her or to give him the silent treatment whenever something is not to her liking. It's a disgusting form of manipulation to get her own selfish way.

"I guess you could call that the seventeen commandments of a disagreement, June."

"I'd like to add one, Aunt Emily."

"Sure, go ahead."

"18. Don't have debates in front of the children. Husbands feel threatened or humiliated, especially if the kids take up sides with Mom. If it's just a family conference or friendly discussion about where everyone would like to go on vacation, that's fine; but strong disagreements should be discussed in private."

"Well said, June."

Emily proceeded, "There's another picture in the Bible which describes the one-flesh aspect of marriage—that of being yoked together. This is a type of the Church being yoked together with Christ. He bears the weight of our burden, but we are pulling together with Him. As husband and wife, we should be pulling together in the same direction. This is why the Lord said 'Be not unequally yoked together.' He knew that a believer and an unbeliever have a whole different philosophy of life. They can't really pull together. In Deuteronomy 22:10 God said, 'Thou shalt not plow with an ox and an ass together.' It's an unequal yoke. It's the same way in a marriage; the couple has to pull in the same direction, or they're pulling against one another.

"For the woman with an unsaved husband it's going to be harder, but God will give her grace. If there's going to be oneness, someone has to give in. There's often room for discussion and the wife is equal before God and man, as a person; but just as the Church says, 'Yes, Lord,' we say 'Yes, dear.' It avoids all sorts of endless arguing and ill feeling. If we have to have our own way, we'd better search our hearts and find out why."

"It's like I tell my kids, Aunt Emily, 'Of pride only cometh contention.' "

"That's plain, isn't it, June? The Scripture is always plain.

"O.K., then, June, the wife gives the husband the ministry of her mind rather than a piece of her mind. The Church is told in Philippians 1:27:

> ... That ye stand fast in one spirit, with one mind striving together for the faith of the gospel;

"And also in I Corinthians 1:10:

> ... And that there be no divisions among you; but that ye be perfectly joined together in the same mind and in the same judgment.

"That message is written to the Church, but how much more should the husband and wife be of the same mind. This is a good godly soul tie.

"Let's hurry on," said Emily. "The mind is like a computer; what you put in is what comes out. That's Scriptural too: 'As a man thinketh in his heart so is he.' Read Matthew 12:34 and 35 for us please."

> ... For out of the abundance of the heart the mouth speaketh.
>
> A good man out of the good treasure of the heart bringeth forth good things: and an evil man out of the evil treasure bringeth forth evil things.

"There are two opposing personalities seeking to help us program our minds—God and our adversary, the Devil. God once had to destroy all mankind, except for Noah and his family, because man's mind was so degenerate. Genesis 6:5 says that God saw 'that every imagination of the thoughts of his heart was only evil continually.'

"God created us with an imagination, but He wants to program it. He does not want us to have a passive mind. I used to have a very passive mind. It's still an area which I need to guard carefully."

"You?"

"A passive mind doesn't mean one that doesn't work. In fact, sometimes it works too much, but with the wrong program. Passive means it receives anything that comes into it without filtering it. The 'immigration office' is closed and alien thoughts sneak in unobserved. The idea of a passive mind is that it is acted upon rather than acting of itself. It sits there waiting for some thoughts to march through rather than actively directing the thoughts. The passive mind soaks up good and bad thoughts like blotting paper, and the result is confusion and doublemindedness.

"A housewife is especially susceptible to this because much of her daily work does not require concentration. Her 'computer' becomes a target for programs of self-pity, suspicion, resentments—all sorts of negative material. A passive mind is characterized by talkativeness, gossip, slander, foolish jesting, fantasies (especially about one's own importance), insomnia, and doublemindedness."

"I think that's what Trent calls a scatterbrain."

"That's graphic enough. If we let our minds run without discipline, the Devil will fill them with a fast-pace set of interesting programs designed to steal and to kill and to destroy. Everyone and everything that comes along is afforded a listening ear. The passive mind does not examine the Scriptures to see whether these things be so. People with passive minds vacillate between two opinions; they can never seem to make a decision. Choosing a pair of shoes is an act of Congress."

"Like the people in Elijah's day, Aunt Emily; they were trying to serve God and Baal. Elijah asked them, 'Why halt ye between two opinions?' "

"That's a good example, June. There are other symptoms of a passive mind such as memory recall. That's when Satan won't let you forget some sinful situation or a tragic accident. You keep on living the scene over and over in your mind until you're so depressed you can hardly move. The other side of the coin is forgetfulness."

"Uh oh, now you're getting on *my* case."

"Lack of concentration is another symptom."

"Oh dear."

"Mind racing is another. I'm referring to flashing thoughts that run unhindered through your mind. They come rumbling through like a subway train and rumble back out leaving a few passengers and picking up a few."

"I can identify there, Aunt Emily. I had an awful experience some years ago when we lived in an old farm house out in the country with no phone. We were five miles from town and Trent worked the afternoon shift. We were buying a house in the city from an elderly lady. We had discussed prices with her and she had somehow misunderstood what we said. She wrote us a letter accusing us of trying to cheat her out of $600.00. I was very upset and since I had to go into town to do errands, we agreed that I should call her and try to explain the misunderstanding to her.

"I poured all the money I had from my change purse out on the shelf in the phone booth so I could pick out the coins I needed. When I finished the call, I still had not been able to make her understand. I was hurt and upset. Trent had to get to work and I still had to fix his dinner and pack his lunch. He had held me up all morning so I had to fly like mad to get everything done. I felt the pressure of time breathing down my neck. I scooped up the left over change into my purse and hurried home, my mind still in a turmoil because I couldn't get this lady to understand and I was afraid I would make Trent late for work.

"I breathed a big sigh of relief as he headed off to work on time. Then it hit me. I had left all the paper bills—forty dollars—sitting on the shelf in the phone booth. I had no car and no phone. I knew nobody in town; besides, it would no doubt be gone by now. That was a lot of money to us. Trent's factory had been on a nine-week strike, and we were trying to save money for a down payment on the house. Talk about mind racing. My head was on a marathon until Trent got home that night.

"First I hated myself. Then I assumed Trent would be angry, so I hated him right back and defensively blamed him for holding me up and making me do so much in so little time. I cried and grumbled and talked to myself. I had a whole defense case built up for when I had to face my heartless accuser. Then the Holy Spirit nudged me, 'Where do you think this is coming from?' Immediately I realized where this barrage of thoughts originated. 'Satan is just trying to attack our relationship!' I almost said it out loud. Maybe I did speak out loud when I told him where to get off. All the ugly emotions melted away right there. A terrible weight lifted and I felt free.

"When Trent came home, I calmly explained what happened and he felt sorry for me, because he knew how bad I felt. He was very understanding and gentle and a real comfort. I still felt bad about losing the money, but I dread to think about what kind of scene would have ensued had my emotions 'crescendoed' through the entire evening to burst into a grand finale upon my poor husband's ears as he entered his castle that night. I told him how Satan had tried to attack our relationship, too.

"Occasionally we still have a good chuckle over the whole thing and it's done us good. When one of us begins to build a case in our head against the other, all we have to say is, 'Well, you know where that's coming from' and the plot is exposed."

"It's a good thing the Lord woke you up, June. Many women never do see what's happening. It gets worse instead of better. This is the type of thing I'm talking about when I say a passive mind. You clapped a filter on your thoughts before there were any disastrous effects; many women never do. They don't direct their minds; their minds direct them. We have to filter everything that comes into our minds through the Word of God.

"The mental gymnastics of a passive mind can sap a person's physical strength. It drains a person to feel anxiety, hatred, grief—all those negative emotions. That's why God said 'a merry heart doeth good like a medicine.' "

My eyes took in Emily's radiant face. Her heart always seems merry, I thought.

"Another problem area is lustful thoughts," Emily continued. "Satan takes all the unclean material he can imagine and programs these thoughts slyly into our minds and then reruns them in different series. Then he's always on the look out for new material.

"We need to get the jump on Satan and program our minds before he gets a chance to poke in his trash. We prepare our 'computer' so it refuses the material we don't want with a 'reject this' command. If we pre-program our minds with Scripture, and a list of 'reject this' items, it will save us a lot of time, effort, and heartache. Once those lustful ideas are received and become ensconced in our heads, they're much harder to remove because they become entwined with our emotions and our will.

"We're told in the book of Daniel that Daniel, as a youth, purposed in his heart that he would not defile himself with the portion of the king's meat. Women need to purpose in their hearts that they will not defile themselves. This means a commitment to the Word of God. It also means they need to read it so they know exactly what they're committing themselves to. For example, as we read the Word, we purpose in our hearts: 'God hates slander; therefore I purpose in my heart never to slander anyone.' 'God hates lust;

therefore I purpose in my heart that I will not open myself to books, magazines, TV, movies, or anything else that will stir up lust in me.' As we read God's Word, we purpose to obey; then we don't have to think it through; we've already determined what we'll do when Satan tries to tempt us. This is the opposite of situation ethics.

"The media is always screaming lust. It's like Sodom and Gomorrah. No wonder Lot's soul was vexed from day to day. I'm vexed too. We're blitzed by the spirit of Babylon. Harold calls the TV the Babylon Box."

"You don't have a Babylon Box, do you?"

"No. When they first came out, we talked about getting one. Harold was over at a friend's house and they had just gotten a nice set. There was a lovely travelogue on with a man fishing. All of a sudden the man's fish got away and he cussed a blue streak. Harold's embarrassed friend turned it off, but they had already heard it all. That was when they wouldn't allow any profanity on the air. Someone was asleep at the switch."

"Or maybe they were testing the public, Aunt Emily, to see how much evil they would tolerate before they complained. The American people are sometimes too tolerant and polite about having ungodly language and behavior foisted on them. When we don't complain, Babylon's crowd assumes we don't really mind. There was a day, not too long ago, when decent people were in charge of things and indecent people were embarrassed if they exhibited their evil behavior. Now the indecent people have grown bold. I really don't think the immoral people are in the majority, but they have taken such an aggressive stand that if you're not one of them, they try to intimidate you. I think this is the influence of the Babylon Box. We don't have one either."

"You're right, June. We're supposed to be the salt of the earth, but the salt has lost its savor and it's being trodden under the foot of men. This is why I say we need to guard our thoughts; we're surrounded with a propaganda program which is geared to defile our minds.

"Each morning in my prayer time, I ask God to put a hedge of angels around my mind to protect it from evil thoughts. I place the blood of the Lord Jesus Christ on my mind. Then I ask God to loose His ministering spirits of wisdom from Joshua 34:9 upon me and my family and also the seven spirits of God from Isaiah 11—the spirit of the Lord, the spirit of wisdom and understanding, the spirit of counsel and might, the spirit of knowledge and of the fear of the Lord!

"Throughout the day, I bind evil spirits when I detect them, and ask the Heavenly Father to loose upon me ministering spirits as I see the need. The binding and loosing is the negative and positive sides of guarding your mind. For example in II Timothy 1:7 it says:

> For God hath not given us the spirit of fear; but of power and of love, and of a sound mind.

"Fear is an evil spirit. Power, love and a sound mind may very well be ministering spirits from the Lord. Scripture talks about a spirit of adoption, a spirit of holiness, a spirit of wisdom, a spirit of truth—look up the word *spirit* in Strong's; there's a whole string of them.

"Psalm 104 says, 'Who maketh his angels spirits; his ministers a flaming fire.' This verse is quoted again in Hebrews 1:7. Hebrews 1:14 says, 'Are they not all ministering spirits, sent forth to minister for them who shall be heirs of salvation?' We don't worship angels, but we can surely appropriate the ministrations God provides through them.

"I begin my day feeding Scripture into my 'computer.' Harold and I read through the Bible every year together; then on our own we do different studies like this one about the ministry of a wife. Each morning I write out a verse on a 3x5 card and memorize it, then feed it like a time release vitamin to my mind throughout the day. Sometimes the Lord gives me a melody to go with it. By starting out right, I've been able to have victory over a passive mind. I also received prayer for deliverance from a spirit of Passivity."

"So you're saying, Aunt Emily, that on the negative side, you avoid the stream of pollution oozing out of Babylon, namely the degenerate TV, radio, magazines, and books."

"Right, June, these things stir up lasciviousness. (Defined by Wycliffe's as '. . . unbridled lust, debauchery, licentiousness, wantonness, shamelessness . . .[7]). Lasciviousness often culminates in fornication or adultery. Romans 8:5-7 says:

> For they that are after the flesh do mind the things of the flesh; but they that are after the Spirit the things of the Spirit.
>
> For to be carnally minded is death; but to be spiritually minded is life and peace.
>
> Because the carnal mind is enmity against God: for it is not subject to the law of God, neither indeed can be.

"Paul told Timothy to 'flee youthful lusts,' " I added.

"Yes, and today it takes a lot of dependence upon God to be *in* the world but not *of* it. Our whole environment is saturated with lust. Paul spoke of a renewed mind in Romans 12:2:

> And be not conformed to this world: but be ye transformed by the renewing of your mind, that ye may prove what is that good and acceptable, and perfect will of God.

"Here's another good book, June, by Larry Christianson called *The Renewed Mind.* He does a beautiful job of explaining how we can live a holy life by a dependence on our holy God. I'll add this to your pile of books to read while you're here."

"Aunt Emily, where do you find time to read all these books?"

"I read about fifteen minutes to half an hour each evening. In a week or two I've read a whole book. Sometimes I read books to Harold if he's tinkering on something that's quiet. Reading Christian books is like hearing sermons, and it actively fills your mind with Scriptural type program material. You have to filter what you read by the Word of God, though; there are so-called Christian writers who sound good but are crafty in heresy. Everyone should pray for the gift of discernment these days.

"You know, June, most women read a lot, but they read the easy, sensual variety of fiction—romances or science fiction. This sets off a whole array of passions that are not conducive to a good marriage. This kind of reading doesn't take much thought; it's like sliding down hill. A woman doesn't have to utilize her mind to read this variety of material, she just relaxes with it. It carries her along, sort of off guard. She identifies with the woman in the story, feels what she feels, and begins to pick up her feelings and attitudes."

"Is that what you mean by transference of spirits?"

"Exactly. We can pick up spirits of the authors of these books and I don't think, from what they write, that a Christian woman would want those spirits. I picture it like a naive lady paddling around the edge of a river on a rubber raft. While she's basking in the sun with her eyes closed, the raft moves out into the main stream where she's carried quickly down the river and over the dam.

"If a woman reads enough of this destructive literature, she'll find her personality making unwholesome changes. I've seen it happen. Sometimes spiritually healthy reading is not easy to read, but the end result in our personality and commitment to the Lord is worth the added exercise of our brain cells. Harold says if we don't keep stirring our brains, they'll set up like head cheese. Our minds can atrophy from lack of use."

"My mind will be doing push-ups all next week if I read all the things you've dug out for me."

"You'll go home with a renewed mind.

"Tim LaHaye's book, *How to Win Over Depression* also has a good explanation of how to handle your mind. He describes the imagination as a screen onto which you project your thoughts. If your thoughts are negative, your feelings will follow and you'll become full of self-pity, worry, etc., resulting in depression. The answer is to allow only positive thoughts to come on the screen.[9] Philippians 4:8 says:

> Finally brethren, whatsoever things are true, whatsoever things are honest, whatsoever things are just, whatsoever things are pure, whatsoever things are lovely, whatsoever things are of good report; if there be any virtue, and if there be any praise, think on these things.

"In another book by Tim LaHaye and Bob Phillips, *Anger Is a Choice*, we're given further insights on how this works. Our will cannot control our emotions; but it can choose the thoughts upon which our mind will dwell. Our emotions correspond to what we're thinking about, so we must actively will our minds to think only on a Philippians 4:8 level.[10] For some reason, many of us find it easier to think wrong thoughts instead of right ones, easier to sin than to walk with God. We have to struggle to keep our minds clear of the things that oppose God. We're not talking about mind power or some kind of occult control power which uses demonic powers to direct our thinking processes; we're talking about self-discipline. It's a spiritual battle but as one wise fellow said, 'You can't keep the birds from flying over your head, but you can keep them from making a nest in your hair.' Read II Corinthians 10:3-6 for us please."

> For though we walk in the flesh, we do not war after the flesh:
>
> (For the weapons of our warfare are not carnal, but mighty through God to the pulling down of strong holds;)
>
> Casting down imaginations, and every high thing that exalteth itself against the knowledge of God, and bringing into captivity every thought to the obedience of Christ;

"Actually, our struggle, June, is to keep turning everything over to the Lord—to depend on Him to handle our worry, fear, lust, hatred, jealousy, and all the other non-Philippians 4:8 thoughts that parade to the door of our minds. It's pride that makes us think we can handle it ourselves. We need to rest in Jesus like Hebrews 4:10 and 11 say to do:

> For he that is entered into his rest, he also hath ceased from his own works, as God did from his.
>
> Let us labour therefore to enter into that rest, lest any man fall after the same example of unbelief.

"We don't rest in the Lord passively; we rest in Him actively. We make a commitment to the Lord to have a Philippians 4:8 mind. We choose to think only that style of thoughts, depending on the Lord to work in us both to will and to do of His good pleasure. Our emotions will then follow our pleasant frame of mind. A passive mind doesn't do this; only an active mind does.

"When I say we don't think negatively, I'm not talking about a positive mental attitude. There are times when we have to examine negative things. We have to weigh certain decisions or face the reality that we have been cheated by a business person, that we have made a terrible mistake, or even committed sin. There are times when we have to say no and be very negative when we're faced with certain decisions. This may be negative thinking, but how we respond to these realities is where Philippians 4:8 must be applied.

"Another thing that's necessary for maintaining an active mind is meditation. Now I'm not talking about transcendental meditation—that's the ultimate of a passive mind. Anytime you empty your mind of everything and open it passively for so-called spiritual thoughts, you'll get lots of spirits, but they won't necessarily be from God. The insane asylums are full of glazed-eyed meditators who are talking about God."

"So how are you supposed to meditate?"

"You meditate in the Word of God. First find out what a passage really says. Look up the words in Strong's, Vine's—any good Bible dictionary or encyclopedia or lexicon which will help you know word for word what the verse actually says. Commentaries are helpful, but remember that is man's interpretation. Ask yourself, who was the God inspired human writer addressing? What was the culture and philosophy of that day? What did he mean? What is the context of the whole chapter? The whole book?

"I often lay out several translations of the Bible and compare them. The ideal, of course, would be to take Greek and Hebrew and do it right. There are Bible school correspondence courses that offer Greek. It doesn't take any more time than watching television. Greek and Latin were both taught as a matter of course in the earlier years of our country. The Hebrew is a bit more difficult, but then the women's libbers are hollering that the housewife has no intellectual challenge. Let the women learn Hebrew and teach their children the very depths of the Old Testament.

"I also run the chain references. In the center column of my Bible is a footnote section referring to other verses which pertain to the same subject. When you look up that verse, you may find another reference that the first verse didn't have. In this way you can often get a much wider picture of what the Lord is saying in that one passage."

"What you're saying, then, Aunt Emily, is that meditation is a form of deep Bible study, right?"

"Not exactly. Meditation applies the Scripture to your own personal life. It uses Bible study to get all the facts necessary so it can be applied. Bible study can be a cold, sterile, and almost useless endeavor unless it uncovers knowledge and then applies it so that it can change our lives. And I might add, if we're not willing to change, we aren't going to get much out of either study or meditation. We'll just stagnate like that green algae pond down the road from us."

"Not exactly a well of water springing up into everlasting life is it?"

"No. Read Joshua 1:8 please."

> This book of the law shall not depart out of thy mouth: but thou shalt meditate therein day and night, that thou mayest observe to do according to all that is written therein: for then thou shalt make thy way prosperous, and then thou shalt have good success.

"That's a good reward for meditation isn't it, June? There's a similar passage here in Psalm 1:1-3:

> Blessed is the man that walketh not in the counsel of the ungodly, nor standeth in the way of sinners, nor sitteth in the seat of the scornful.

> But his delight is in the law of the Lord; and in his law doth he meditate day and night.
>
> And he shall be like a tree planted by the rivers of water, that bringeth forth his fruit in his season; his leaf also shall not wither; and whatsoever he doeth shall prosper.

"Malcolm Smith has written an excellent book, *How I Learned to Meditate*. My copy is loaned out, but I highly recommend that you buy a copy and share it with your ladies. He has a good handle on meditation."

"Aunt Emily, it's hard for me to concentrate on Scripture or try to pray while I'm working. I make valiant efforts but it's difficult. I try to pray for the boys and Trent as I mend their socks or iron their shirts, but it's a battle."

"Of course it is. We're in a conflict over the territory of our minds. Remember what it says in Ephesians 6:12? I'll read that:

> For we wrestle not against flesh and blood, but against principalities, against powers, against the rulers of the darkness of this world, against spiritual wickedness in high places.

"This is a very important battle to win, June, because it affects our entire life. If we don't win it, the enemy can destroy us mentally, emotionally, and spiritually—even physically. A sick mind soon sickens the whole body—usually through the stress of our sour emotions. Let me give you a few more verses here about the mind and then I want to move on. Titus 1:15 says:

> Unto the pure all things are pure: but unto them that are defiled and unbelieving is nothing pure; but even their mind and conscience is defiled.

"Ephesians 4:17 says:

> This I say therefore, and testify in the Lord, that ye henceforth walk not as other Gentiles walk, in the vanity of their mind,

"Romans 1:28 shows us the depravity to which an unguarded mind can descend:

> And even as they did not like to retain God in their knowledge, God gave them over to a reprobate mind, to do those things which are not convenient;
>
> Being filled with all unrighteousness, fornication, wickedness, covetousness, maliciousness; full of envy, murder, debate, deceit, malignity; whisperers,
>
> Backbiters, haters of God, despiteful, proud, boasters, inventors of evil things, disobedient to parents,
>
> Without understanding, covenant-breakers, without natural affection, implacable, unmerciful:
>
> Who knowing the judgment of God, that they which commit such things are worthy of death, not only do the same, but have pleasure in them that do them.

"June, I have seen women, over the years, soak up a steady diet of intellectual smut. As new brides, they were sweet, good girls who were always in church. They passively read romance novels, watched TV, especially soap operas, and thought nothing of going to one of Hollywood's suggestive movies. I've watched them slowly drift away from church, away from the Lord, and two of them have also drifted away from their husbands. Sensual fantasy can only produce lust and lust is selfish—'What can I get?' It only destroys the marriage relationship. Love says, 'What can I give?'

"I tried to warn them as kindly as I could, but they just thought I was old fashioned and out of touch with today's society. They were right; as Christians we should be. Jude 23 tells us to hate 'even the garment spotted by the flesh.'

"So much for the lust aspect. Anxiety is another troublesome problem for women. Isaiah 26:3 says, 'Thou wilt keep him in perfect peace whose mind is stayed on Thee.' We're not supposed to worry about things. Matthew 6:25 tells us:

> ... Take no thought for your life, what ye shall eat, or what ye shall drink; nor yet for your body, what ye shall put on. Is not the life more than meat, and the body than raiment?

"Verse 33 says:

> But seek ye first the kingdom of God, and his righteousness; and all these things shall be added unto you.

"I Peter 5:7 says:

> Casting all your care upon him; for he careth for you.

"Philippians 4:6:

> Be careful for nothing; but in every thing by prayer and supplication with thanksgiving let your requests be made known unto God.

"Worry, anxiety, complaining, murmuring, fears—any form of negative expectation—are destructive thoughts in the mind. They produce destructive emotions, which in turn cause a large proportion of the destruction of our bodies. Stress causes ulcers, high blood pressure, heart problems ('men's hearts failing them for fear'), nervous disorders, hives, headaches, back and neck pain. I could go on all day. Doctors call this psychosomatic illness. The problem in many instances is that the will does not tell the head to think with the mind of Christ."

"We're back to 'a merry heart doeth good like a medicine,' aren't we, Aunt Emily?"

"Correct. Again, a passive mind allows runaway thoughts that throw us into fears and worries. How would Jesus think? Did He express self-pity? Jerusalem rejected Him. He wept, but not out of self-pity; He wept out of compassion for the lost. His own brothers didn't believe in Him, but He trusted the Holy Spirit to bring them around. The letters of James and Jude indicate that His expectations were not in vain. He forgave His enemies on the cross and prayed for them. He was totally unselfish in His outlook.

"If we knew all the tragedy that would befall us during our lifetime, we'd come unglued. Jesus knew what He was facing, but He was at peace. He totally trusted His Father. All the fretting and stewing and worrying that we do indicates that we don't trust God. It's an insult to His benevolent character. It's unbelief and doubt. That's what the children of Israel were doing. That's why they died in the wilderness and never saw the fulfillment of what God had in store for them. We may also miss a great deal of blessing from God when we don't trust Him.

"I might add, too, June, that we need to trust God to supply through our husbands. We trust our husbands, yes; but we trust beyond them to our Heavenly Father to provide through them. Our complaining says to both our husbands and to the Father that we don't believe they will meet our needs. This is not how the Father wants His handmaidens to behave. In several passages God tells us to be quiet. That's the opposite of noisy and restless and troubled. I Thessalonians 4:11 says: 'And that ye study to be quiet, . . .' We'll have lots more to say on this one when we talk about the tongue tomorrow."

I groaned, "I think I have to go home tomorrow, Aunt Emily."

"Just be *quiet* and read I Peter 3:4."

"O.K., O.K.

> But let it be the hidden man of the heart, in that which is not corruptible, even the ornament of a meek and quiet spirit, which is in the sight of God of great price.

"Here's part of Isaiah 30:15. I have this on a plaque in our bedroom. 'In quietness and confidence shall be your strength.' June, you read Ecclesiastes 4:6, please."

> Better is a handful with quietness, than both the hands full with travail and vexation of spirit.

"Christians today are always talking about the tremendous pressures Christian young people are under, but not many people are very sympathetic to the pressures being laid on today's woman."

"What are you referring to specifically, Aunt Emily?"

"The world, the flesh, and the Devil. The whole world system—the world's philosophy, their religion, their psychology, their education, their economy, politics, the job market, the food, clothing, and household shopping. (I call that one the cry-at-the-counter syndrome). Every move a woman makes, she has to sort out all of this and seek her husband and the Lord for advice and wisdom. Some try to manage very independently and fall flat on their faces.

"The flesh calls out in all the advertising media, 'Let's all indulge ourselves. Indulge yourself in sex, food, clothes, cars, luxury items. You deserve it. Whatever appeals to the eyes, or the flesh, or the pride of life, indulge in it.'

"There's the pressure of time. The wife has to work her schedule around everyone else in the family. This can really get hectic if her husband works swing shift or travels. And when the kids hit those active teen years, the time pressures seem to multiply by how many kids you have. (Of course the kids should also be of some real help by then). A woman almost needs a degree in business management to properly utilize the fleeting hours of the day.

"Some women are overwhelmed by the pressure of having to do things quickly and efficiently, because they've never learned to do this as they were growing up. Girls aren't learning to keep and manage a household at school, and quite a few are not learning it at home either. Many go into marriage totally ignorant of how to cook, clean, wash, iron, sew, shop, budget, decorate, and meet the physical, social, spiritual, and emotional needs of their families. This is one of the reasons we have Fellowship Day; so our young girls can learn these skills.

"Then we have another type of person who is capable and efficient, but she's a workaholic. She goes and goes, sort of like the dog chasing his tail, and never seems to get everything done. She drives herself and then she drives her family."

"Aunt Emily, have you been talking to my family lately?"

"I've been guilty myself. We knew a couple, when we were living in town, who were fairly well off. They owned a nice home and he had a decent job, but she wasn't satisfied; she wanted another house in a better neighborhood. She pushed, she worked, she pushed him, they moved and he had a heart attack. Some of the kids fell away from the Lord into drugs, unwed motherhood, even the occult. She was a lovely person and she loved the Lord, but it seems she was pushing the wrong things.

"Men are quite often materialistic, but I've often seen their materialism grow out of the desire to satisfy their wives' insatiable desire for things. When a woman pushes for material things, she often pulls her husband away from spiritual pursuits. That's what Paul was getting at when he said, in I Corinthians 7:33: '. . . He that is married careth for the things that are of the world, how he may please his wife.' Marriage doesn't have to make our husbands handicapped spiritually; it should increase the effectiveness of both of our ministries. Hebrews 13:5 says, '. . . be content with such things as ye have.'

"Some women feel guilty sitting down to rest or read. They've got to be moving. They're nervous when they're quiet, and they're nervous when their husbands are relaxing as well. He should be mowing the lawn, fixing the washer, calling the insurance man. She's got a hundred projects lined up and she comes on like a sergeant."

I was beginning to feel uncomfortable. "Aunt Emily, this is making me say 'ouch' inside. I am decidedly not quiet on the inside. Sometimes I've got a knot in my stomach from all the turmoil. My neck hurts and I can hardly turn it. I keep thinking of the Israelites who were a stiffnecked people.

"The day before I came down here, I looked up the word *stiffnecked* in *Wycliffe Bible Encyclopedia.* It said, in effect, that this word came from the idea of a rebellious and stubborn ox which refused to receive the yoke. It's used metaphorically of stubbornness or obstinacy along with arrogance relating to their unbelief in God and rejection of His revealed will.[7] It said to look up hardness of heart, which I did. I copied it down in my notebook.

"But let me backtrack here to give you the whole picture. Some years ago I asked one of the elders at church to pray for me because I had a lot of pain in my lower back. As he prayed, he discerned that I had a spirit of Fear. Now it took me quite a while to figure out what I could possibly be fearing. I wasn't afraid of the dark, or storms, or dogs, or bugs. I'm just not a 'scaredy cat.'

"This brother also felt that I had a spirit of Silent Rebellion. Rebellion? I had just told a friend of mine the day before that is was easy to obey Trent because he wanted to do God's will. It was just like obeying God. So I had to do some real heart searching. I knew if the Devil was gaining a foothold, I'd have to remove his grounds, so he had nothing to stand on.

"I finally realized that the two spirits—Fear and Silent Rebellion were linked together. I feared Trent wouldn't be able to lead the family the way I thought it should be led, so I pushed and drove and planned. The rebellion was in trying to usurp Trent's leadership. I was fearing bills wouldn't get paid, the house wouldn't get painted before winter—anything and everything. I worked my socks off and Trent's too. When I realized this, I made a concerted effort to cease and desist, and I did much better. That's where I first encountered these spirits.

"Now let me read to you what I wrote here from Wycliffe's on hardness of heart: It said hardness of heart described a 'certain moral attitude and firm set of mind. This stubbornness, impenitence, and impenetrability of man's heart as a condition is caused by wickedness and sin.' It goes on to say that it 'signifies the dryness or stiff, unbending quality of mind in the realms of both faith and practice.'[7] Then it discusses God hardening hearts that men had already hardened themselves, like Pharaoh. I thought to myself, 'Boy, I sure don't want God finishing up a heart-hardening on me!

"About half an hour after I read these things, and I was still trying to figure out how I might be rebellious and stubborn, our friend Larry called. He's a chiropractor and also an ordained minister. We got into a discussion about how physical problems are related to spiritual problems, so I told him about my little study. He had worked several times on my neck, but it didn't take very long for it to get all out of whack again. I told him I wasn't able to see how I was being rebellious and stubborn, but I did know the area where I was up-tight, hurt, bitter, and worn out physically—my kids!

"I complained away to him about how Trent had goals and I could foresee how this and that had to be done to implement his goals, but the boys wouldn't budge. I felt like a mule skinner. They did a lot of work when Trent was home, but they goofed off all day while he was at work. (Now that you've read me that Jezebel tract, I can see that all my hollering and nagging was what made them balk. They were reacting to me because they sensed that Jezebel spirit.) At the rate the boys were going, I knew Trent's goals would never be achieved, so I kept pushing every day. I was exhausting myself.

"After unburdening myself, Larry kindly added the insight I needed: 'The people of Israel were murmuring and complaining and they entered not into His rest because of their unbelief.'

"Here was that same old fear popping up in a different place, like a poison in the bloodstream. A boil pops up so we treat it and then it pops up in another place because the blood is carrying the poison through the whole body. That same fear and silent rebellion that I had uncovered some years back had popped up in a new place—in the area of the kids. I was afraid Trent couldn't or wouldn't handle it so I'd do it for him. Before it was the house or the finances; now it was the kids. That's unbelief in God, Aunt Emily.

"I made excuses—Trent's always busy working at his job, repairing the car, fixing the house. When something came up, it seemed like just one more thing too much for him to handle. He didn't worry about it; I did. It was really a lack of trust that God can direct him and lead him as the head of our home. When I saw it, I found a real healing, but that spirit of Fear was popping out in other areas. Finally last week I recognized that this fear had to be dealt with, not just treated on the surface. I believe I have finally 'cleansed the bloodstream.' I really got down to business with the Lord that day. Let me read you the poem I wrote afterward. I think it expresses the victory:

## RELAX

A fear gripped my heart as I thought of the day,
And listed the duties all coming our way.
I don't see how all of the work will get done,
Unless we all work until setting of sun.

A fear gripped my heart as I thought of the day,
And long grew the list and I started to say,
"Come, children, and help or we'll never get through
With all of the work that's before us to do."

A fear gripped my heart as I thought of the day.
I prodded my husband to hurry and say,
"The children must help us so we can get done
With all of the work. Let us run; let us run."

A fear gripped my heart as I thought of the day.
I feverishly plotted and planned what to say,
To drive them and nag them and push them along.
But no one was moving! Something was wrong!

Then one day these actions became quite absurd.
The Lord said "Relax; you're missing my Word.
Your husband can channel these energies best.
Please trust Me to lead him; I'll handle the rest."

So gradually I learned what He meant when He said
To labor to enter His rest with my head.
My day starts with trusting and resting and prayer.
He takes all my burden and all of my care.

It wasn't too easy to make the transition.
For years I had taken my husband's position.
But one day I noticed his plans were achieving,
The projects were done about which I was grieving.

When fear grips my heart as I think of the day,
I say to the Devil, "You must go away!"
I'm ceasing my works before ever I start
And entering God's rest with all of my heart.

Now no fears can grip me as I face my day.
I rest it in Jesus, I sing and I pray.
Then do all the work that's within my own realm,
And leave them the rest, knowing God's at the helm.

"I like that," said Emily. "You're getting a deep cleansing this month, aren't you?"

"I hope so. I've been praying for revival, and I know it has to start with me. Unbelief is sin no matter how subtle it is. When we can't trust God to lead our husbands, how can we say we trust Him at all?"

"That's true. If you find yourself still battling this same area, you may need to have those spirits cast out. When we go through a spiritual commitment—a crisis, so to speak—we remove the grounds for these spirits, but until they are forced to leave, they often lie low for awhile and then manifest again when we're weak or lax. You can command these spirits to come out yourself, in the name of the Lord Jesus Christ, but usually it's good to have a couple friends help you. This is a regular ministry in our church. Sometimes when we remove the grounds, the demons know they can't cause any more damage, so they just slither away, but more often they're just waiting for another opportunity where we won't recognize them so easily."

"I'll put that on the back burner. I have had some deliverance, but there may be more to go, or more grounds to remove."

Emily returned to our lesson, "I have several more verses here on quietness. Let's start with Isaiah 32:17:

> And the work of righteousness shall be peace; and the effect of righteousness quietness and assurance for ever.

"Another aspect of quietness, June, is waiting. Read Psalm 130:5 and 6 for us."

> I wait for the Lord, my soul doth wait, and in his Word do I hope.
>
> My soul waiteth for the Lord more than they that watch for the morning: . . .

"This is not passive waiting. It's expectant waiting for God to do His will on our behalf—to show us what to do or our husbands what to do. Psalms 62:5 says, 'My soul wait thou only upon God, for my expectation is from Him.' "

"One of the things I did, Aunt Emily, was write down every verse about trust in the Scripture.. A lot of these verses are about people who trusted in something other than the Lord, and the sad results. It has been a real eye-opener to observe the contrast between trusting in the Lord and leaning on the arm of the flesh."

"Next you might want to go through the verses on hope. Hope means an earnest expectation."

"That should be good."

"Waiting is based on hope because we have a sure expectation that he is going to come through. Hope is built on trust; trust is built on belief, and Jesus said, '. . . This is the work of God that ye believe on him whom he hath sent'. The bottom line is believing. How do we increase our faith, June?"

"'Faith cometh by hearing and hearing by the word of God (Romans 10:17).' "

"So we saturate ourselves with the Word and wait for God to move. We do at the moment what we know we should be doing and we are at peace about it. When the peace lifts, we pause and examine what's wrong.

"Oh, there's Snappy, announcing Harold's return. We're about half done with this lesson. Let's get dinner on the table. We'll finish this lesson tomorrow morning after breakfast. Harold will be here all day tomorrow. He may have some good things to add from the male viewpoint."

Emily began handing me things from the refrigerator to put on the table.

"Hello," said Harold happily as he gave Emily a peck on the cheek. "I see my favorite dessert is awaiting the weary traveler."

"Sure thing," returned Emily.

Harold gave an extra exuberant thanksgiving prayer, as only a tired, hungry man can, then he filled us in on all the details of his day.

Emily took her turn, "We've been going through the third lesson, Harold—the one about ministering to your husband with your mind. We're about half finished with the material I gave the class."

"Does that mean you ladies are going to continue tomorrow with only half a mind?"

"Just for that, Uncle Harold, I have half a mind to give you a piece of my mind."

"I'd have it coming," he chuckled.

Emily and I made quick work of the dishes, and I bid them both good evening.

Upstairs I spread my notes out on Ruth's bed again. deciding not to put together my outline until we had covered the remainder of the lesson, but I did kneel and pray the following prayer. Perhaps you'd like to pray it with me:

Dear Lord, I surrender my mind to You. Cleanse it, sanctify it unto Your use that it may be free from passivity. Right now I cast down every imagination and high thing that exalts itself against the knowledge of God, and I bring my thoughts into the captivity of the obedience of Christ. Give me an active mind. Help me to discipline my mind to think Philippians 4:8 type thoughts. Enable me to rest in You, Lord, so I can cease from my own works. In Jesus Christ's name. Amen.

# 5. THE MINISTRY OF OUR MINDS (CONTINUED)

Emily's bird friend, Barnabas, awakened me heralding, "Good cheer! Good cheer!"

"Thank You, Lord, for Your feathered messenger," I responded. "You have indeed overcome the world. Help me to be in such fellowship with You that I too am an overcomer. Help me to overcome the strongholds of the world, the flesh, and the Devil in my mind."

I dressed and then washed myself with the Word. As I finished the chapter, I heard Uncle Harold's truck pull out of the driveway.

Hurrying downstairs, I met Emily at the foot of the stairs.

"Did I oversleep, Aunt Emily?"

"Oh no, Harold just forgot he needed some fence wire. He'll be back in a little while. Let's get some granola; then we'll pick some green beans while it's still cool. We can pop them in the freezer and then pick up where we were in the lesson on the ministry of our minds."

"Sounds great!"

We were soon done with Emily's morning work and settled with our Bibles at the kitchen table. She wasted no time.

"The next point I had in my notes was a trusting mind, which we had just touched on somewhat when we stopped yesterday. We need to trust our husbands as the Church trusts Christ. It's harder because no man is perfect like our Saviour, but we trust God to work in them, to provide through them."

"Ouch. I'm still not walking in total victory in that area."

"I know Trent is not a bungler, June, but many husbands bungle everything because no one believes in them; then *because* they bungle, no one believes in them. It works in a vicious circle. It is difficult to encourage a bungler, but it can be done. When he's successful, his wife should brag about his accomplishment. Encourage him to try things and never laugh at him. She should get him started with easy things. She should go gently and not apply too much pressure. Never nag. I've seen women build up their husbands' confidence so they felt they could do almost anything."

"Is that called husband psychology?"

"No, it's called edification. This is what edification is all about. It means building up someone as opposed to tearing down that person. A man who really succeeds, usually has a wife or mother who believes in him and he can believe in himself. Also, he doesn't want to disappoint her. This covers wide ground. This dependent trust upon our husbands is just another picture of the Church and her Lord. Who gets the greatest blessing, the one who depends upon the Lord, or the independent person who makes plans to do a great work for the Lord and then asks the Lord to bless those plans?"

"Oh, the 'leaner' gets the blessing. I've always loved the description of John the disciple leaning on Jesus breast. That's why we named our first son John, because we wanted him to be that close to Jesus. That makes sense concerning our relationship with our husbands, too, doesn't it? If we are independent of them and try to do everything for ourselves and for them, we aren't nearly as close to them as we would be if we depended on them to do what God intended for them to do. I understand that we have our own responsibilities, like conquering the kitchen sink, but I for one, have tried too many times to take over his responsibilities."

Aunt Emily continued, "We trust them to handle the money, the repairs, the proper discipline, the spiritual leadership, their job or business. We trust them to be faithful to us. They need our trust. It challenges them to fulfill that trust. Not trusting a man only causes him to feel worthless. If he was going to fail, he'd do it a whole lot sooner when he knew his wife expected him to fail than if he felt he was letting her down. Sometimes I think some wives are so sure their husbands can't do anything right, that they're almost disappointed when they *do* achieve success."

"Is that what it means in I Corinthians 13, Aunt Emily—'. . . rejoiceth not in iniquity, but rejoiceth in truth; Beareth all things, believeth all things, hopeth all things, . . .'?"

"Let's finish the verse—'endureth all things.' That's for when he *does* fail. We all do. That's one way we all learn—from our mistakes. Husbands are no exception. We have to trust them, knowing they might make mistakes, that they'll learn from them, and that all things will work together for good as Romans 8:28 says it will.

"This brings me to the next point–give him a humble mind. 'Think not more highly of yourselves than you ought to think.' There's a tendency in women, more today than ever before, to compare themselves with their husbands and disdain them for a number of reasons. They may look down their noses in pride at their husbands' jobs. This can demolish a man. His job is to him like your house is to you. How would you feel if your kids said, 'I don't want to bring anyone home; this house is not nice enough. It's decorated ugly and it's messy and dirty'?"

"I would dissolve."

"Sure you would. And every woman needs to praise the Lord for her husband's job. Many men don't even have a job. She needs to see his work from his viewpoint. Maybe he hates his job too, but he's making a sacrifice for his family because it earns more money than the job where he would be doing something he enjoys doing. Then she needs to hate it with him and let him know how much she appreciates his sacrifice.

"She needs to work with him to achieve his financial goals, so he can extricate himself from what he loathes and do what he enjoys. Perhaps he has a certain skill, but there are only a few places where his skill is needed. He likes what he's doing, he's proud of his ability, but he does not like the place where he's working. His wife must be sympathetic and encouraging, but never condescending and proud.

"Perhaps he's looking for her approval to launch into a business of his own—moonlighting until it gets off the ground. It definitely will take sacrifice on her part too. It could very well flunk. I read somewhere that 90% of all businesses fail. She might help him consider the cost before he 'builds the house.' The timing may be wrong, but the idea great. If it's honest, righteous employment, the wife should do all she can to encourage her husband in doing work he can enjoy.

"Take Joe Doe; he loves being a carpenter. It's not always super money, but it pays all the bills, and besides he built his family a beautiful home. What more could the little woman ask for? But Flo Doe's father was a stockbroker. She went to a very elite college and her parents expected her to marry a rich pencil pusher. Now Joe is no dummy (most good carpenters aren't). He could have gone to college, but he doesn't like to study or push pencils or shuffle papers. He loves it outdoors in the sunshine—even the rain. He likes to be physically active. He doesn't mind getting dirty or having sawdust in his hair. In fact, he loves the smell of fresh-cut pine. He feels productive and creative. He's not afflicted with a love of money; he's content that the bills are paid; they eat well; the family is well dressed; and the car runs.

"If it weren't for Flo's attitude toward his job, he'd whistle his way through work every day. But there's a certain heavy feeling—a feeling of inadequacy, because he can sense that Flo feels his job is beneath her dignity. The children catch her attitude, too. 'I'll never marry a carpenter,' announces his daughter, 'I'm going to marry a business man with lot's of money.'

"Here again, 'godliness with contentment is great gain.' Flo can begin to praise the Lord and be grateful for Joe's job, see it through Joe's eyes, and be content. When she can realize how selfish and proud and grasping she is, she can repent and accept Joe as he is and his job as it is. *His* contentment will be *her* contentment. Then she can begin to be a helper suitable for her husband. It might help her to remember that Jesus was a carpenter, not a corporate executive."

"What if the husband's work is ungodly like dope-peddling or selling liquor?"

"Pray. God will move. That wife needs to examine herself to see if she has a covetous craving for things that compels him to supply these things by means of illegitimate or fast-money schemes. Her pride may have instigated his poor choice. Expressing gratefulness and appreciation to God and our husbands for their provision is usually destructive to our pride. However, our husbands thrive on being appreciated.

"The wife of a dope pusher might point out to her husband that drugs are sorcery and that God Himself puts a curse upon the sorcerer. With a meek and quiet spirit, she can express her concern for him not only concerning what the law enforcement officials will do to him, but God himself. Then encourage him to find something to employ his real talents.

"The wife of the man selling liquor can, with a meek and quiet spirit, point out Habakkuk 2:15:

> Woe unto him that giveth his neighbor drink, that putteth thy bottle to him, and maketh him drunken also, that thou mayest look on their nakedness.

"She also can express her concern about what will happen to him and the family if he continues in this activity upon which God has proclaimed punishment.

"She may not even have to address the negative aspect; just poke around in his dreams and push his button: 'You've always wanted to be a computer repairman? I think that's great! Where could you get the training?' Don't manipulate, but do encourage.

"All I'm trying to say, June, is that a woman must not disparage what her husband does for a living or make him feel like a good-for-nothing in her eyes. A poem or a love note in a lunchbox can express our appreciation that they've gone off to the 'salt mines' for another long day when they'd rather be playing golf. Most men will do exploits for a sincerely grateful wife.

"There are other areas where pride causes trouble besides deprecating his work. Ridicule also comes out of a proud mind. I Corinthians 13, the love chapter, says, in verse 4:

> Charity suffereth long and is kind; charity envieth not; charity vaunteth not itself, is not puffed up.

"If hubby isn't handy, ask if you can call a repairman when things fall apart. Perhaps that can be made a part of the household budget which he delegates to you so that when the sink sprouts a leak, you can immediately call a plumber. There must be a lot of other husbands who can't or don't have time, or who choose not to fix things, because the service industry is a booming business. Appreciate what he can do and don't call attention to what he can't do.

"The loving wife will never ridicule his paunch, his bald head, or his teeth because they come out like the stars at night. She needs to accept him like he is; that's how God accepts him. If he does foolish things, she should determine to pray for him more. If she writes down all the foolish mistakes she's made lately, that should humble her. We need to guard our minds against pride. Proverbs 13:10 says, 'Only by pride cometh contention: but with the well advised is wisdom.'

"Our pastor was talking about pride last Sunday. He advised us to humble ourselves, as God said we should, rather than wait for God to do it. He said, 'Is humility just thinking less of yourself? No, it's not thinking about yourself at all.' That's the answer to the whole issue of humility—put your attention on serving God and other people, your husband being second in line to God only.

"You can spot pride in a woman when you see her put her husband down so she can exalt herself. This self-exaltation is the basis of what Satan did when he rebelled against God. Remember, putting down is the opposite of edification, which means building up. We are told in Romans 14:19:

> Let us therefore follow after the things which make for peace, and things wherewith one may edify another.

"How does one edify her husband, Aunt Emily?"

"Well, let me say first what it doesn't mean. *Edify* means to build up, right? So it doesn't mean to correct, criticize, belittle, disparage, ridicule, teach, set straight, baby, pacify, protect, mother, or anything else which does not really build up a husband, but which makes him feel useless, immature, and inadequate. When we make his improvement a project, we cannot really help him. As we said, each woman needs to accept her husband as he is, including his faults and failures. That's unconditional love such as our Saviour has for us.

"If she has no faults, God should have translated her long ago like He did Enoch. Most of us need to work on the beams in our own eyes which cause us to be spiritually farsighted. Some folks can only see somebody else's faults way over there and can't see up close where they just might notice some spiritual pride if they could get a good look at themselves."

"Or a critical or judgmental spirit?"

"Right. Now you're 'seeing.' O.K., we accept our husbands, we admire them, we express this admiration, we encourage, and we express appreciation for everything we can. We verbalize our gratefulness and we make an effort to recognize his talents. We teach this admiration to our children. We respect him and instill this respect in our children. I guess the key words here would be a positive encouragement in opposition to a negative discouragement. Make him feel like he's needed, he belongs, he's appreciated, he's loved, and he's not under scrutiny to determine whether he can remain in this status in the future."

"I don't think women realize how important that encouragement is to a man, Aunt Emily. Trent had a falling out with a friend some years ago, and it was very upsetting to him. I was praying for him one day, and the Lord told me to be to him as a cheerful bird in the nest so he would have that comfort in the midst of his sorrow. He's expressed many times how glad he is to come home. But I do tell him from time to time when he does something I think is wrong."

"I don't mean to say, June, that a wife should never confront her husband with anything negative. She needs to point out some of his blind spots occasionally (that's edifying too), but it's her attitude and how she does it that makes it helpful or destructive. The Bible tells us how to correct in order to edify, whether it be our husbands, our children, or even our pastor. We mentioned this verse when Fran was here, but it bears repeating. Read Galatians 6:1-3, please."

> Brethren, if a man be overtaken in a fault, ye which are spiritual, restore such an one in the spirit of meekness; considering thyself, lest thou also be tempted.

> Bear ye one another's burdens, and so fulfill the law of Christ.
>
> For if a man think himself to be something, when he is nothing, he deceiveth himself.

"Pride is destructive; humility is constructive. My parents always told us 'Don't offer any criticism unless you can suggest a better way—a solution.' As we mentioned before, that's the difference between the way the Holy Spirit convicts us and the Devil condemns us. The Holy Spirit gives us a solution, but the Adversary only accuses. The Holy Spirit doesn't attack our personhood, He's after the specific thing that's wrong. Satan just makes us feel like a total 'reject.' We need to be cautious, when we admonish our husbands, that we imitate the methods of the Holy Spirit, not the Accuser of the brethren. And that's probably enough said about giving our husbands a humble mind.

"Next on the agenda is a creative mind. I think I could write a book on this one. This covers so much ground, but I didn't spend much time here; instead I stirred up each woman's creativity and sent them home to use the imagination God gave them. Our Fellowship Day encourages creativity so our ladies aren't too remiss in this area. Let me just say we were created in the image of God Who is the Creator. He created us to be creative and He enjoys our creativity and so do we. Doing creative things wipes out boredom. Pagans are not very creative. The people in the jungles who worship demons don't usually invent things; it's usually Christians or people influenced by the Gospel who are inventive.

"Creativity is decorating a home so it's comfy and beautiful. It's buying an odd collection of old furniture and painting it an antique white with gold striping for your teenage daughter. It's learning calligraphy so you can letter Bible verses on parchment or flowered stationery and then making a beautiful frame for each one. It's finding a pleasant way to keep the neighbor kids from making a path through the corner of your lawn, or sparrows from building a nest on your porch. It's drying your clothes on a snowy day, when the dryer breaks down, instead of complaining. It's making rainy days entertaining and pleasant for six kids under ten, buying food for five people for the same amount of money your mother spends for two. It's creating a banquet with candlelight and flowers, elaborate appetizers, and the most elegant dessert your husband's boss and his wife ever enjoyed. It's knowing when to leave your husband alone so he can concentrate on bills and bookkeeping and when to chatter cheerful small talk to keep him from becoming anxious on the way to the dentist. It's making something out of nothing, fun out of drudgery, freedom out of chains, challenge out of disaster. In short, it's using your head to figure out the best way to do something and doing it with a cheerful spirit."

"Aunt Emily, you make me feel like going home to renovate my house. All of a sudden I have dozens of ideas."

"Next on our list is to give our husbands an informed mind. I do think today's woman is more interested in what is going on in the world outside the home than when I was a young woman."

"Is that good?"

"Yes and no. The Christian woman should filter what she reads and hears through the filter of the Word of God and through the godly counsel of her husband and their church leadership. Remember, Adam wasn't deceived; Eve was. Women tend to be more naive and trusting. That's a quality God created into them, but if they're not under the protective love of their husbands, that quality can become a handicap. This is evidenced by the way women have gobbled up the whole ERA package. They've been thrown a hook with freedom bait on it and they've swallowed the whole thing—hook, 'lie,' and sinker. Just like the fish, they never get to have the bait. ERA takes away most of a woman's freedoms and gives her nothing she doesn't already have. I'd better not get started on this subject now; we'll cover this in the last lesson—the attack against our ministry. "It is necessary, however, for women to know what's going on. The Lord told us to watch and pray. I believe the watching includes knowing where that 'roaring lion' is and what he's up to. We need to be aware so we can pray for our children, our grandchildren, our husbands, our neighbors, our friends, the lost, our government leaders, church leaders, and ourselves.

"Our pastor shocked me right out of my lethargy a few weeks ago. He said in effect: 'Jesus is at the right hand of the Father praying for us, the believers; and the Holy Spirit is making intercession for us as well. That leaves us, as believers, to pray for the lost!"

"Wow! What a tremendous responsibility!"

"I'm sure the Holy Spirit will help us, but it is an overwhelming thought, isn't it?

"Here's just an example, June, of what I mean when I say women need to be knowledgeable. Think of what the philosophy of humanism is doing in our society. Humanism believes that man is the ultimate deity. Harold read me a not-so-funny definition of a humanist. He's a self-made man who worships his creator. Evolution plays a big part in this philosophy, dismissing God as creator and taking man from a single cell all the way to the ultimate man—the antichrist."

"That's evolution or dev—illusion?"

"Whatever. Remember Satan's lie in the garden? 'Ye shall be as gods.' It's the same tune all over again. Oh yes, and 'ye shall not surely die.' That's now called reincarnation by the humanist. This philosophy drips from the TV screen and is cleverly incorporated into the educational materials in our government schools and libraries.

"Humanism has also affected our modern church theology. Or maybe I should say infected. A man goes to church, behaves himself, is nice to his neighbor, and then he has some hope of heaven. Who, pray tell, has provided this man's salvation?"

"He has, Aunt Emily. According to that brand of teaching, Jesus died in vain because man is his own saviour. It's salvation by works, not by Christ's death on the cross. That concept totally ignores the grace of God and His love in sending Jesus to die for us. But I never thought of works salvation as humanistic. It is, though, isn't it?"

"Yes, it is. And there are multitudes of people in the churches today who think they're Christians when they're not. Acts 4:12 says:

> Neither is there salvation in any other: for there is none other name under heaven given among men, whereby we must be saved.

"But worse yet, the folks in the church down the street, where they *are* being taught the Word of God, don't realize what doctrine of devils their dear neighbors, friends, and relatives are being taught. With no one to warn them and pray for them, they will slide to hell from a church pew. Many real believers have no idea what is going on around them. They think because their neighbor goes to church, he's probably a true believer.

"As I said before, the public schools are feeding this philosophy to the children, June. They have the children six hours a day, and in some areas they play rock music on the school buses. You are probably aware of the subliminal backward masking in much of that music."

"They don't need much backward masking on some of those records, Aunt Emily; the words themselves are full of adultery, violence, and rebellion. And the country western music is worse than what we heard when we were kids. It's a message of adultery and broken hearts. It's not allowed in our home any more than the rock music. Music reflects the thinking of society, and I would say, as depraved as the music is, we desperately need a revival."

"That's true. The schools play the rock and western but seldom any good music in the lunch rooms as well. Then when the children get home, they catch the humanistic philosophy on the TV. After supper Dad reads them a chapter from the Bible. Does that one fifteen-minute insert in the midst of all that propaganda help combat the day-long indoctrination? I guess it's better than nothing, but we really need to do better than that. Many women aren't even aware that there is anything wrong. I find there are many Christian women who are totally ignorant of the philosophy their children are learning from their text books and from many of their teachers.

"They haven't the faintest idea of the inroads the socialists have made in the legislation that has been passed to take away our freedom—freedom to worship, to preach, to have Bible studies in our homes, share our faith, or raise our children the way the Bible tells us to do.

"Not many Christian mothers, in the last half century, have encouraged their sons to become godly statesmen and judges. Christian young people have not been given a vision to be the leaders in government such as their forefathers were. Instead, we're leaving the governing of our lives to the ungodly and then boo-hooing because they legalize abortion, side-step the pornography issue and ban prayer and Bible from the schools. What happened to the Biblical admonition to be salt and light?

"What bothers me more than anything else that they've done is that some states have legislated that the child actually belongs to the state. As I understand it, if the parents have a state marriage license, the state is a third party in that marriage and has a right to the progeny of that marriage. The state can take the child away from the parents if they feel the parents are not raising it the way the State wants it done. If they feel the parents are forcing religion upon that child or if they spank their child, they may try to place the child in a foster home.

"One mother was put in a mental hospital because she was fasting, and the State took the children and put them in a foster home. Other parents have had their children taken away because they sent them to a Christian school or taught them at home. We're losing our freedom rapidly and most Americans are blind to what's happening."

"You make me feel guilty, Aunt Emily. I know a lot about what's happening around us, but I haven't shared a whole lot about these things with my ladies' class because I felt it was my job to just teach them the Scripture. But I'm seeing this whole thing in a new light. We should teach the Word in relation to the age in which we live—applied practical living where all of us have to live. We shouldn't be adapting the Scripture to the culture; we should be adapting the culture to the Scripture."

"That's being salt and light."

"All right, Aunt Emily, let's take Sally, a mother of three small children and expecting a fourth. What can she do to be salt and light?"

"She can learn what's going on. Read when and where she can, ask questions of her husband, listen to the news instead of trashy music and fantasy programs. I'm amazed at the women who claim they don't have time to be informed about what's going on in America, yet they can tell me about the latest affairs on the soaps or some incident from a cheap paperback novel. They know about pac man! We've got to come out of Babylon's system! We're in the world, but we don't have to be of it. We do need to know what they're doing to erode our freedom or we'll soon be in a land where we don't have the choices of separating ourselves, and especially our children, from their evil system.

"For instance, right now we can send our children to a Christian school, but some rascal legislators are working on sneaky bills to do away with Christian schools. The Christian schools are training children to be leaders in this country, and those kids are not learning the philosophy of humanism. They are not planning on a Global 2000, one-world government. They are being taught a love for God, His Word, and also a love for their country, because when the United States loses its sovereignty, we will also lose the freedom which goes with it. Whenever the communists have 'annexed' another country, they have exterminated millions of people—mostly Christians.

"I'll be covering this subject in more detail in our last lesson—the attack against our ministry. Suffice it to say here that women need to cancel some of their subscriptions to the magazines that are saturated with lust and foolishness and fill their minds with the Scripture and some sensible information which will enable them to watch and pray and occupy 'til the Lord comes back. After the last lesson, I'll be giving the class a list of books which will be helpful reading both in the area of marriage and in the area of social-political awareness.

"I want to mention another aspect of one of Satan's lies in the garden: 'Ye shall be as gods, knowing good and evil.' I believe there's an evil spirit of Humanism feeding phony data into our thinking apparatus. It works like this: 'This is such a little thing; it's not sin. It doesn't hurt anyone.' What this spirit says, in effect, is: 'I am as God and I make my own standards. I don't have to heed God's standards which are laid down in His Word since that book is old fashioned and outdated. Nor do I have to obey the authorities which He places over me.'

"Humanism's doctrines teach that there are no absolutes. There is no right and wrong. If it feels good, do it! This means there is no truth, as we know it. With a wave of the hand, they brush away all the foundations upon which a man or woman can live in security, peace, and joy."

"Aunt Emily, it would be like living in a society without rulers, scales, or clocks."

"Not exactly; it's like having no standard weights and measures. Every merchant could weigh your hamburger or apples on his own 'homemade' scale. The service station could pump out gallons which were pint size on one corner and half-gallon size on the next corner."

"What chaos!"

"You get the picture. That's why we have such confusion in our society today. That's one reason suicide is the #2 killer among our young people. That's why we have fighting, murder, stealing, adultery, misery, and bedlam pervading our whole social scene. We're reaping the harvest of the doctrine of humanism.

"June, remember the situation in Israel during the time of the Judges? As long as they had godly people to tell them the Word of God, they did fine; but when the judge died, they forgot God and His Word. Judges 17:6 and 21:25 says: 'In those days there was no king in Israel, but every man did that which was right in his own eyes.' "

"Look here in Judges 2:19, Aunt Emily, at the end of the verse: '...and they ceased not from their own doing, nor from their stubborn ways.' "

"And they suffered—until they returned to God," concluded Emily. "This nation is in for a lot of self-inflicted suffering unless we see a revival.

"Let's wind up the need to give our husbands an informed mind and move on. Each woman needs to be informed not only so she can help her husband protect the family and be able to watch and pray intelligently, but so she can converse with him on an intellectual level. An exclusive conversational diet of baby's teething problems, Billy's grades in school, her aches and pains, her friend Millie's tupperware party is all 'womanspeak' and tends to bore most men.

"On the other hand, they don't want to talk 'shop' when they come home either—not on a competitive level anyway. Wives need to learn what their husbands want them to learn.

"This brings us to the next subject—give him a sharing mind."

"Oh, boy; this should be good. This is where my ladies are really having problems, especially the ones with unsaved husbands. They're on two different wave-lengths."

"Communication is one of the most important areas of marriage. If we're not in a close friendship, we can't really move ahead in any other area either. If we're not really relating, we're living under a pretense and a sham. The bottom line for real communication is complete truthfulness and openness—no secrets (unless you're talking about a surprise party or something of that nature).

"This is very difficult, June, if the husband or wife is laboring under the burden of sin. His guilt, or hers, can block any openness. However, if the husband knows his wife is receptive toward him and is offering forgiveness regardless of what he's done, he'll very likely come around. The wife needs to be very sure her conscience is clear with God and that there is nothing between her and her husband such as bitterness and resentment. This is where the confrontation issue comes in. It's better, usually, to bring it out in the open than to pout or suffer in silence. We should cleanse anger away, not hide it or suppress it. Controversy, confrontations, disagreement, and arguments—all those unpleasant elements of communication should be a very minute part of our sharing with our husbands. It is usually because we are not communicating that we have negative situations.

"The husband and wife need to explain their expectations to one another. If the husband doesn't know the wife expects him home at 5:00 to eat supper, he may do errands, stop off at the neighbor's to chat, and wonder why his wife is all up-tight when he whistles in at 6:30. On the other hand, if hubby is starved by 6:00 and he comes home to find his darling Polly on the phone while dinner is still in the freezer, things could get real noisy around there. He needs to share when he wants supper. She needs to share when supper would best fit in with the children's activities and agree with him on a time. Then they should subject themselves one to the other. That way it's clear what is expected of each of them.

"All our expectations should be clearly spelled out. If our husbands don't tell us clearly what they expect from us, we should ask them. Some fellows are afraid they will appear demanding or bossy or fussy, but when the wife falls short of his expectations, he may resent it or be annoyed. We should gently pry until we know everything our husbands like or dislike. And if our memory is short, write it down. This is especially true in the first couple years of marriage.

"As wives, we should express our likes and dislikes too. Being a phony is burdensome anywhere, but in a marriage it's disastrous. If a woman doesn't like flashy costume jewelry, her husband should know so he doesn't come home on her birthday with brightly colored dangles and spangles and expect her to wear them."

I added, "Some men really get their feelings hurt when they buy something for their wives and they don't like it. From then on they're afraid to get anything for them."

"This is why it's so important early in the marriage to talk a lot about likes and dislikes, expectations, goals, dreams, longings, aspirations. This kind of sharing prevents disappointments and misunderstandings. When we constantly assure our husbands of our acceptance of them as a person and our abiding love regardless of their faults and foibles, we can discuss our differences without them feeling put down personally. I have found you can be very frank with someone if they know you deeply love them and are loyal to them no matter what happens."

Emily glanced at the clock. "It's almost noon. Harold's stomach will be sending him in the house shortly. I'd better put some cheese sandwiches together for us. Will you get the celery and carrots out and scrub them up, please?"

"Sounds good."

Emily was right. Harold's stomach kept good time.

"Uncle Harold," I teased, as he opened the screen door, "did you swallow a timer when you were a boy?"

"No, I guess I'm just a grown boy. My mother used to tell me a boy was a hungry noise with dirt on it."

Harold washed the dirt off and then gave thanks.

Emily explained to Harold, "We just got into the importance of communication between husband and wife."

"I've told Emily she could make lots of cheesecakes and I'd be happy. I also told her to never fix eggplant 'cuz I wouldn't eat it. How's that for communicating?"

I laughed, wondering if any men liked eggplant.

"Aunt Emily, what responsibilities does the wife have in particular concerning communication?"

"She needs to be open and honest."

"She doesn't have to tell him he's homely though," teased Harold. "It's not necessary to tell him everything that's on her mind—might hurt his feelings for no reason at all."

Emily smiled and continued. "Most of all she needs to schedule her husband into her day. This may sound silly, but if a woman doesn't make a schedule and just does what comes to hand, God and her husband will get pushed out by chores, children, and church. Whatever or whoever clamors loudest gets attention as it comes about. The ministering wife must arrange her day and train her children so she has definite blocks of time alone with her husband. I firmly believe youngsters should go to bed early enough so their folks can have about an hour together to talk and pray and share with one another. This is another reason we don't want a television. It destroys that sharing time and leaves loose ends that can lead to misunderstandings and strife."

"What about teenagers?" I asked.

"Well, after we had supper and family devotions and shared together as a family, we sent the kids upstairs to do their homework. In the summer they usually went back outdoors until dark. On the weekends they went to school functions or church activities. This is an advantage some of the newer homes have with a family room. Mom and Dad can sit in the living room and the kids can play games and have their friends over in the family room. Harold paneled a room in the basement and bought a ping-pong table and a dart board. Our basement soon became the neighborhood club house. Of course, we often did things with the children or went to see them play in a sports activity or listened to them at a band concert. They never felt that we didn't want them around, but they also knew we wanted some private time to discuss things together, and they have always respected that."

Harold added, "It's important, for the sake of the children, that Mom and Dad have time to understand between them how they're dealing with each child. They must present a united front before the kids. Every child I've ever known is interested in getting his own way at least some of the time. If Mom and Dad don't agree, he'll be quick to sense this and work to get the one favorable to his cause to rally on his side against the other partner. This puts a wedge between the parents.

"If the sympathetic one is usually the mother, and the father gives in, the child will learn to disrespect the father because he appears too weak to stand his ground. Later, he will despise his mother because she took away his father's authority. It may be that the husband is only trying to keep peace in the household. He may be unsure of his decisions because he's not around the children as much as his wife. When she comes on strong, he may yield to her wishes, thinking she's more knowledgeable. However, some mighty poor decisions have been made this way. The whole mess can be easily avoided by discussing each issue through while they're alone so the couple can come to a firm agreement without giving the children the opportunity of making them feel they're taking sides. Emily and I caught on pretty early to this game. We agreed together that we would not let the children drive a wedge between us.

"Anytime one of the kids would come to her and ask if they could go somewhere that was not a routine, O.K.'d situation, she would say, 'Your Dad and I will discuss it.' They were eager for us to have some private discussion time so they could get their answers. There was no game of pitting Mom against Dad. It made our kids feel secure. They never worried about whether Emily and I might get a divorce. If kids have parents who deeply love each other and who love the kids and agree on how to discipline them, those kids are not too likely to turn out bad."

"Well, Uncle Harold, yours are a pretty good example.

"Aunt Emily, what if a husband won't communicate? I've known gals who have no idea what their husbands are doing half the time, let alone what their goals and dreams are. These fellows have conversational 'lock jaw,' unless they feel like complaining. They seem like strangers in the same house and their kids are suffering as well."

"There are several reasons why men won't talk to their wives. One, their wives talk and never listen."

"Motor mouths," interjected Harold.

"They interrupt, contradict, argue, bury their nose in a book, or ridicule—any number of things which indicate they're not interested in hearing what he has to say. If they exhibited the same rude manners to one of their friends or neighbors, they'd probably never see that person again. Good listening manners are also important in a marriage.

"Another reason is a breach of confidence. The husband shares with his wife something about a fellow employee or a friend (usually a difficult relationship with which he's struggling), and she tells this personal news all over town. This can be very destructive, especially for a pastor. When he can't share the flock's problems with his own wife to get her perspective and prayer support without her broadcasting the problem through the whole church, he definitely won't continue sharing. No one wants to seek counsel from a man who publishes their confidences.

"It's true that some situations should not be shared with the wife, especially if the person confiding the information has asked the pastor not to share it. However, women do have a different perspective than men, and their God-given insight into certain problems can enhance their husbands' ministry, if they can be trusted to control their tongue. The same holds true for the wives of doctors, lawyers, or any other men who deal with the public. We have to keep everything we hear in strict confidence."

"I get to put in my two cents, too," said Harold. "I know some fellows who won't tell the little Mrs. what they're planning to do because it will inevitably cause an argument. It seems whatever they want to do, the little woman is opposed to it. She either doesn't want them to spend the money or go where they're going or to do what they're planning to do. Rather than have the hassle, they just peacefully go their way. Tell your lady friends to quit trying to run their husbands. Let the men do their dumb stunts and fall flat on their faces. If they're responsible for their own actions, they won't view the wife as a jailer and will be more willing to share their plans.

"I know a fellow who wanted to invest in some real estate. His wife fussed until she talked him out of it—too risky. If he had gone ahead, he'd have been a millionaire. He died poor as a church mouse and most of their lives they had it kind of rough. He lost everything he had anyway during the depression and had to start over again."

"What if you see he's heading for disaster, Uncle Harold?"

"Tell him. But let him make the decisions. When a woman tries to lead her husband, he knows he's being pushed out of his rightful place of leadership and he resents it. He'll react in several ways. If he dislikes confrontations, he'll clam up and live his own life with a little corner fenced off for the wife and kids when he cares to communicate. On the other hand, he may rant and rave, and most women aren't interested in that kind of communication."

Harold continued, "Now there's another type of communication problem I hear a lot about. Good old John Doe received a promotion, the doctor told him he's got to have a hernia operation, and the boss's secretary keeps making passes at him. His wife has put the little papers that separate the cheese slices right along with the cheese on his sandwiches for the last two days, and his thermos doesn't keep the coffee hot.

"He comes in the door after work dying to talk all these things over with his wife. Five neighbor kids are giggling and hooting with his five kids. Dear wife is doing a wash, cooking supper, and at the same time trying to keep some order. He decides he can dismiss the multitude later and talk after supper.

"However, after supper, Sally has piano lessons; Mark has a little league game; and, of course, Mom is taking them. It's now eight o'clock and everyone is home again. The TV is on and the whole family gets involved in some mystery plot, then a comedy, then the news, and it's bedtime. Dad turns off the TV, Mom yawns, and when poor John tries to unburden his heart, she mumbles, 'We have to get up at six, honey; it'll keep until morning.' But breakfast is too hectic and what he wants to share is for her ears only. Imagine the following scene:

> JOHN: Could we go out for dinner tonight, Susie?—Just you and me? You can get Elaine to come and babysit.
> SUSIE: Aren't we going to prayer meeting?
> JOHN: Oh sure. I forgot it was Wednesday. How about tomorrow?
> SUSIE: Mark has his big game tomorrow. Aren't you coming?
> JOHN: Oh sure. Friday night?
> SUSIE: Bible school program.
> JOHN: Saturday?
> SUSIE: The Bible school picnic.
> JOHN: Hmmm. Well, sometime I'd like to talk with you.

"I can read the next lines, Uncle Harold. At work the next day, the boss's secretary excitedly congratulates him on his promotion and inquires why he's going to be off for a week and sympathizes with him about his operation, shares with him a hot cup of coffee from her thermos, plus homemade cookies, and *listens* to him."

"There you go, June. It shouldn't happen, but it does, especially when a man is rethinking his goals and determining whether he's made something of himself or not. He needs a lot of encouragement and patience, a lot of sympathy and understanding."

Emily added, "A good wife will keep her finger on her husband's emotional pulse. She can detect if he's feeling down and carefully lift him up. She'll make a way to provide them time alone to talk and pray. This is what I'm referring to when I say the wife gives her husband a sharing mind. She shares her thoughts, but she also gives him an attentive mind so he can share his thoughts. If it doesn't work both ways, the communication will soon cease."

Emily continued, "There are other ways that a woman silences her husband. If she ridicules his plans or ideas, especially in front of others, or treats him like a dumb-dumb, he probably won't share his ideas again.

"Some men are just naturally quiet. They don't talk much to anyone, but when they do, they usually have carefully thought through what they have to say and can usually condense it very well in a few sentences. Their wives must be especially good listeners. Such quiet men need to be drawn out wisely—not with any attention drawn to the fact that they resemble a clam."

Harold piped up, "Besides, you're after the pearls in there, aren't you? So you bait him with questions and you hang on his answers so he knows, when he does say something, it's respected, appreciated, and really heard.

Harold continued, "I heard a woman ask her husband something and she never listened enough to know whether he answered her or not. He opened his mouth to answer her, but before he could get a word out, she started talking about something else. Her mind jumped like a frog from one thing to another. Ten minutes later she asked him the same question, accusing him of never answering her. He just looked at me and shrugged his shoulders. The dear lady talked so much he couldn't communicate anything if he tried."

Emily smiled. "We'll be talking more about the tongue tomorrow in lesson four."

"Oh, dear," I moaned.

"Believe it or not, June, Harold used to be a bit on the shy side."

"That *is* hard to believe."

"One thing a woman can do to draw out her husband is to turn the conversation over to him, especially when friends are over. I could say, for example, 'Well, I'd better let Harold explain that to you; he understands it much better than I do,' or 'Did you see the beautiful job Harold did to repair the garage after that tree limb fell on it?' or 'I don't want to steal Harold's thunder; I'll let him explain what happened at the meeting last night.' When you're alone, you might say something like 'A penny for your thoughts, dear.' or 'If you could do anything you wanted to do, what would it be?' "

"A man needs to share his dreams and his goals—maybe his fears and his weaknesses too, or his temptations. That's sharing. I might add, they'll be much more interested in listening to our problems if we give them our full attention when they talk."

"I'll add this," said Harold. "There's nothing more annoying to a man than trying to talk to his wife when she's dividing her attention between him and a magazine or a TV program. This really irks most men."

"Women too, Uncle Harold."

"I know, I know," he admitted. "But right now we're cracking open male clams.

"Some men have irkitis," Harold continued. "That's a malady which is brought on by being irked repeatedly in a short period of time. It's symptoms are like that of lock-jaw. The only thing that cures it is discovering what irked them in the first place. Some are admittedly oversensitive sometimes, but it won't kill a wife to uncover the offense and ask forgiveness. Some husbands pout when they're offended, and then they feel sorry for themselves because she doesn't even notice he's hurt or else she doesn't care. Usually just a few humble words can put the train back on the track again."

Emily added, "A discerning wife will not let irkitis go very long. It must be treated at the very onset of its symptoms; otherwise it develops a root of bitterness, and resentment moves in too. These negative emotions can kill a man as well as real lock-jaw; it just takes a little longer."

"Here," said Harold, "let me read Matthew 5:23 and 24:

> Therefore, if thou bring thy gift to the altar, and there rememberest that thy brother hath aught against thee;
>
> Leave there thy gift before the altar, and go thy way; first be reconciled to thy brother, and then come and offer thy gift.

"The Scripture says, 'Let not the sun go down upon your wrath.' Emily and I almost always pray just before we go to sleep. If either of us sense bad feelings between us, we get it straightened out before we pray."

Emily was nodding agreement as she started clearing the table. "I guess we could elaborate on the area of communication for many more hours. Let's suffice it to say, if you're not communicating, you're not walking as one."

"Amen!" agreed Harold. "In fact, Emily is my best friend and she says I'm her best friend. I think that's the way it should be."

"O.K., here's the last one," said Emily, running her dish water. "Give him a sensible mind. The word for *sensible* in the King James is *prudent*. Proverbs 19:14 says, 'House and riches are the inheritance of fathers: and a prudent wife is from the Lord.' " Emily dried her hands. "Here, let me read what Vine's says about the word *prudent*:

> . . . To have understanding (phren, the mind), denotes practical wisdom, prudence in the management of affairs. It is translated "wisdom" in Luke 1:17; "prudence" in Eph. 1:8. . . .
> Understanding is rendered "prudence" in I Cor. 1:19, R.V. . . . It suggests quickness of apprehension, the penetrating consideration which precedes action.[5]

"*Discreet* has a similar meaning. This is what Vine's says:

> . . . Of sound mind, self-controlled (for the deviation, see DISCIPLINE), is translated "sober-minded," in its four occurrences in the R.V. . . .
> . . . lit. mind-possessing (nous, mind, understanding, echo, to have), hence denotes discreetly, sensibly, prudently. Mark 12:34.[5]

"In Titus 2:5 the aged women are told to teach the young women to be discreet. Harold, please read us Proverbs 24:3 and 4."

> Through wisdom is an house builded; and by understanding is it established:
> And by knowledge shall the chambers be filled with all precious and pleasant riches.

"Here's one about a lack of discretion," continued Harold. "Proverbs 11:22:

> As a jewel of gold in a swine's snout, so is a fair woman which is without discretion.

Emily talked as she washed the dishes and I divided myself between drying dishes and taking notes. "We didn't say too much about this area," said Emily, "though it could be a whole study by itself. We talked about the Scripture as the source of wisdom. For example, Psalm 119:99 says, 'I have more understanding than all my teachers: for thy testimonies are my meditation.' If we read and meditate and obey the Word of God, we become sensible. We may not be intellectuals, but we will make wise and common-sense decisions.

"A fool is a person who lacks sense or judgment—a silly person. Paul talks about silly women in connection with lust in II Timothy 3:6."

"I'll read that," Harold volunteered.

> For of this sort are they which creep into houses, and lead captive silly women laden with sins, led away with diverse lusts.

Emily took it up again: "Notice, June, these women are not liberated, they're captives. The so-called women's liberation would like us all to be captives. Please read Proverbs 31:26 to us, Harold. We're going to do an expository study on this chapter and go into more detail about financial wisdom tomorrow, so we only mentioned financial wisdom and tabled it. Go ahead, Harold."

> She openeth her mouth with wisdom; and in her tongue is the law of kindness.

Emily spoke again, "The eighth chapter of Proverbs personifies wisdom—as though it were a woman named Wisdom. Proverbs 9:10 says, 'The fear of the Lord is the beginning of wisdom: and the knowledge of the holy is understanding.' In chapter 8 it tells us something about the fear of the Lord."

"I'll get that," said Harold, "it's verse 13:

> The fear of the Lord is to hate evil: pride and arrogancy, and the evil way, and the froward mouth do I hate.

"James 1:5 says:

> If any of you lack wisdom, let him ask of God, that giveth to all men liberally, and upbraideth not; and it shall be given him.

"Now the Devil likes to counterfeit anything God has," said Emily, emptying her dish water. "He makes the world's people proud about their worldly wisdom, but God says the 'wisdom of this world is foolishness with God . . .' The world doesn't comprehend God's wisdom because they're subjects of another kingdom.

"We have a strange phenomenon here on planet Earth. All of us live in the same physical place, but spiritually there are two kingdoms, the kingdom of light and the kingdom of darkness. Each person is in one or the other—either a servant of Jesus Christ in the kingdom of light or a servant of Satan in the kingdom of darkness. We behave much like the master of the kingdom to which we belong. The best choice must be God because Lucifer wanted to be like Him—'I will be like the most High.'

"The last chapter of the Bible tells us how the story ends. '...And He (Jesus Christ) shall reign for ever and ever.' The Devil and all his kingdom will be cast into the Lake of Fire. God's handmaidens would do well to stop casting their eyes over into the kingdom of darkness like Lot's wife did. They need to be pillars in the Church, not pillars of salt over in Sodom.

"We had an exciting experience in our class when I taught this lesson. One of the ladies had a cousin visiting with her who was involved in witchcraft. She told us later that she had turned down a promotion to the next level of witchcraft because she would be required to offer a human sacrifice."

"You mean kill somebody, Aunt Emily?"

"Right!"

"No wonder God said 'suffer not a witch to live' (Ex.22:18)."

"*Wicca* means Wise Ones. They believe, because they use occult powers, they are wiser than others, especially the people against whom they're using their witchcraft."

"I'm glad there aren't too many of these folks around."

"That's just the trouble," said Harold. "There *are* too many of these folks around. They've taken over the media. Emily's washer broke down last winter, so I toted her and the wash over to the laundromat in town. While we were there, two separate programs about witches came on. They were comedies, but witchcraft, nevertheless. Children watch several witchcraft type programs every week. The spooky mystery programs are often loaded with occult practices.

Harold proceeded, "The drug scene is also sorcery. Revelations 18:23 says concerning Babylon: '...For by thy sorceries were all nations deceived.' That word *sorcery* is the Greek word *pharmakeia* which means medication—in other words, drugs. Those who smoke pot or pop pills are involved with sorcery. Witches regularly use drugs to open themselves up to demons for the purpose of receiving occult power.

"In many of our government schools," continued Harold, "the teachers tell the kids to go home and look up their horoscopes. Some schools even teach astrology courses. College kids are all hyped up on Dungeons and Dragons, which is a craftily planned course in witchcraft geared to getting our nation's youth involved. Cases are being reported from different parts of the country of young people committing suicide after getting involved in Dungeons and Dragons. It is sometimes used in gifted and talented programs without the parents' knowledge.

"Ouija boards are sold by the thousands. It's not a toy; it moves by demonic power. Transcendental meditation is taught in some of our schools, even though it was declared a religion by the Supreme Court. We had a teacher right here in one of our local schools who hypnotized the kids in his class and did magic for them.

"Constance Cumbey says the New Age Movement is a loose network of hundreds of organizations made up of tens of thousands of people, and it's foundation is the occult. Many of the people involved in their programs do not realize this, but their work in these organizations is forwarding these occult goals. One of these goals is to usher in the Antichrist and his one-world religion, government, and economy."

Emily finished wiping the counter. "Thank you for drying for me, June. You'll have me spoiled. Harold helps me once in awhile if I get behind. He calls my dish-drain rack the leaning tower of pieces."

"Can't walk by without dishes falling all over the place. I think she designs that tower to do that so I'll help her," teased Harold.

"Let's all go in the living room," said Emily.

Once we were settled, she picked up the conversation again. "Last summer we had a video tape at an extra meeting at the church. It was from a TV program called 20-20. They had done a documentary on witchcraft and how it was affecting children. They didn't show the children's faces, but they were interviewing children who had repeatedly stabbed other children, under adult witches' direction, and then eaten their flesh. Then they showed some of the practices of Satanism. There is a real increase in witchcraft covens and Satan worship throughout the country. What makes me sick is that so much of it is creeping into our churches. Christians are wearing occult jewelry like Italian horns and good-luck charms. Sometime, look up the word *charm* in the dictionary. They even wear pentagrams, calling them the star of David. Witches use that star to cast spells. Unicorns and rainbows are symbols of the New Age Movement."

"I guess it is a lot worse than I thought. I've known a lot of what you're saying, but I never put it all together. I guess I don't think a whole lot about it because it's such an unpleasant thought."

"Happily," said Emily, "the girl Nancy, who was a witch, responded to the Word, so I threw out the net with Colossians 1:12 and 13. I'll read it:

> Giving thanks unto the Father, which hath made us meet to be partakers of the inheritance of the saints in light:
>
> Who hath delivered us from the power of darkness, and hath translated us into the kingdom of his dear Son:

"We had the privilege of leading Nancy out of the kingdom of darkness and into the kingdom of light. Now she can have God's wisdom, which is not phony and which will bring her eternal rewards instead of eternal punishment."

"I get goose-bumps every time I hear about someone getting saved. But I'm still thinking about all those curses and spells coming at us."

"We can combat that," said Harold. "I frequently include in my prayer time what I call a boomerang prayer:

> In the name of Jesus Christ, I now rebuke, break loose myself, and my family from any and all evil curses, charms, vexes, hexes, spells, jinxes, psychic powers, bewitchments, witchcraft, and sorcery that have been put on me or our family line from any persons or from any occult or psychic sources, and I cancel all connected and related spirits and command them to leave us and return upon the one who sent them bringing upon them the evil meant for us your anointed ones. In Jesus Name, Amen.[11]

"This is a prayer from the Warfare Prayers put out by H.B.C. Publications. We are definitely in a war, you know."

"I see that. It's good I can write fast, Uncle Harold. This prayer makes me feel like I've got some protection against 'the Force' anyway. I'm sure the witches don't like their little packages returned."

Emily opened her Bible. "We could spend a whole year studying wisdom, but we concluded with James 3:17:

> But the wisdom that is from above is first pure, then peaceable, gentle, and easy to be entreated, full of mercy and good fruits, without partiality, and without hypocrisy.

"And that concludes lesson 3."

"Let's see if I have everything down in my notes, Aunt Emily. We should give our husbands:

1. A united mind—one with God and with him.
2. A mind that is active rather than passive.
3. A mind that is pure rather than lustful.
4. A mind that is disciplined instead of undisciplined.
5. A mind that is peaceful instead of anxious.
6. A mind that is creative as opposed to lazy.
7. A mind that is trusting as opposed to suspicious.
8. A mind that is humble rather than proud or critical.
9. A mind that is informed instead of ignorant.
10. A sharing mind rather than one which is withdrawn and self-centered.
11. A mind that is sensible as opposed to foolish.

"Is that everything, Aunt Emily?"

"Somewhere in there should be a positive mind. That does not rule out all negative aspects, however. We cannot confront our husbands with their faults or differences of opinion without being negative. However, the negative aspect should be the exception rather than the rule. When we do express some negative aspect, we serve it up with a meek and quiet spirit sandwiched between two thick slices of love and/or forgiveness. Turn to Luke 17:3. Read 3 and 4 for us June."

> Take heed to yourselves: If thy brother trespass against thee, rebuke him; and if he repent forgive him.
>
> And if he trespass against thee seven times in a day, and seven times in a day turn again to thee, saying, I repent; thou shalt forgive him.

"Our general attitude," Emily concluded, "should be positive—expecting God to work in us and in our husbands for His glory."

I jotted down number twelve:

> 12. A mind that is positive instead of negative.

Then I stood and scooped up my Bible and notebook. "Well, I wasn't much help this time with the dishes, but I sure have a lot in my notebook. I think I'll leave you two alone so you can communicate. If you'll excuse me, I'm going upstairs and communicate with the Father. When you get ready to fix dinner, give me a shout and I'll come and help you."

"We'll take up lesson 4 tomorrow morning," said Emily. "I'm sure your head is stuffed full today."

I walked slowly upstairs into Ruth's old room and dropped to my knees with my notes before me on the bed.

This is so much, Lord; I can never do it without Your help. You said, 'Ye have the mind of Christ,' so please help me guard my thought life. Give me the wisdom I need to be a good wife and mother. I surrender my mind to You. Cleanse it, renew it, and fill it with Your Holy Spirit.

Perhaps you'd like to pray something similar.

# 6. THE MINISTRY OF OUR EMOTIONS

I awoke early Wednesday morning feeling a happy anticipation. "Well," I thought, as I finished reading Proverbs 8, "the Lord has begun renewing my will, my mind, and today, no doubt, He'll begin the job on my emotions. I surely wasn't expecting a complete overhaul, just a few ideas for my ladies' Bible class. Thank you, Lord."

I heard Harold and Emily singing, so I tiptoed quietly down the stairs. The aroma of something baking met me on the stairway. They finished their song just as the timer on the stove went off.

"That sounds good, folks. I've never heard that song before."

"That's because it's never been published," said Harold. "That's one of those new songs the Bible talks about that the Lord put in Emily's heart."

"I like it."

"A bird came here in our yard a couple years ago singing the first part of that melody," said Emily. "The rest of the song just fits in with it. As we said yesterday, God gives creativity to His creatures so we can praise Him better."

Emily headed for the oven. "Do you like blueberry muffins?"

"Sure do."

We enjoyed a hearty breakfast together. Then Uncle Harold went out to putter in the garden while Aunt Emily and I wisked through the house with vacuum sweeper and dust cloth.

"Whew!" panted Emily. "It's getting too warm for all this exercise. I'm glad I had you to help me."

"Your house doesn't get as dusty as mine, Aunt Emily."

"That's because there are only two of us to track in the dust. Let's make some lemonade and sit down with lesson four."

"Great. I'll get my notebook and Bible."

"Now, then," said Emily, once we were settled down at the kitchen table, "God wants a woman to minister to her husband with her emotions—just the good ones, though. It's a little hard to separate a person, even for a discussion of these areas, because our mind, emotions, body, and our will are so interrelated. For example, the word *heart* in the Scripture sometimes refers to the mind, sometimes it's referring to the seat of our emotions, sometimes to our will, and sometimes it's all-inclusive. In several places the Scripture refers to the heart as the source of our conversation, which we'll cover later in some detail."

"Oh, me."

"When the Scriptures refer to the soul, it also discusses the mind, will, and emotions. As I said yesterday, when we talked about the mind, you can control your emotions by what you choose to think. Our will should tell our heads to think good thoughts and discard the bad thoughts. Our emotions respond to what's in our thoughts. It's because people have passive minds that they don't control their thoughts and subsequently their emotions.

"This is just one more reason we didn't want a television set in our house. When you're constantly receiving information and attitudes and never responding to them, you're training yourself to have a passive mind. It programs you to disengage your thinking and reasoning faculties and just soak up what's on the screen. It becomes a form of brainwashing. Emotions are easily picked up from a sad movie or a scary one. The viewer identifies with the actor or actress and picks up on their attitudes and emotions. Talk about transference of spirits! The same thing is true about people you rub shoulders with every day."

"Oh, I know that's true, Aunt Emily. I had a friend who was always whining and complaining. Pretty soon I found myself doing the same thing. I finally just leveled with her from the Scripture. We prayed together and both of us did a reverse."

"That's the problem, June. Most women don't even notice what's going on because their reasoning powers have been dulled. They flow with whatever is happening around them.

"Our emotions are also affected by how we feel physically. If we're tired from lack of sleep or overextending ourselves or under a great deal of stress, we may be crabby or blue.

"We'll talk a bit about nutrition when we get to lesson 5, about the ministry of our bodies. It's enough to say here that our emotions will be affected by how our body feels, and how our body feels will be affected by the kind of food we eat. The kind of food we feed our family will also affect our family's emotions. We can also make ourselves and everyone around us miserable by not getting enough exercise or sleep."

"The weather affects our bodies as well," Emily added.

"Or our plans."

"It can be both. Rainy, snowy, or cloudy weather seems to affect most people in a negative way, whether it's the extra work of putting on protective clothing, the cancelled plans, or the extra mess to clean up when all that mud and snow gets tracked in. Just the atmosphere of a gray day seems to make us feel down. But we don't need to let our bodies run us. Paul was in charge of his thoughts, which were in charge of his emotions, and he's the one who wrote Philippians 4:8. No one suffered much more than Paul with fastings, shipwreck (in stormy weather, by the way), beatings, rejection, snakebite, and countless other trials. It was he that was stoned and left for dead. It was also Paul and Silas that sang praises in the prison with their feet in stocks while the blood ran down their slashed backs.

"King David was very prone to depression. He was pursued for years by Saul, who was relentlessly seeking to kill him. But David had the answer to his depression. The Psalms are great reading when you feel depression sneaking up on you. In one situation, David and his soldiers returned to the city of Ziklag to find that the Amalekites had gone off with all their wives and children and burned the city. David's men spoke of stoning him. I Samuel 30:6 says, '. . . But David encouraged himself in the Lord his God.'

"Moses also went running to the Lord when things got hectic. He knew he didn't have all the answers. If we operate on a humanistic level, we say, 'I can handle this.' But if we're wise, we run to the Father with all our problems."

"Before it gets us down," I added.

"Right. If we're smart, we can sense when a situation is becoming a problem before it does.

"God expects us to control our emotions. The world's people often try to control tears, especially the men, but they consider it a form of strength to get angry. Yet the Bible says, 'Rejoice with them that do rejoice, and weep with them that weep.' (Romans 12:15) Jeremiah was known as the weeping prophet. Weeping is usually a healthy outlet, unless we let it go to extremes, but anger is an unhealthy outlet in most cases. We need to submit our emotions along with our minds and our bodies to the Lord. There's a healthy balance that we can maintain if we walk in unselfish obedience to the Lord. Let me emphasize those two words—UNSELFISH OBEDIENCE.

"Our emotions don't just affect us; they affect everyone we live with. There are times when we should control our emotions, and there are times when we should release our emotions. The balance is maintained through unselfish obedience to the Lord.

"One extreme is the person who lets fly whatever she feels. One moment she's giddy with delight. Then something or someone comes crashing into her rosy world, and she crashes with it. She feels anger so she screams and throws things and everyone runs. Maybe she collapses in sobs and remains depressed for two weeks—unconsolable.

"The other extreme is the person with bound-up emotions. Perhaps she was hurt in childhood or her teen years, so she has built a wall around her. She's unable to reach out to anyone—even her husband or children, because she's afraid of being hurt. She buries any new hurts down inside, rather than let anyone see a show of emotions. This is a good way to develop ulcers or colitis. If there's a spirit of Unforgiveness there, it invites in Bitterness and those two demons bring in Resentment. These spirits open the door for Cancer, Arthritis, and other degenerative diseases. This is what doctors call psychosomatic illness. The majority of sickness is caused by wrong attitudes."

"Aunt Emily, what are you supposed to do with hurts and disappointments?"

"Forgive! As soon as possible. Our minds have a way of multiplying each hurt and hashing it over and exaggerating it, which opens us up to self-pity over even the smallest thing. Some hurts are purely our own imagination."

"You mean 'the Devil made us think it' type?"

"Right. Let's say the neighbor doesn't wear her glasses when she goes out to get the mail. She doesn't see Susie, let alone know Susie waved to her. But Susie feels rejected and hurt. If Sue would just forgive and forget, except to pray for her neighbor, and go out of her way to love her, the whole problem would be solved.

"Some women think everyone they know should be falling all over themselves trying to show consideration and attention towards them, or they feel rejected. People, including husbands, *do* have other things on their minds. Paul said in Romans 12:3 for a man 'not to think of himself more highly than he ought to think.' "

"One of the men in our church preached about forgiveness a few years ago, Aunt Emily. He said that as we mature in the Lord, we are less easily offended. When we're young Christians, we tend to say, 'I'll let the Lord get even with them because He said, "Vengeance is mine; I will repay.' " We want them to get back some of the hurt they caused us. Then we advance to 'Father, forgive them they know not what they do.' But the level of maturity for which we need to strive is the level where we don't get concerned over the things people do to hurt us. Offenses go over us like water off a duck's back. Psalm 119:165 says, 'Great peace have they that love thy law; and nothing shall offend them.' I can't say that I've arrived at that place, but I'm improving as I fill myself with God's Word."

"We need more messages like that. Sometimes, however, it's necessary to confront someone when they've offended you, not only for *your* sake, so they don't continue this behavior, but for *their* sake so they develop better character in their lives. It may be best for a wife to say to her husband, 'It hurts me when you say this or do that.'

"The key here again is unselfishness. Has he, or maybe the children, corrected you and it hurt? Correction does hurt, but the Word says, '. . . Godly sorrow worketh repentance.' Here, humility is necessary. We should consider when someone corrects us, 'Well, how can I change this and become the kind of person I should be?' A person who can't be corrected is unteachable. There are two kinds of unteachable people that I know about. One is the person who will not accept any kind of rebuke, criticism, or even a very kind suggestion for improvement."

"I know the kind, Aunt Emily. 'Don't tell me ANYTHING! I'm *always* right. I'm *never* wrong. *You're* wrong, not me!' "

"That says it, June. The other kind is just as bad and is more often found in women. If some correction is offered, she goes to pieces and dives to the bottom of an emotional sea. She's like an anchor. Anchors are steadily pulling down and allow no forward motion. A husband needs a wife who will flow with him and buoy him up, not anchor him down. The husband of that kind of woman can't communicate his likes and dislikes for fear she'll fall apart. By reacting like that she cuts off all negative communication coming from her husband. If he can't express what annoys him or angers him, how will she eliminate these things in order to please him. If these irritations continue, he may become bitter. He'll avoid the areas of confrontation, but the rancor will build up inside of him, and their relationship will suffer. Has it ever occurred to you what Paul means when he tells the husbands to love their wives and then admonishes them not to be bitter against them?"

"I often wondered about that. So we should allow them to communicate without the stop action of 'boo-hoos.' Aunt Emily, I'm pretty stable, but sometimes even I break down and cry."

"All of us feel shattered sometimes when the one we love the most comes down on us. I just tell Harold, 'Go ahead; don't mind me. I'm just watering your words in my heart so they won't die.' That let's me express myself, but relieve him—unless what he's saying is unfounded and wrong. If he's just expressing anger, and I'm the closest one at hand, he'll come to a sudden stop. Harold seldom gets angry, but once in awhile he behaves quite human.

"In every marriage there are occasions when a husband feels he should correct his wife. For example, some years ago Harold told me, 'You should wash clothes every day in the summertime, so these clothes don't get full of mildew sitting in the hamper.' He was right. Our summers are very humid and a couple of his favorite shirts had mildew stains on them. So I washed almost every day. At least, I hung things on a rack in the laundry room so they could air out if I couldn't wash them. Now I could have gotten all excited about this and felt attacked. He was upset about his shirts and wasn't altogether pleasant when he said it, but his purpose was not to make life miserable for me; he just wanted me to keep our clothes from being ruined."

"Aunt Emily, some men come on like a sergeant, barking orders and grumbling about everything."

"Yes, and I feel sorry for women with churlish husbands; but I know some of those men are like that because they can't get their wives to do what they want done without yelling at them. Some wives are lazy and neglectful, and then they feel put upon when hubby is ugly about it. Now I know you're going to say some men are ornery no matter how diligent their wives are. All I can say is pray for him and give him lots of vitamins and minerals to ease his hypertension, and then bind up evil spirits in him. Sing or play quiet Christian music like David did to quell Saul's evil spirits. Having two people out of sorts won't help matters anyway, so it's best to keep sweet yourself. The Bible says, 'A soft answer turneth away wrath,' and I've seen it work many times.

"We're not responsible for our husbands' behavior, but we are responsible for ours. We just need to be sure our husbands have no cause to grumble. Some women frustrate their husbands nearly out of their minds by being contrary and then seem surprised when they roar. All of us dread being bawled out by our husbands or even our children, but we need to examine what they say and thank them for correcting us. Gratefulness for their correction gives them a respect for us and it destroys pride in us.

"At any rate, we must avoid the one extreme of unfettered emotions and the other of bound-up emotions. Both can destroy our health and our relationship with our husbands. If we're unselfish in expressing our emotions, we'll probably be well balanced.

"For women who have built emotional walls around themselves, I recommend that they pray, asking the Father to tear down these barriers. Then they should get deliverance prayer from spirits of Fear of giving and receiving love, Inability to give and receive love, Fear of failure, Fear of hurt, Rejection, Deep hurt, Wounded spirit, and Self-rejection. Often Rebellion and Stubborness are part of this bunch. There may be more with this nasty little package, but that's a good start.

"Next, we addressed some specific negative emotions and how we could handle them. What do you think is the most destructive of our negative emotions?"

"Anger."

"That was the general consensus of the class. I think anger is a problem for most of us. Anger expresses itself in many ways. Some pout; some get quiet and won't speak; some scream and shout; some get violent; some think up revenge; some just feel sorry for themselves; some laugh it off; and some cry."

"Aunt Emily, you were saying before that tears were a *healthy* release."

"Usually. I'm sure you have heard a two-year-old, on one occasion cry because he was hurt and on another occasion cry because he was having a temper tantrum."

"Oh, yes, indeed. The first cry you run to hug him, but the second cry you know is anger; it's selfish, and more than likely, he needs an application of the golden ruler to the seat of learning. A mother can usually tell."

"Exactly. Our crying may be a release of real hurts or a selfish explosion because we can't have our own way. Two-year-olds learn to manipulate their folks if they can get away with it; and some women who have never grown up will manipulate their husbands with angry tears to get their own way.

"Every woman has her own means of expressing anger. How we were raised as children and how our parents and brothers and sisters expressed their anger affects us greatly."

"Can anger be inherited?"

"Sort of. The Bible speaks of the sins of the fathers being visited unto the third and fourth generation. The Insititute in Basis Youth Conflicts published the testimony of a woman who had trouble with a terrible temper. When she confessed the sins of her father, who had a violent temper, as well as her own sin, she was able to have victory over her own problem with anger. Win Worley's book, *Eradicating the Hosts of Hell*, has a whole section about the sins of the fathers. This goes for any sin or circumstance with which we're suffering. We need to ask the Lord to show us the sins of our ancestors. Remember

God holds the husband or the father responsible for the sins of his wife or daughters, so your mother's or grandmother's sins are considered to be the sins of the fathers."

"Does this mean if I sin, my father, and then my husband, catch it from God because of what I've done?"

"I've never thought about that, but I guess that could be so. It would make an interesting Bible study, wouldn't it? Anyway, if we sin, our children suffer from it later down the line. They can also reap what we sow.

"Jesus was made a curse for us on the cross, so we can appropriate His death to deliver us from the curses brought upon us by the sins of our fathers. As it says in Ezekiel 18, we don't bear the iniquity of our fathers. We're not going to be lost for eternity because they sinned, but there are consequences for sin which do affect our circumstances in life. There are curses which carry down to the fourth generation. Read Leviticus 26:40-42 for us, June."

> If they shall confess their iniquity, and the iniquity of their fathers, with their trespass which they trespassed against me, and that also they have walked contrary unto me;
>
> And that I also have walked contrary unto them, and have brought them into the land of their enemies; if then their uncircumcised hearts be humbled, and they then accept of the punishment of their iniquity:
>
> Then will I remember my covenant with Jacob, and also my covenant with Isaac, and also my covenant with Abraham will I remember; and I will remember the land.

"The meaning of confession is that we agree with God that a certain action is wrong. Repentance is turning away from it. By confessing the sins of the fathers, each succeeding generation is reminded that what their fathers did was wrong and brings unpleasant consequences. When we suffer for their sins, our uncomfortable circumstances cause us to agree with God that what our fathers did was wrong, and we will want to forsake those sins, rather than follow in their footsteps. We can pray something like this: Father, I confess the sins of my fathers in having a bad temper (or whatever). I also confess my own sin of anger. Forgive us of this sin and deliver me from the consequences of the sins of my fathers because of the work of Jesus on the cross. I also ask that You will remove the consequences of our sin upon my descendents. In Jesus' Name. Amen.

"I would say, June, that some of the most serious curses that come upon the third and fourth generation are from the fathers' involvement with the occult. It was this idolatry which caused Israel to lose their land and the benefits of the covenant which God had made with them.

"We may not know all the sins of our fathers. We can confess their sins in areas where we think there may have been problems just in a general way, but the more specific we can be, the more cleansing there will be. What's important is the heart attitude: 'Lord, we don't want this sin to continue in our family any longer.'

"Now let's go over several verses on anger. God's Word says in Proverbs 16:32:

> He that is slow to anger is better than the mighty; and he that ruleth his spirit than he that taketh a city.

"He says in Proverbs 29:22:

> An angry man stirreth up strife, and a furious man aboundeth in transgression.

"Psalm 37:8 says:

> Cease from anger, and forsake wrath: fret not thyself in any wise to do evil.

"Ephesians 4:26 says:

> Be ye angry, and sin not: let not the sun go down upon your wrath:
>
> Neither give place to the devil.

"Verse 31 continues:

> Let all bitterness and wrath, and anger, and clamour, and evil speaking, be put away from you, with all malice:

"Notice the list of evils which includes wrath in Galatians 5:19-21. Read that for us please, June."

> Now the works of the flesh are manifest, which are these; Adultery, fornication, uncleaness, lasciviousness,
> Idolatry, witchcraft, hatred, variance, emulations, wrath, strife, seditions, heresies,
> Envyings, murders, drunkeness, revellings, and such like: of the which I tell you before, as I have told you in time past, that they which do such things shall not inherit the kingdom of God.

"Now then, we can conclude, June, that anger, wrath, and strife, which are all first cousins, are a decided 'no-no' for any believer. It would be a good project for your Bible class to go through *Strong's Exhaustive Concordance of the Bible* and look up all the verses on anger, wrath, strife, bitterness, and resentment. Have them each write out all the verses in a notebook. Look up the definitions of these words and then discuss ways you can overcome anger. Have them write their conclusions in their notebook. Oh, yes, add grudges, vengeance, and reviling. You can probably think of more."

"That sounds profitable."

"Tim LaHaye and Bob Phillips have written an excellent book called *Anger Is a Choice,* which I think I mentioned in the last lesson in connection with the mind. You could use that in connection with this study. They list a lot more of the verses of course. I just mentioned a few to show that God expects us to overcome anger.

"Anger is a problem for both genders, but here's a verse in Proverbs 21:19 specifically for women:

> It is better to dwell in the wilderness, than with a contentious and an angry woman.

"You know, Aunt Emily, I just happened to think, the women who espouse the feminist movement, ERA, National Organization for Women and all the abortion and lesbian groups, as a rule, look angry. Pictures in the newspapers and magazines usually show them with a hostile, bitter countenance. In fact, they have written articles about how male chauvinists want women to be pleasant and smile all the time, and they don't want to oblige them."

"No one could help but notice their unhappiness, or their arrogance in some cases," agreed Emily. "But whenever you see a picture of Phyllis Schlafly or Beverly LaHaye or Marabel Morgan, they look as though they thoroughly enjoy life as a feminine woman. They look fulfilled. The women's liberation folks shouldn't really be called feminists because many of them deplore true femininity. They should be called masculinists because many of them want to make women like men. We'll get into this more in our last lesson."

"Oh, good. I didn't mean to get us off the track of anger. Go ahead."

"Well, you're correct; a good many of these women *are* angry, and in connection with that last verse we read, many of them are also alone. No man wants to come home to an angry and contentious woman.

"Another thing I want to mention in regard to anger is that it is sometimes related to drinking. For all that the Scriptures say about drinking, the churches, on the whole, in the United States have become very lax in their position concerning drinking. More and more Christian people are sliding over into the world's camp with so-called moderate drinking. But I'm beginning to hear of one tragedy after another, such as Christians becoming alcoholics and teenage drinking in so-called Christian homes."

"Kids always seem to do in excess what their parents do in moderation," I interjected. "Or maybe it's the sins of the fathers visited unto the third and fourth generation."

"That's probable. The connection of drinking and wrath is mentioned in Proverbs 20:1:

> Wine is a mocker, strong drink is raging: and whosoever is deceived thereby is not wise.

"We've found, June, that when people drink, they open themselves up for evil spirits of Rage and Mockery. It's similar to what happens when people smoke marijuana, or take drugs in other forms; they give grounds for evil spirits to enter them."

"Even legal drug store-drugs, Aunt Emily?"

"It's possible even for legal drugs to do the same thing. Even the kids will remark, 'Hey, my Dad takes prescription uppers to stay awake, and my Mom takes prescription downers to go to sleep. What's the difference if I pop a few pills?' And, I'm sorry to say, they're probably right; there's not a whole lot of difference. You'll remember yesterday, when we were talking about witchcraft, we said the word *sorcery* in the *Strong's Concordance* is the Greek word *pharmakeia* from which our words *medication* and *pharmacy* stem. Not everything sold in the drug store is related to sorcery, but many of the drugs could be, especially the mind-altering ones. Most mind-altering drugs don't cure anything; they only mask the symptoms or make them more bearable. All of the 'substances,' controlled or uncontrolled, are suspect to me. I avoid anything that's addictive—even caffeine products. I don't need to be in any bondage, whether it's socially approved or not.

"Back to the drinking problem. Whenever I counsel someone who has a problem with violent anger, I always ask them if they drink or if they drank before they were saved. Quite often, I get a surprised reply of 'Yes. How did you know?' From there, we deal with the area of the demonic, and I also suggest that they confess the sins of their fathers concerning drinking, supplying liquor to others, and rage."

"Aunt Emily, I'm still somewhat dense about what you do with your anger. If you don't let it fly and you don't hold it in, what do you do with it?"

"Harold and I put together a list of practical means to overcome anger. First, don't let it get a start. Anger is like a fire. You can blow out a match, but not a forest fire. Recognize anger as sin and confess it as such, even if you think the other person is in the wrong. Having a wrong attitude is wrong also, and two wrongs don't make a right. Immediately forgive the other person. Pray as if you were reaching for a fire extinguisher. Keep very short accounts with God.

"Secondly, do something constructive with that anger while it's only a mild irritation. If someone has angered you, examine carefully whether you're at fault, and make the thing right. If the other person is clearly wrong, tell the offender in a meek spirit, or with a show of humor, how they've offended you. We discussed in lesson two how to settle disagreements with your husband in a good way. Sometimes joking about something that has bothered us can ease, not only the other person's tensions, but ours too.

"A third option, if you can't dissolve your anger by gently expressing it with self-control, is to give it to the Lord like any other burden. Write it on paper and hand it to the Lord to make it graphic. My friend Alice gets out butcher paper and pretends she's wrapping her problems in it. Then she gives them to the Lord. Ask the Lord to forgive the person, and to bless him. Then *you* forgive the person as well. Then leave the problem with the Lord for Him to handle. Ask the Lord to cleanse your heart from anger, resentment, hurts, or bitterness. We read a few minutes ago from Ephesians 4:26:

> Be ye angry, and sin not: let not the sun go down upon your wrath:

"We mentioned this before, but Harold and I almost always pray before we go to sleep at night and again the first thing before we get up in the morning. Matthew 5:23 and 24 says:

> Therefore if thou bring thy gift to the altar, and there rememberest that thy brother hath ought against thee;
>
> Leave there thy gift before the altar, and go thy way; first be reconciled to thy brother, and then come and offer thy gift.

"If one of us is grumbled about something, one or both of us apologize. Or if it's a disagreement, we agree to table it for discussion and agree to love each other with a forgiving attitude until it's settled. It's usually the unforgiving attitudes over which people can't sleep, not the disagreement itself. If one of us is out of sorts, it's expected at the dinner table that the angry one give thanks for the food. How can you pray before you straighten things out? Frequent prayer makes you keep short accounts with God. We know that an unforgiving attitude is ugly in God's sight, so we repent and apologize. That way we don't build any walls between us, and our fellowship with God is not broken either. To pretend nothing is wrong doesn't fool anyone, not even ourselves. We only show that we're proud, stubborn, and implacable."

"Why do you have to make that so plain, Aunt Emily?"

"And besides 'stubborness is as idolatry.' That's plainer yet.

"Fourth, thank the Lord for the experience. He tells us in I Thessalonians 5:18:

> In everything give thanks: for this is the will of God in Christ Jesus concerning you.

"And He says in Romans 8:28 that, '. . . all things work together for good . . .'

"Nothing happens to us by mistake. Hard things build character into our lives; if nothing else, patience. God tests us with hard things in our lives. If we flunk the test, He just puts us through a review of the lesson again and repeats the test. When we pass the test, we go on to something a little harder. That's growing, and that's how we become mature. Some people keep going through the same bad routine because they never learn the lessons and pass the test. We need to ask the Lord to teach us what we're supposed to be learning in all of this trial. Our reactions may be at the bottom of all our troubles.

"Fifth, put your mind on other things, as Philippians 4:8 commands us to do, and rest in the Lord. Trust God to handle it in His way and in His time."

"Aunt Emily, you're purposely not limiting this to the anger the wife feels towards her husband."

"As I mentioned before, June, anger opens the door for resentment and bitterness. A woman can have a bad relationship with her dad and bottle it all up inside. She's never handled it, so it pops to the surface years later, and her husband gets the action of this 'floating bitterness.' She needs to write down all the offenses and then forgive her dad, or whomever. It could be her mom, an old boy friend—anyone. She needs to forgive them and ask God to forgive them and bless them. Some people have a floating anger much like a submarine—just a little below the surface. Every little thing anyone does or says is interpreted as aggression of the enemy. The old anger surfaces and fires on them. Kids catch a lot of floating anger carried over from Mom and Dad's childhood, and unfortunately, they do the same thing—save it inside for their spouse or kids."

"The sins of the fathers again?"

"Yes, ma'am, perpetuated on and on to the Devil's delight. Oh, yes, let me mount my soap-box again. The next time you're obliged to watch the Babylon Box, observe how much anger is exhibited. Tell me a woman doesn't absorb some of that hostility when she's soaking up soap operas all day and detective stories all evening.

"Another thing we can do with angry attitudes is picture them as old ragged and dirty clothes. The Scriptures offer a good description of this in Colossians 3:8-10. Read that for us, please."

> But now ye also put off all these; anger, wrath, malice, blasphemy, filthy communication out of your mouth.
>
> Lie not one to another, seeing ye have put off the old man with his deeds;
>
> And have put on the new man, which is renewed in knowledge after the image of him that created him:

"I'll read verses 12-17," said Emily:

> Put on therefore, as the elect of God, holy and beloved, bowels of mercies, kindness, humbleness of mind, meekness, longsuffering;

> Forbearing one another, and forgiving one another, if any man have a quarrel against any: even as Christ forgave you, so also do ye.
>
> And above all these things put on charity, which is the bond of perfectness.
>
> And let the peace of God rule in your hearts, to the which also ye are called in one body; and be ye thankful.
>
> Let the word of Christ dwell in you richly in all wisdom; teaching and admonishing one another in psalms and hymns and spiritual songs, singing with grace in your hearts to the Lord.
>
> And whatsoever ye do in word or deed, do all in the name of the Lord Jesus, giving thanks to God and the Father by him.

"And the next verse, Aunt Emily, is about wives submitting to their husbands."

"That's a good observation, June. See, the new garments are so much nicer; it's best to take off the old rags and toss them in the rag bag. They're not even good enough to give away. Here in Proverbs 31:25 we find another description of proper wearing apparel:

> Strength and honor are her clothing; and she shall rejoice in time to come.

"Read I Timothy 2:9-10, June."

> In like manner also, that women adorn themselves in modest apparel, with shamefacedness and sobriety; not with broided hair or gold or pearls or costly array;
>
> But (which becometh women professing godliness) with good works.

"In Isaiah we're told that Jesus was anointed to give us, among other things, 'a garment of praise for a spirit of heaviness.' Read I Peter 3:3-5 for us, please."

> Whose adorning let it not be that outward adorning of plaiting the hair, and of wearing of gold, or of putting on of apparel;

> But let it be the hidden man of the heart, in that which is not corruptible, even the ornament of a meek and quiet spirit, which is in the sight of God of great price.
>
> For after this manner in the old time the holy women also, who trusted in God, adorned themselves, being in subjection unto their own husbands:

"This is interesting, Aunt Emily. The three New Testament passages about a woman putting on spiritual apparel are in the context of submission to her husband, and they're each describing different types of spiritual clothing."

"That *is* interesting isn't it? Remember what we read from Wycliffe's about meekness?"

"I still have a difficult time understanding meekness. I connect it in my mind with obsequiousness—being a doormat, and I know that's not God's concept."

"Meekness suggests controlled and bridled strength, Wycliffe says. It's self control in which we humble ourselves under the mighty hand of God so He can accomplish His will in a given situation. A meek and quiet spirit is a lovely garment in God's sight."[7]

"I guess I'll have to renovate my entire spiritual wardrobe."

"Think of it this way, June: the Church is getting ready for the Bridegroom, and when He comes for her, she'll be without spot or wrinkle. The Lord Jesus may need to do some last minute spot cleaning. In fact I think He's attempting to clean up the Church right now with revival, and He wants His Bride to be working on all her spots and wrinkles in preparation for His return. As wives, we're a lesson to other people when they see us adorned in the spiritual garments He tells us to wear.

"We can't do this in our own strength either. We're told that 'all our righteousnesses are as filthy rags.' We must become leaners, leaning on the Lord for every need—even our spiritual clothes.

"Well, June, does that give you some constructive help on how to overcome anger?"

"Yes, that gives me a way to go—a *long* way to go."

"Another aspect," continued Emily, "is that when a person entertains these sinful attitudes of anger, they soon entertain the evil spirits that accompany them. An angry person gives legal grounds for demons to reside in her, and then those evil spirits invite in other spirits also. These need to be cast out as well as repenting of the sin and dying to it according to Romans 6-8. The longer a person has been harboring bitterness and resentment, the stronger the bondage will be.

"The Church, as a whole, avoids this ministry. Some feel a demon can't dwell in the same temple with the Holy Spirit. Do they think the Holy Spirit is instigating dear Susie to throw dishes at John? She may indeed be struggling with her old sin nature, the flesh. But if she has seriously surrendered herself to the Lord and reckoned herself dead indeed to this sin of anger and the compulsion of anger still persists, one must consider the need for deliverance from demonic spirits. Demons did not go away when Jesus ascended into heaven. Nor did they go away when the Canon of Scripture was completed.

"I think, June, that the list in Ephesians 3:31 includes most of the different forms of anger. You might add strife, contention, argumentation, and rage. Hatred and murder would probably be at the bottom of the pile—the ultimate result of not gaining victory and deliverance over anger. I John has a whole lot to say on hate versus love."

"And the impression love or hate has on an observing world that views the Church," I added.

"True. Or the marriage, which is a type of Christ and His Bride, the Church.

"Well, let's go on. What do you think is the next most destructive emotion, June?"

"Fear."

"I'll agree. Read II Timothy 1:7, please."

> For God hath not given us a spirit of fear; but of power, and of love, and of a sound mind.

"I John 4:18 says:

> There is no fear in love; but perfect love casteth out fear: because fear hath torment. He that feareth is not made perfect in love.

"I read a little verse years ago that has really helped me. Two lines have stuck with me:

> Fear is faith in Satan;
> Faith is fear in God.

"What's the difference in those fears, Aunt Emily? I've always had a question there. How can one fear be good and another fear bad?"

"Pick up *Wycliffe's Bible Encyclopedia* again and look up the word *fear.* Read it to us, please. Just skip the Bible references and the Greek or Hebrew words; you can put them in your notebook later."

> Fear. A term used both in the O.T. and the N.T. in several very significant ways. The Scriptures speak of the following kinds of fear.
>
> 1. A holy fear . . . which amounts to awe or respect for the majesty and holiness of God, a godly reverence. . . . David speaks of fear as clean and pure;. . . Job and the psalmist, as the basis or beginning of all true wisdom. . . . This fear is God-given and enables man to respect God's authority, obey his commands, turn from evil, . . . and to pursue holiness. . . . Gentile converts to Judaism who believed in God were called God-fearers.
>
> 2. A filial fear . . . which is based upon the proper reverence of the child of God for his heavenly Father. . . .
>
> 3. A fear for unforgiven sin which is caused by the work of the law written in the heart . . . and the knowledge of God's Word; e.g., Adam's fear when he sinned; . . . Felix as he heard Paul preach; . . . that of men who reject the preaching of the gospel. . . .
>
> 4. A fear, dread or terror . . . of God's holiness on the part of the wicked at the Lord's coming. . . . Along with this we may consider a fear of His people that God places in other men's hearts to protect His own. . . .
>
> 5. A fear of man is also mentioned in Scripture. This may either be a proper respect for those in authority, . . . or a senseless dread. . . .
>
> 6. A fear for others and the danger in which they stand. . . .
>
> 7. A terror of the unknown . . . or of the uncanny. . . .
>
> 8. Cowardice or timidity, . . . as in "A spirit of fear" . . . and "let not your heart . . . be afraid". . . .
>
> Fear is sometimes falsely assumed to be the origin of religion, but fear alone in the sense of dread is not the positive force that draws men to God with an attitude of reverence, worship, and respect.

> The Kierkegaardian concept of *"Angst zum tode,"* that anxiety which pursues man right through life until his death, falls under the third classification above, since it expresses the nagging anxiety which besets the unsaved. This fear, and the dread of appearing before a holy God, is eliminated—or ought to be—in the lives of believers, . . . though the fear of reverence and of respect for authority remains.[7]

"Does that help cure your wonders, June?"

"Yes, that clarifies a lot of things. I've been telling my ladies' class that they should ask the Lord to expose their fears so they can see them and get rid of them. One lady was so afraid of the dark, she had to sleep with the night light on. We encouraged her to think through her fear rationally and prayerfully. 'What can darkness do to you? Did something happen to you in the dark as a child? Is there something in the dark of which you're *really* afraid? Can you trust the Lord to protect you in an automobile? Can you see that being afraid of the dark is saying to God that you trust Him to take care of you everywhere but in the dark?'

"That night she prayed, committing herself to the Lord, and turned out the light. She was a little uneasy at first, but kept praying and repeating Scripture until she fell asleep. The next night was a snap. She overcame her fear and was delighted."

"That's wonderful."

"However, another lady did the same thing with her fear of dogs and it flunked. She lives next door to a family with two large Dobermans, and they snarl and bark at her every times she goes out in the yard. She's so filled with terror every time she sees them, she shakes all over. She waits for the kids to come home from school so they can carry out the garbage or clean the yard. She can't enjoy her flowers, a lawn party—nothing outside. She feels like she's in prison. She acknowledges that the dogs are behind a high fence and there's no way they can get at her. She's committed it to the Lord, she's prayed and trusted God to take care of her, but everytime she sees those dogs, she freezes. It fills her with a lot of doubt and depression."

"Does she have other fears too?"

"Loads. None of which she seems able to overcome."

"She may very well have spirits of Fear. She may have been born with them. Demons don't respond to reason; they have to be forced out by the Name and authority of Jesus Christ. She may have picked up these fears from her parents. One spirit of Fear seems to pick up other kinds of fear spirits.

"Fear is one of Satan's biggest tools. It blocks us from sharing our faith, destroys relationships, and hinders us from ministering to others. You mentioned the other day about how you were afraid Trent couldn't handle the organization of the family work. See what damage it did to your relationship with your whole family? Satan must dance with glee when he can fill people with fear, because it immobilizes them, torments them, and even kills them. Luke 21:26 speaks of men's hearts failing them for fear. Satan steals, kills, and destroys.

"Fear can totally destroy a marriage. Satan will throw Fear of failure on the husband and Fear of poverty on the wife. She needles him and reinforces his fear, so he fails worse and reinforces her Fear of poverty. As wives, we have to get our eyes off the waves, put our hand in the Lord's hand, and trust Him to help us walk on the water in the tempest. We trust our husbands, yes, but the underlying trust is in our Lord. We trust Him to help our husbands. That's what a believer is—a truster. 'The fear of the Lord is the beginning of wisdom.' To fear other things or people is the beginning of foolishness. 'Fear not' is a frequent command in Scripture, often followed by 'I am with thee.' That's the promise part."

"I've noticed something else, too, Aunt Emily; the people who don't fear God, and are very flippant about sin, are often full of the wrong kind of fears."

"Sure. 'The wicked flee when no man pursueth, but the righteous are as bold as a lion.' That's Proverbs 28:l. The Lord supplies courage and boldness to his people in hard places.

"There's another aspect of fear, however, which I want to discuss here. One reason God created us with the capacity to fear was so we could remove ourselves from danger. If I see a truck bearing down on me as I cross the road to the mailbox, I scurry out of its path. I fear I'll get run over if I don't move quickly.

"If I lived in Colorado, and a rattlesnake slithered up, my adrenalin would flow, and I'd be gone like a flash. If I had a hoe, I might try chopping off his head, especially if the children were near by. But if Harold was anywhere around, I would call upon him to protect me from a real danger. Men are the ones God put in charge of defending the family from real dangers and some of the imaginary ones too. God built into the man special strengths in his body, mind, emotions, and will that enable him to respond efficiently to danger.

Men usually enjoy their role as protectors of the family and wives should not deny them this role."

"Now if Harold is in town and a tornado comes through here, I'm not going to stand here paralyzed and wait for Harold to rescue me. However, if he's near, I'm not going to act like I'm his mother and protect him or independently dive for the fruit cellar. I'll look to him to protect me. He'll feel like a man and I'll feel like a cherished wife.

"Too many women try to be a fearless Wonder Woman, which makes their husbands feel useless. The 'Macho Mom' role robs a man of his God-given responsibility to protect the family.

"If a husband tells his wife not to go out alone on a long trip or into a certain part of town where there may be real danger of being molested, she should realize this is his God-given instinct to protect, and she shouldn't argue with him about it. If he fusses over unlocked doors on the house or car, it's because assaults on women are very real dangers. She should cooperate with him and let him know she appreciates his protection of her, even if these are not things that worry her.

"If she has fears, she should confide them to her husband so he can help her overcome them. This will also strengthen the protective instincts which fortify his masculinity. These fears are not always unbelief. If we didn't fear for our children, we'd let them play in the traffic. That would be tempting God, not trusting Him."

"Does this apply to the nonphysical dangers, like mortgage forclosures and bankruptcy?"

"That's a tough one because probably the husband and wife are both scared. 'Now what will we do?' She needs to encourage him in every way, but not allow him to feel that she can handle it but he can't. When a man faces failure, the best way to encourage him is to assure him of your love and trust. He needs a super measure of affection—'You look like you need a hug and a kiss.' It might be best to express her fears; it may jolt his protective instincts and fill him with courage so he can calm *her* fears. But she needs to walk gingerly here. If she's totally distraught, the trauma may be too much for him to handle. She has to share not only her fears, but her confidence that he will be able to make a new start, benefiting from the lessons of the past.

"He will feel unworthy to make love, but he needs it. This is one of those times the wife may need to be the aggressor. This picture is not, 'O.K., Bud, you've been a colossal failure, but don't you fear, I'll hold you up through the mess and help you put the pieces back together again.' Rather, 'I'm scared, but I love you more than all these things, and I know you can rebuild our lives. We have each other and that's what really counts.'

"Even millionaires have gone bankrupt and have become millionaires again. It can draw a husband and wife closer together than they have ever been before. When Dr. Walter Wilson, that beloved physician, who was so well known as a soul winner, lost everything during the depression, his wife said something like this: 'Well, now we'll have the opportunity to see what God can do for us when we have nothing.' Dr. Wilson knew she trusted in God and in him."

"So you're saying, Aunt Emily, that if you have fears, let him help you get rid of them. If he has protective fears, let him protect you. In the main, however, fear is unbelief, and you should overcome it."

"Right. I'd like to address another kind of fear at this point—a fear of loss or a fear of being alone. Many women fear their husbands will run off with another woman, that he'll be unfaithful to her, that he'll abandon her, or that he'll lose interest in her. This kind of fear causes her to cling to him like a parasite. She doesn't want him to go anywhere or do anything without her. Suspicion is hard to conceal, and it is an insult to a man that his wife doesn't trust him, even if he's not trustworthy. On the other hand she may fully trust him but just doesn't want him to leave her alone at home. "The natural response of a husband to this clinging vine is to get loose from it. He feels smothered and entangled—controlled. A man resents feeling trapped by a marriage. The more she clings, the more he pulls away. It isn't right, but it is human nature.

"It's also human nature for the wife to center her life around her husband. Her ministry is to minister to her husband, so she plans everything around him, including her affections. The answer to this problem is to center her life in the Lord and consider her ministry to her husband as flowing from that center. Her security, then, is in the Lord. Her affections flow from the Lord through her to her husband as she ministers to him as unto the Lord. When her husband no longer senses a possessiveness, he can relax and enjoy her company. They can be best friends as well as marriage partners.

"If she has misgivings about her husband's faithfulness, she can pray that the Lord will put a hedge of thorns around him.
I'm not saying that the woman who trusts the Lord with her husband will never have an unfaithful husband or will never have a husband who leaves her alone frequently. What I am saying is that a woman who centers her life around her husband makes an idol of him, and God is in the business of removing our idols."

"So the way to avoid smothering your husband is to rest in the Lord and then rest your husband in the Lord as well."

"Exactly."

"So how do you deal with the other fears, Aunt Emily?"

"You handle them much the same as anger. First you confess your fears as unbelief and sin, and ask God to forgive you and help you overcome them. As you told your class, think each fear through and make yourself face it head on. Most fears are totally irrational. Ask yourself, 'What's the worst thing that can happen?' The worst thing that can happen is that we'll all die. Then we'll go to heaven, right? Christians shouldn't fear death. Death is the beginning of a wonderful new life with Jesus Christ. We'll be absent from the body and present with the Lord.

"If someone is fearful of where they'll spend eternity, they need to ask themselves, 'On what am I basing my salvation? My works? Then I'm my own Saviour; I'll never make it to heaven! On the Church? The Church cannot be my Saviour.' Jesus said, 'I am the way, the truth and the life, no man cometh unto the Father but by me.' They need to see that God as a judge cannot lay aside justice for mercy and retain His holiness and His Godhead, so He sent His own Son to pay our debt. 'The wages of sin is death.' With the penalty paid, He could extend pardon and forgiveness. We can't do a thing to save ourselves. All we can do is receive God's pardon and His salvation through Jesus. The price was paid for all mankind, but each must come personally to receive the free gift before he is saved from condemnation. When we do receive His gift of eternal life, He adopts us as His own child and the Holy Spirit bears witness with our spirit that we are the children of God. If we're sure we're saved, we're sure we're safe when we die.

"As I said before, if all that reasoning doesn't remove a person's fears, she probably needs deliverance from demons."

"Aunt Emily, that poor fearful girl I told you about is no doubt in need of deliverance. How can I help her?"

"Read through Win Worley's books and there's another book that will be helpful too—*Pigs in the Parlor* by Frank and Ida Mae Hammond. She and her pastor should read the books as well. If her pastor doesn't believe Christians can have demons, the demons may claim they don't have to leave because she's under his spiritual authority. I've seen that happen. You or your friend may need to talk with her pastor. If he wants everything God has for us in His Word, he'll no doubt be willing to help you, but if not, she may have to find a pastor who desires to work all the works of Jesus, or at least give his blessing, before she can get free of all those fear spirits."

"She's very depressed."

"Depression is the next negative emotion we covered in class. Do you see how the negative emotions all tie together and the positive emotions all tie together? If we're angry, we tend to be depressed."

"Or vice versa."

"Right. And if we're fearful of something, we tend to be depressed, especially if it's nonphysical things like Fear of failure, Fear of loss, Fear of poverty. These fears are described as anxiety or care in Scripture, and when these fears come, we get depressed. If we're fearful, we may also find ourselves angry and hateful. We tend to seek out someone on whom we can blame our troubles.

"There are other times when depression moves in on us like an overcast sky during the night. In fact, sometimes the weather makes us feel depressed, as we mentioned in the lesson on the mind. You'll remember, David wrote many of the Psalms when he was feeling blue."

Emily continued, "Now it may seem repetitious, but with anger, fear, or depression, you must nip it in the bud before it gets too big for you to handle. If you blow out the match, you won't have to fight the prairie fire.

"There are a couple books your ladies may want to read: *Spiritual Depression: Its Causes and Cure* by D. Martyn Lloyd-Jones. and *How to Win Over Depression* by Tim LaHaye. There are probably many other good Christian books on the subject, but these two should be enough help.

"Jones elaborates on Psalm 42:11, noting that David talked to himself instead of allowing his 'self' to talk to him. Here, I'll read a few lines to you."

Emily went to the bookcase in the living room. "This woman has a remarkable memory for her age," I mused. "Must be the combination of healthy physical and spiritual food."

"All right," she proceeded, "let me read this to you:

> Have you realized that most of your unhappiness in life is due to the fact that you are listening to yourself instead of talking to yourself? Take those thoughts that come to you the moment you wake up in the morning. You have not originated them, but they start talking to you, they bring back the problems of yesterday, etc. Somebody is talking. Who is talking to you? Your self is talking to you.

> Now this man's treatment was this: instead of allowing this self to talk to him, he starts talking to himself, 'Why art thou cast down, O my soul?' he asks. His soul had been depressing him, crushing him. So he stands up and says: 'Self, listen for a moment, I will speak to you.'

"I'm skipping a bit here," said Emily.

> . . . Exhort yourself, and say to yourself: 'Hope thou in God'—instead of muttering in this depressed, unhappy way. And then you must go on to remind yourself of God, Who God is, and what God is, and what God has done, and what God has pledged Himself to do. Then having done that, end on this great note: defy yourself, and defy other people, and defy the devil and the whole world, and say with this man: 'I shall yet praise Him for the help of His countenance, who is also the health of my countenance and my God.'[12]

Emily continued, "Now let me add here, June, the negative thoughts we have of this nature, are not always only our own thoughts within us as the author expresses, but the harassment of demonic spirits. We can address them, binding them and telling them that we refuse to listen to them and command them, in Jesus Christ's name, to leave us alone. We apply the blood of Jesus the Lamb to our minds. James says, 'Submit yourselves therefore to God. Resist the devil, and he will flee from you.'

"Mr. Lloyd-Jones also brings out the fact that sin will make you depressed. We must confess it and forsake it or we cannot shake our misery. I think this is more true for Christians who fall into sin, because they've experienced the joy of having their sin burden removed, and they miss the fellowship with the Lord when guilt moves in on them again. The contrast is more obvious than for one who has never felt God's cleansing in her life."

"Aunt Emily, sorrow isn't always a bad emotion is it?"

"Oh, no; we feel sorrow when a friend is sick or suffering. That's where 'weep with them that weep' comes in. However, we must not let ourselves be overcome with much grief. We overcome the grief as we look to God and His promises. We may weep for the unsaved as in Psalm 126:6:

> He that goeth forth and weepeth, bearing precious seed, shall doubtless come again with rejoicing, bringing his sheaves with him.

"But our weeping comes to an end when we're assured God has heard us. If we're forever in misery, what sinner would ever choose to adopt this new life in Christ?"

"A long face sure isn't much of a selling point, is it?"

"No, our neighbors might observe us and say, 'If being a Christian is that painful, I sure don't want any part of it.'

"We mentioned Tim LaHaye's answer to depression in the lesson on the mind: let your will tell your mind what to think and your emotions will follow your thoughts.

"We need to send our thoughts through God's immigration office. All undesirable aliens must be deported.

"Again, if a woman cannot shake depression after seeking to overcome it in a practical Scriptural fashion, she will probably need deliverance."

"Aunt Emily, you mentioned a second ago about a woman getting depressed over her failures, but what about the poor girl whose husband has not achieved his aspirations? He feels like a failure and she feels it with him. As you said before, his fulfillment is her fulfillment. His failure makes her feel like a failure too."

"As we've mentioned before, a lot of men get really depressed, especially around forty or fifty, because they feel they haven't accomplished anything in their lives. And some really haven't. But let's discuss for a minute what success really means. A man is successful if he has obeyed God. Noah didn't accomplish much in terms of modern evangelistic standards. He preached for over 100 years and had only eight souls aboard the ark when God shut the door. And they were all part of his family. However, he's mentioned in the Hebrews 11 'Hall of Faith.' Jonah preached to Ninevah and the whole city repented, but he didn't accomplish his goals; he wanted God to destroy the city and God spared them instead. He obeyed God."

"After strenuous nudging," I commented.

"Yes, but he was depressed when he shouldn't have been. God accomplished what *He* desired through Jonah, not what Jonah wanted.

"Jesus Christ wouldn't be considered very successful if we measured Him by his earthly possessions. He didn't have a good salary, though he may have worked as a carpenter before he began his public ministry. He didn't have a posh house or a condominium. He didn't even have a place to lay his head that he could call his own. He preached such hard lessons that the crowds left him. Even his disciples abandoned him when he was arrested. So by what do we measure success?"

"Well," I answered, "Jesus told the parable of the talents. The man who invested what God gave him and doubled it received praise—'Well done, thou good and faithful servant: thou hast been faithful over a few things, I will make thee ruler over many things: . . .' "

"That's a good example, but some men work a job that just pays the bills and apply the rest of their energies to spiritual endeavors. They're laying up treasures in heaven. Other men, trading in material talents, are laying up big treasures down here, but neglecting the eternal storehouse. Who is going to hear the 'Well done'?

"Then too, some men are doing all sorts of spiritual exercises in the arm of the flesh. Paul talked about building with wood, hay, and stubble; in the end it will all go up in smoke. Some men are just plain lazy; they accomplish very little materially or spiritually. The key to a successful life is whether that man has been obedient to God and his Word.

"Every wife, June, needs to encourage her husband when he's discouraged. Proverbs 12:25 says, 'Heaviness in the heart of a man maketh it stoop: but a good word maketh it glad.' She can help him think through his goals and by gentle questioning help him discover that he really hasn't failed; he's just had very high goals or maybe too many goals for one man to accomplish in a lifetime. If he really has failed, she can best help him by being cheerfully content with what they have. His biggest fears are probably that she and the children will suffer from the privations and lose respect for him. She needs to unselfishly assure him and help him think Philippians 4:8 thoughts. The key word is EDIFY—build up.

"Another reason some men fail, June, is because their wives have always lived their lives for them. These men have never been allowed to assert themselves without criticism of some kind. If they want to go to trade school or college, change jobs, go into business for themselves, the little woman has a tizzy fit."

"Why? I've seen it too. In fact I've seen it in me, I'm ashamed to say."

"Fear for one. She feels insecure. As we mentioned before, she doesn't trust God to supply their needs through her husband. When she doesn't trust him, he senses this. It makes him feel inadequate even if she doesn't say much. A wife's trust in her husband makes him feel confident. As long as he knows she believes in him, he'll believe in himself."

"She inspires him rather than expires him."

"There you go. There are also evil spirits that work back and forth between the husband and wife to establish and perpetuate failure. Laziness, Passivity, Automatic failure mechanism, and Fear of failure may work in the husband, making him say the wrong things, do the wrong things, break things, and essentially bungle everything he does. The demons instigate her to react in fear and anger. She criticizes and nags. If she has a Jezebel spirit, she'll ride him like a broomstick.

"The essence of what I'm saying here is for the wife to stop trying to direct her husband's life and allow God to lead him. If she's in the way, God cannot work in his life. Her interference is hindering her husband from interacting with God. Pray tell, how can he listen to God and her too? Matthew 6 :33 says:

> But seek ye first the kingdom of God, and his righteousness; and all these things shall be added unto you.

"God's righteousness includes, among other things, loving our husbands in the midst of their failures. The material things will follow when we allow our husbands to function the way God intended them to do.

"I might add, if a man doesn't love himself, he can't reach out in love to his family, friends, or a lost world. If his wife loves and respects him and lavishly expresses this to him, he will eventually learn to love himself. I'm not talking about selfishness or self-centeredness, but rather self-acceptance. When a man loves himself, he doesn't feel threatened by rejection and he can give and receive love. Ephesians 5:33 says:

> Nevertheless let every one of you in particular so love his wife even as himself; and the wife see that she reverence her husband.

"You see, whenever we invest love, it almost always brings good returns. Conditional love is loving someone on the condition that they perform a certain way. Conditional love throws fear and insecurity into a marriage and it builds walls. 'God commendeth His love toward us, in that while we were yet sinners, Christ died for us.'

That was unconditional love. Marriage isn't a reform school. God will work out the bugs in our husbands. Our responsibility is to just exude unconditional love."

Emily shifted gears. "We've talked about what emotions we shouldn't give our husbands. Now let's talk about the ones we need to give our husbands. Read Galatians 5:22 and 23, June; that's a good list for us all."

> But the fruit of the spirit is love, joy, peace, longsuffering, gentleness, goodness, faith,
>
> Meekness, temperance; against such there is no law.

"Now these are fruits which come out of our lives if we abide in the vine, Jesus Christ, as it says in John 15. And our fruit shall remain. These fruits develop as we grow by reading the Scriptures, praying, fellowshipping and worshipping with the Church, sharing our faith, and working the works of Jesus. Here in verse 25 it says, 'If we live in the Spirit, let us also walk in the Spirit.'

"When we exhibit these pleasant fruits, we cheer the whole household and lift everyone's spirits. Our husbands are glad to come home, and the kids are glad to be home with their parents. The neighbor kids and their parents flock to our house because they feel the joy of the Lord there. It becomes a place of hospitality and an opportunity for soul winning.

"Let me add just a word here: foolishness is the Devil's counterfeit for joy. A constant diet of silliness, levity, foolish jesting, giggling or stupidity becomes obnoxious to God and an intelligent husband.

"Isaac sported with Rebekah his wife in such a way that Abimelech knew she was his wife and not his sister. Sport, according to Strong's concordance, means to 'laugh outright in (merriment or scorn) . . . laugh, mock, play, make sport.'[1] However, America has gone overboard in pleasure seeking and entertainment. Recreation is great for a family if it's not the central focus of their lives. I don't recall reading in the Gospels about Jesus going from one game to another."

Emily stood and stretched. "Say, how about some lunch? Then we'll talk about the tongue."

"I was afraid of that. I suppose Uncle Harold will razz us through it all."

"He might," she chuckled. "How about it if you go out and ask him to cut some lettuce for us and we'll make a big fruit salad."

"Yum."

I carried out my errand and made a plea to Emily: "Would you mind if I ran upstairs to pray for a few minutes before lunch?"

"Go right ahead, June."

Kneeling by Ruth's bed, I poured out the following prayer. Maybe you'd like to pray the same thing with me.

Dear Lord, after this lesson, I know I need a renewed heart as well as a renewed mind. I need to be crucified with Christ in the area of my emotions and raised to newness of life. Right now, I reckon myself dead indeed unto anger, fear, and depression. Pour through me the fruits of your Spirit. Lord, help me to cling to You as a vine on the branch, drawing my life from You. Work in me both to will and to do of Your good pleasure, so I can minister to my husband with good emotions.

In Jesus' Name. Amen.

# 7. THE MINISTRY OF OUR EMOTIONS (CONTINUED)

As usual, Emily's culinary creation was refreshingly delicious, and we were soon settled down with our Bibles, Uncle Harold's company, and a cold glass of lemonade to the second part of lesson 3.

"Mmmmm," hummed Harold, "this lemonade's got pucker power. I like it tart."

"See, he's easy to please, June. Now let's get to the Scripture on the tongue. We'll try to make this as painless as possible. However, I think anyone who reads the Scripture honestly is convicted when he comes to the passages about the tongue because the tongue is a constant troublemaker for all of us."

"I seem to have foot-in-mouth disease," I confessed.

"You mean you open your mouth only long enough to change feet?" teased Harold.

"See, I told you so, Aunt Emily."

Smiling, she proceeded, pretending not to hear me. "Look at Matthew 12:34-37. Please read that for us, Harold."

> O generation of vipers, how can ye, being evil, speak good things? for out of the abundance of the heart the mouth speaketh.
>
> A good man out of the good treasure of the heart bringeth forth good things: and an evil man out of the evil treasure bringeth forth evil things.
>
> But I say unto you, That every idle word that men shall speak, they shall give account thereof in the day of judgment.
>
> For by thy words thou shalt be justified, and by thy words thou shalt be condemned.

"June, will you please read Luke 6:45 for us?"

> A good man out of the good treasure of his heart bringeth forth that which is good; and an evil man out of

> the evil treasure of his heart bringeth forth that which is evil: for of the abundance of the heart his mouth speaketh.

"So you see, the tongue gets blamed, but the heart is the real culprit. Let's turn to James 3. That's the classic passage about the tongue. I'll read this one; we'll start with verse 2:

> For in many things we offend all. If any man offend not in word, the same is a perfect man, and able also to bridle the whole body.

"He goes on to tell how we tame horses with a little bridle and control ships with a small rudder, but the tongue, though it's small, is like a match that starts a forest fire, we can't tame it. Let's skip down to verse 11:

> Doth a fountain send forth at the same place sweet water and bitter?
>
> Can the fig tree, my brethren, bear olive berries? either a vine, figs? so can no fountain both yield salt water and fresh.
>
> Who is a wise man and endued with knowledge among you? let him shew out of a good conversation his works with meekness of wisdom.
>
> But if ye have bitter envying and strife in your hearts, glory not, and lie not against the truth.
>
> This wisdom descendeth not from above, but is earthly, sensual, devilish.
>
> For where envying and strife is, there is confusion and every evil work.
>
> But the wisdom that is from above is first pure, then peaceable, gentle, and easy to be entreated, full of mercy and good fruits, without partiality and without hypocrisy.
>
> And the fruit of righteousness is sown in peace of them that make peace.

"Now what do you suppose that fountain is, June?"

"The heart. James says, 'If ye have bitter envying and strife in your hearts . . . ' "

"Good. Let's read Proverbs 4:23. Harold, will you read that please?"

" 'Keep thy heart with all diligence; for out of it are the issues of life.' "

"June, how do you suppose we keep our hearts?"

"By keeping in close fellowship with the Lord, in prayer and in the Word."

"You get an A. When Harold and I read through the book of Proverbs together, I wrote down a smattering of verses about the tongue. I'll just read them off:

"Proverbs 19:13: 'A foolish son is the calamity of his father: and the contentions of a wife are a continual dropping.' "

"Like a leaky faucet, " interjected Harold. "The Chinese water torture."

"21:19: 'It is better to dwell in the wilderness than with a contentious and an angry woman.'

"21:23: 'Whoso keepeth his mouth and his tongue keepeth his soul from troubles.'

"25:24: 'It is better to dwell in the corner of the housetop, than with a brawling woman and in a wide house.'

"18:6: 'A fool's lips enter into contention, and his mouth calleth for strokes.'

"27:15: 'A continual dropping in a very rainy day and a contentious woman are alike.'

"12:18: 'There is that speaketh like the piercings of the sword: but the tongue of the wise is health.'

"10:11: 'The mouth of a righteous man is a well of life: but violence covereth the mouth of the wicked.'

"13:10: 'Only by pride cometh contention: but with the well advised is wisdom.'

"15:l: 'A soft answer turneth away wrath: but grievous words stir up strife.'

"15:7: 'The lips of the wise disperse knowledge: but the heart of the foolish doeth not so.'

"15:17: 'Better is a dinner of herbs where love is, than a stalled ox and hatred therewith.'

"15:23: 'A man hath joy by the answer of his mouth: and a word spoken in due season, how good it is!'

"15:26: 'The thoughts of the wicked are an abomination to the Lord: but the words of the pure are pleasant words.'

"15:28: 'The heart of the righteous studieth to answer: but the mouth of the wicked poureth out evil things.' That means thinking before you talk," Emily interjected.

"16:23: 'The heart of the wise teacheth his mouth and addeth learning to his lips.'

"16:24: 'Pleasant words are an honeycomb, sweet to the soul and health to the bones.'

"17:l: 'Better is a dry morsel, and quietness therein than an house full of sacrifices with strife.'

"17:14 'The beginning of strife is as when one letteth out water: therefore leave off contention, before it be meddled with.'

"There are two more verses about having a gracious tongue.

"Ecclesiastes 10:12: 'The words of a wise man's mouth are gracious; but the lips of a fool will swallow up himself.' "

"See," said Harold. "That's a person with his foot in his mouth. Swallows it too."

Emily finished her list. "Colossians 4:6: 'Let your speech be alway with grace, seasoned with salt, that ye may know how ye ought to answer every man.' "

"Remember," said Harold, "salt purifies, preserves, and flavors."

"Well, there are lots more," said Emily, "but we can't cover them all. I suggest you do a thorough study on the tongue with your ladies. Have them go through the concordance and put all the verses on 3x5's, categorizing them under topics like strife, levity, talkativeness, and so forth. The 3x5's can then be put in their file for memorization."

"Oh boy, you're going to have us busy."

One could read Harold's face like a book. He looked like he'd pop if he didn't say something, but was afraid he'd be guilty of 'gendercide' if he did, so I prodded him, "Uncle Harold, what are some of the things about a woman's conversation that aggravate men?"

"Too much is too much! Women can go on and on without saying anything or taking the conversation in any one direction. They can small talk for hours and then nag their husbands because they didn't get anything done all day. The neighbor down the road calls it prattle. It gets on a man's nerves to listen to chatter all day, especially if it's full of things she wants him to do. Emily isn't that way. When I put in my order for a wife, I asked God to make her with just a little key so she wouldn't wind up too tight. Proverbs 10:19 says: 'In the multitude of words there wanteth not sin: but he that refraineth his lips is wise.' "

Emily continued, "I may as well read a couple more verses about talkativeness.

"Proverbs 17:27: 'He that hath knowledge spareth his words: and a man of understanding is of an excellent spirit.'

"Proverbs 17:28: 'Even a fool, when he holdeth his peace, is counted wise: and he that shutteth his lips is esteemed a man of understanding.'

"Then the last part of Ecclesiastes 5:3 is: '. . . And a fool's voice is known by multitude of words.' "

Harold felt encouraged, so he continued with zeal: "Another crime that women commit is sarcasm. Some women can cut through a crowd as fast as Jonathan and his armour bearer went through the Philistines. That kind of gal is especially artful at cutting her poor husband in little ribbons at a church dinner or a get-together with relatives."

"Is that because she gets so much practice at home?" I asked.

"I guess," responded Harold, shaking his head sadly. "I once heard a preacher say, 'Many a marital grave was dug by a series of little digs.' A marriage gets nibbled away like an all-day sucker—one lick at a time. When it's gone, there's nothing left but the memories—bad memories."

"And a bitter after-taste," I added.

"I'm afraid so," sighed Harold. "Emily has another verse, I see."

"It's Proverbs 12:18, which we read a few minutes ago, but it bears repeating here: 'There is that speaketh like the piercings of a sword: but the tongue of the wise is health.' You can cut people by just blasting them with the truth too. There's a time to confront someone and a time to keep still and pray. That's why we need to walk in the Spirit. Our pastor has said several times that we don't need to say everything we know. To do so sometimes hinders what God is trying to say to that person.

"And sometimes a sarcastic or cutting remark may not be true, but only a false accusation. Women and men alike assume things falsely and make accusations that can cause deep hurts which will destroy a marriage in one outburst of the tongue. Once words are out, you can never recall them. You can ask forgiveness, but sometimes the damage to the husband's emotional structure can never be rebuilt."

"Yep," continued Harold, "some gals need a padlock on their lips, and the only key that would open it would be a pleasant disposition. When they feel pleasant, they can talk. That would be good for the men folks as well, I think. I ought to have one of those on me sometimes. Emily doesn't need one. Every morning she prays Psalm 141:3, 'Set a watch, O Lord, before my mouth; keep the door of my lips.'

"Back to the false accusation thing, where's that verse about evil surmisings, Em?"

"I Timothy 6:4. I'll read it. 'He is proud, knowing nothing, but doting about questions and strifes of words, whereof cometh envy, strife, railings, evil surmisings.' "

Harold proceeded, "You know, some men who have wandering feet would never have strayed from home if their wives had trusted them and not made false accusations from the basis of a suspicious imagination (evil surmisings).

"I heard a story on the radio that blessed my heart. A young man had been pretty wild and had sown a lot of wild oats and then he got saved. He met a lovely Christian woman, who had been a good Christian for some time, and they got married. She had the love and wisdom to tell him that she would always trust him, but if he ever did fail in his faithfulness to her, she would forgive him and he would never have to fear losing her love. The young man told the preacher who was telling the story, 'Who would ever betray a trust like that?'

"Now I realize that in these last days there are some men who are so depraved that they would be unfaithful to a really good wife, but if she's careful to observe all that Emily has been teaching in these lessons, he'd have to be really full of the Devil to do so."

"In which case," Emily added, "she can bind up those unclean spirits and cry out to God to work a change in his life. She can also pray a hedge of thorns around him as in Hosea 2:6-7."

"And she shouldn't cry on her best friend's shoulder, either," said Harold. "That kind of information can telegraph across town quicker than Western Union. You've probably heard that old pun—telegraph, telephone, and tell-a-woman. No husband wants to feel that his wife is talking behind his back, especially about intimate matters in their personal life. A wife is one flesh with her husband; to talk about him to others is divisive. It's treason, mutiny, a form of unfaithfulness in itself. That kind of disloyalty will kill even a good marriage.

"Which brings me to my next pet peeve—gossip. Women who sit for hours on the phone and talk about the neighbors, the preacher, their relatives, and anyone else they can rake over the coals are not only wasting the precious hours of the day, but sowing seeds that they'll have to harvest in a short time. Whenever we criticize other people, we will get back criticism. It's just the law of reaping what you sow. We always reap the same thing we sow, later than we sow, and more than we sow. You have the Scriptures for gossip there, Emily?"

"Yes, indeed, Proverbs 18:8: 'The words of a talebearer are as wounds, and they go down into the innermost parts of the belly.' I Timothy 3:11: 'Even so must their wives be grave, not slanderers, sober, faithful in all things.'

"To be honest with you, the word *gossip* is not in the Bible. That's a modern-day word. The *Roget's Thesaurus* lists under gossip: 'busybody, talebearer, chatterer; reports, rumors.—v.i. talk, speculate, report, tattle, whisper.'[16] The dictionary defines a busybody as 'one who officiously or impertinently concerns himself with the affairs of others; a meddler.'[17]

"Another word is backbiter. *Wycliffe Bible Encyclopedia* defines backbite. I'll read it:

> The Heb. word so translated means "to wander about as a slanderer" (Ps 15:3.) Another Heb. word is used in similar manner to describe evil speaking (Prov 25:23).[7]

Harold was ready with Psalm 15:3. "The context here is who shall abide in the tabernacle?

> He that backbiteth not with his tongue, nor doeth evil to his neighbor, nor taketh up a reproach against his neighbor.

"I've got Proverbs 25:23," I volunteered:

> The north wind driveth away rain: so doth an angry countenance a backbiting tongue.

"I'm not real sure who has the angry countenance, the person being bitten or the person having to listen to the backbiting," said Emily. "I think if more of us would give backbiters a dirty look when they commence their evil speaking, there would be a lot less of it. We condone it by listening to it. Here's another verse about slander, Psalm 101:5: 'Whoso privily slandereth his neighbor, him will I cut off: . . .' "

Harold had another Scripture. "Some people make light of the sin of gossip, but God lists it with some pretty dreadful sins. Let me read just part of the list in Romans 1:29 and 30:

> Being filled with all unrighteousness, fornication, wickedness, covetousness, maliciousness; full of envy, murder, debate, deceit, malignity; whisperers,
>
> Backbiters, haters of God, despiteful, proud, boasters, inventors of evil things, disobedient to parents.

"The basis of talking bad about another person," said Emily, "is a heart lifted up with pride. It's the same old game of pushing down someone else so you can be at the top, making the other person look bad so that you look good. The trouble is, it doesn't work. Even inveterate gossips know it's poor taste, bad manners, and downright sin to gossip. Even though they may do it themselves, they will disrespect the person who talks bad about someone else.

"This sin has driven many unsaved people away from the Church. Then, too, that lady who is getting her ears filled is thinking in the back of her mind, 'I bet she has something similar to say about me when my back is turned.' Look at Proverbs 10:18: 'He that hideth hatred with lying lips, and he that uttereth a slander, is a fool.' "

"Now that verse brings me to my next gripe," said Harold. "I shouldn't have to mention this, June, and maybe none of your ladies have this problem, but a lying tongue can sure wreck havoc in a marriage. I hear men fussing time and again because they can't believe their wives. They'll ask them if they did such and such and the little missus will tell them 'Oh, sure!' but it was never done. One fellow took off work to go to the dentist and found his wife hadn't made the appointment, though she had told him she would. Some of these so-called Christian women even steal from their husbands. I can't figure out how these women can be in church every Sunday and never grasp the idea of honesty."

I piped right up, "I think I know the answer to that one, Uncle Harold. I helped a young woman who had that problem. We backtracked from that question—why do people lie? There may be other reasons, but one is that they lie because they don't want to face their responsibilities, and they don't want to face their responsibilities because they're afraid of failure. Whether it is so or not, they feel rejected. They feel they will do the wrong thing—make a mistake. They may not be willing to try anymore so they do little or nothing."

"How about just plain old laziness and lack of self-discipline?" asked Harold.

"That could be a factor too. At least it would appear to be that. It wasn't in this girl's case. We went back to her childhood and dug up the deep hurts buried down inside her. Her mom had sharply criticized her no matter what she did, so she was afraid to do anything for fear she'd do it wrong, and she was afraid she'd be punished if she didn't do what she was told to do. She became a chronic liar to postpone the scoldings or spankings.

"I helped her pray and forgive her mother and also to realize that her bad behavior only made her mother more critical, reinforcing the problem. She was repeating the same thing over in her marriage. She wrote her mom a sweet letter asking for forgiveness, and their relationship is greatly improved, but they have a long way to go.

"Facing the cause for her lying gave her the ability to overcome, not only the lying but the irresponsible behavior. It sure made a big difference in her marriage."

Emily was pointing to a verse in her Bible. "Here in Ephesians 6, where it talks about putting on the whole armour of God, Paul says to gird up our loins with truth."

"More spiritual garments, Aunt Emily?"

"Yes. Our loins are the strong muscles of our bodies. You might say our strength is clothed in truth. And remember what we read in Colossians 3:9: 'Lie not one to another seeing ye have put off the old man with his deeds.' Lying is another garment for the rag bag. Let me just read a few more verses about lying and then we'll move on.

"Proverbs 12:17: 'He that speaketh truth showeth forth righteousness: but a false witness deceit.'

"Proverbs 12:20: 'Deceit is in the heart of them that imagine evil: but to the counsellors of peace is joy.'

"Proverbs 12:22: 'Lying lips are abomination to the Lord: but they that deal truly are his delight.'

"Proverbs 21:6: 'The getting of treasures by a lying tongue is a vanity tossed to and fro of them that seek death.'

"Lying goes hand in hand with a Jezebel spirit. Remember she found false witnesses to testify against Naboth so she could take his vineyard away and give it to her pouting husband. When a woman is driven by that spirit, she will often use deceit in order to manipulate those around her. Often such women are not even honest with themselves. However, when we're not honest with ourselves, we lose touch with reality. That's what they call mental illness."

"You're saying people who lie go crazy?"

"I'm talking about people who refuse to be honest with themselves and with others. They are irresponsible, dishonest, and won't do what they know they should. These people weave themselves into a mess, like a two-year old with super glue. Then they're so filled with guilt and shame, or feelings of failure, they can't face reality. Psychologists are finally admitting, after trying to blame all mental ills on the persons's mother or society, that if that person would confess his sin, repent, and become responsible to God and man, he could make a re-entry into reality. That's an over simplification, I realize, but God gave us the Ten Commandments for our own good as well as the good of society. He didn't call them the Ten Suggestions.

"Let's move on. Another kind of tongue a godly woman should avoid is a disrespectful tongue. A woman should always speak to her husband with conversation befitting his position as the head of the home. Ephesians 5:33 says:

> Nevertheless let everyone of you in particular so love his wife even as himself; and the wife see that she reverence her husband.

"Harold, please take Vine's and read what it says about reverence."

"Well, the meaning relating to Ephesians 5:33 says, '. . . to fear, is used in the Passive Voice in the N.T. ; in Eph. 5:33 of reverential fear on the part of the wife for a husband, . . . ' "[5]

"This is the same good type of fear that we have for the Lord," said Emily. When a woman talks to her husband as though he were one of the kids, bawling him out or telling him rebelliously what she will or won't do, she violates this respect principle. Remember, she's an object lesson of the Church's relation to the Bridegroom. She should speak to him as she would to Jesus Christ. Now we all know our husbands do or say wrong things that our Lord wouldn't, but we entreat them as a father, with utmost respect.

"Our children will also lose respect for us if we are disrespectful to our husbands. In fact, we will have much more respect from our children and anyone else we relate to if we always treat everyone we know with respect and the best of good manners. Children who grow up with respect generally become respectful. Hollering, demanding and threatening produce anger, hostility, rebellion, strife—all the negative responses a woman doesn't really want. Besides, it shows how immature she is and that she's not quiet inside. It's the opposite of a meek and quiet spirit."

"Ouch," I moaned.

"We all fail in this area. I call it heart failure. We fail to keep our hearts pure, so our disposition is sour and so is our tongue. Have you ever wondered why a man calls his wife Sweetheart?"

"I've never thought about it, Aunt Emily. We'd get a shock some day—one of those days when we're complaining or grouching or indulging in self-pity—if hubby came home and called us Sourheart."

"Here's another aspect," said Emily. "A sweet disposition makes you healthy. Remember, 'a merry heart doeth good like a medicine.'"

"Aunt Emily, you've always had such a sweet disposition. Just like the woman in Proverbs 31, you have the law of kindness in your tongue."

Emily looked up from her Bible. "That's interesting, June. What you've just said is an answer to a prayer I wrote down, probably forty-five years ago." Emily reached for the little black notebook that was always with her Bible. "My tongue was always sharp. I always had some come-back, some smart remark, some cutting dig, or a put-down for everyone who knew me. I always winced when I read Proverbs 31. One day I was reading about the Israelites as they came to the bitter waters of Marah. God told Moses to fell a tree into the waters to sweeten them. The Lord drew my mind to James' piercing question, 'Doth a fountain send forth at the same place sweet water and bitter?' So that day I wrote, 'Neutralize my tongue, Lord. Fell Thy cross into my bitter waters of Marah and sweeten them so it will be said of me, "The law of kindness is in her tongue."'

"Whenever God answers a prayer, I write down that it's been answered. See, these pages are full of answered prayer. I feel some of my requests have probably been answered with God's all wise 'No' or are still delayed while He tries to form me into a useful vessel." Emily wrote briefly in her notebook. "I'll put down 'noticeable progress' because I see me at my worst, and I think I still have a ways to go.

"This is my prayer book, June. I pray through many of these pages every day. Some pages are fulfilled and the circumstances change. I take out a whole section occasionally, wrap a rubber band around it and poke it into the bottom drawer of my desk. When I forget how wonderfully God answers prayer, I dig out a couple of these and read them over—so I can remember what He's done for me in the past.

"I start out with praise—that's worshipping God for Who He is, and then thanksgiving—that's thanking God for what He's done for us.

"Next, I have some pages for self-evaluation, or maybe I should say the things concerning which God is dealing with me. Introspection is usually more condemnation from the Devil than a work of God, but as we read the word with a mind to become what

God wants us to be, the Holy Spirit will point out sins in our lives for which we can repent and change.

"I have a page down here for each of the children; they write or call home prayer requests from time to time, and the Lord lays additional things on my heart as well. Parents seem to know the weak areas in their children. Those get the most attention.

"I also have a page for my spiritual children—those I've led to the Lord or those who have come to me for counsel.

"Then there are those prayer requests we get at church. The missionaries we support have another page. When we get a prayer letter, their requests are written in this book.

"Our government has a page. I pray for our government in general and then more specifically for our representatives, our senators, the President and Vice President, his cabinet, and the Supreme Court. I also use the warfare prayers often throughout the week as well.

"Harold and I have a little list hanging by his desk in our bedroom. When we need something or just want something, we put it on the list and then we bring it before the Lord and ask Him to supply it or the money for it, to help us to find the item at a cheap price, and to give us wisdom as stewards as to whether we should buy it at all. It's amazing how many of those things I've found at garage sales or through the classified adds in our little county paper. I bought that beautiful, almost new, blender for $3.00. That toaster oven was $5.00."

"Isn't it exciting to see what God can do in that area?" I added. "I prayed for a stereo and found one at a garage sale for $8.00. Then I found good Christian and classical records for 10 cents apiece."

Harold laughed and added, "I've threatened to buy Em one of those bumper stickers that says, 'This car stops suddenly for all garage sales.' "

"So then," resumed Emily, "we minister to our husbands with our emotions—the good ones, and we learn to control, by unselfish obedience, the destructive ones. We need to keep our hearts pure so that what comes from our hearts does not defile our home. We need to rule over our spirits. 'He that is slow to anger is better than the mighty, and he that ruleth his spirit than he that taketh a city.' The emotions spring from the heart, and the tongue expresses these emotions or feelings. A home can be built or destroyed by a wife's tongue. 'Every wise woman buildeth her house, but the foolish plucketh it down with her hands.'

"Emotional climate or emotional tone refers to the feel a home conveys. Some homes are tense and explosive—unhappy places filled with complaining, bickering, sarcasm, bitterness, ridicule, sassing, defiance, criticism—an underlying feeling of hatred and malice. Others are filled with loving warmth, good humor, understanding, patience and acceptance. The husband is responsible for the atmosphere of the home but the wife can help him or hinder him especially by what she says and how she says it."

Harold spoke up: "There is a type of conversation that makes husbands find some reason for not coming home. I think many an unsaved husband spends the 'Happy Hour' in the bar because the little woman's critical or whining tongue never allows him one happy hour at home. Many times it's the undisciplined children at whom she's screeching. All that confusion and noise is unnerving to a man who has already put in a day's work and looks forward to some peace and quiet at home.

"There's also the kind of atmosphere," Harold continued, "that makes a man look forward with his whole being to coming home to his cozy, clean house to be greeted by a peaceful, loving wife and his happy children. She greets him at the door with a kiss and a refreshing word of gratefulness for his day of work to provide for their needs. She's considerate of his weariness. The aromas from the kitchen start his salivary glands going. Maybe some quiet Christian music is playing or she's singing. She's full of praise to the Lord and also for her husband—lots more edifying than criticism. Her gratefulness probably challenges him too, because he wants to live up to this image his wife has of him. It's amazing how folks will live up to what others expect of them. We would never think of criticizing our Lord. We continually praise Him for His person and His works. Why can't a woman praise her earthly lord? Emily has always lavished praise on me, even when I know I didn't deserve it. I think if women would set aside their critical spirits, they'd see a lot more of the life of Christ in their husbands."

"I've been in both kinds of homes, Uncle Harold. I know just what you mean. It makes a big difference in how the kids turn out too. I think we could safely say a lot of it depends on the little woman's tongue."

"Incidentally," said Emily, "a women needs to remember that she enjoys a little privacy once in awhile, so she shouldn't be offended if her husband also wants to have some time to himself. It doesn't mean he doesn't appreciate his wife. Most men need time to think, to relax, to read. We need to be mindful of this and respect it. It takes something out of a man to make conversation. Some men need a little rest period after they've worked hard all day and driven home through rush-hour traffic. Get him a glass of juice, scratch his back, massage his scalp—it won't hurt to spoil him a bit. Then let him rest if he wishes. Let him set the pace. He may be bursting with things to tell you and want your undivided attention.

"One more item," added Emily. "Extreme emotional expression will shorten our lives, and so will no emotional expression. A vibrant, balanced expression of pleasant emotions will add years to our lives, especially the expression of joy and gratitude. It's kind of like a car; if you run it real hard all the time, you'll shortly burn it out. But if you run it real slow all the time, it will carbon up and deteriorate quickly as well. People will last a good while longer if they will practice temperance in their emotional expressions."

"And, I might add," said Harold, "the people who live close to them will last a lot longer too."

"Thus endeth the lesson on The Ministry of Our Emotions," concluded Emily. "See, you survived!"

"Yes, but this gives me an awfully big package on which to work. Let me see if I've got all the essentials down in my outline. I'll just read the main outline to you, not all the details, though I've got them down in my notes.

1. We control our emotions with our will. The will chooses what we will think and our emotions follow our thought pattern.
2. No matter what affects our emotions, God expects us to control them with His help.
3. We can maintain a healthy balance of emotional expression.
4. We deal with hurts and disappointments by quickly forgiving the offender.
5. We should respond to our loved ones' correction of us with gratefulness and consider what they have said.
6. Avoid the expression of the following three emotions:
    a. Anger.
        (1) Linked to sins of the fathers.
        (2) Linked to drinking.
        (3) Practical means of overcoming:
            (a) Don't let it start.
            (b) Do something constructive with it. Express the offense.
            (c) Give it to the Lord and forgive.

- (d) Thank the Lord for the experience to build character.
- (e) Put your mind on Philippians 4:8 thoughts.
- (f) Put off your anger as dirty clothes.
- (g) Get deliverance from evil spirits.

b. Fear.
- (1) Deal with it before it gets too big to handle.
- (2) Fear can keep you from serving the Lord.
- (3) There are right fears of danger to protect you.
- (4) Allow your husband to protect you.
- (5) Practical means of overcoming:
  - (a) Don't let it get a start.
  - (b) Face fears head on.
  - (c) Get deliverance from spirits of fear.

c. Depression.
- (1) Deal with it before it gets too big to handle.
- (2) Tell yourself to hope in God.
- (3) Get deliverance.

7. Minister to your husband the fruits of the spirit.
8. Continually keep your heart pure so that your tongue doesn't sin.
   a. Keep a pleasant tongue.
   b. Don't talk too much.
   c. Don't be sarcastic or cutting.
   d. Don't make false accusations.
   e. Don't gossip.
   f. Don't lie or deceive.
   g. Don't have a disrespectful tongue.
9. The wife helps the husband set the emotional tone of the home, especially with her tongue."

"Sounds like you've got the meat of the nut, June," said Emily.

"Are you going to do raspberries this afternoon, Aunt Emily?"

"Well, maybe. I need to pick green beans first. If I can get to the berries before the mosquitoes come out, we'll pick those too. Harold said he'd give me a hand today, so if you'd like to think over the lesson, don't worry about helping."

"I think I will run upstairs and spend some time in prayer."

Again, I spread out my notes on Ruth's bed and got down on my knees. Maybe you'd like to join me.

Dear Lord, I ask You to cleanse my heart of all bitterness, anger, hurts, disappointments, jealousy, pride, criticism, or anything else that will cause my tongue to sin. Fell Your cross into my bitter waters of Marah and sweeten my heart so it sweetens my tongue. I surrender my tongue to You to be sanctified unto the Lord's use. Bring me to the place where it will be said of me that she has the law of kindness in her tongue, and enable me to minister to my husband as a sweet heart. Oh, yes, help me not to talk too much, either.

In Jesus' name. Amen.

# 8. THE MINISTRY OF OUR BODIES

Friday morning found me eagerly anticipating Emily's Bible class.

"What time is your class, Aunt Emily?" I asked, as we did the breakfast dishes.

"Normally it's at two in the afternoon, but today we have an extra long lesson so we're going to meet at eleven, have a carry-in lunch, and then finish the second half after lunch. Harold and I are going on a trip at the end of the month, just after the last lesson, so I didn't want to divide today's lesson up into two separate weeks and leave the last lesson hanging until we got back."

"Oh, I'm glad you're doing it this way too. I'd be disappointed if I missed the last lesson."

"I need to do a couple loads of wash and freeze some beans before we leave. If you have some clothes you'd like washed, June, bring them down."

"O.K."

The morning seemed to go slowly, even though I made myself helpful. I was glad when we were finally driving toward the church.

"How many ladies usually come to the class, Aunt Emily?"

"It varies in the summer because of vacations. There are usually around twenty."

"Oh, that's a good-size class. My group is much smaller. Would you say they've been receptive to what you've been teaching?"

"Most are. Some are weighing it, some are struggling with it, some are silently rebelling, and a couple feisty gals are openly challenging what I say. They've soaked up the women's lib program. Unless God, sovereignly changes their hearts, I'm afraid their marriages are going to fail. They have established a life philosophy that's contrary to the Word of God and they don't seem to have any desire to change. Also, there's a strong ungodly soul tie between these two girls, strengthening the evil spirits that are deceiving them. I love these girls, and I continue to pray for them, binding those spirits and asking the Lord to open their eyes to His truth. They claim to be believers, but they're rejecting His Word—not me—God's Word."

"I have a lady like that in my class too, Aunt Emily; it grieves me because I know it grieves the Holy Spirit."

"You'll like the ladies in the class, June. For the most part they're committed Christians who have made up their minds a long time ago that if God's Word says it, they'll obey, depending on Him to help them. They add a lot of good input and a testimony here and there which blesses everyone.

"Turn right at the next corner. The church is at the end of the block on the left."

Emily introduced me to the group after everyone was settled. A new addition to the class was also introduced by the lady who had brought her. The pastor's wife, Wanda, prayed and Emily stepped behind the podium to teach.

"We have discussed so far in this series of lessons the meaning of our ministry, the position of our ministry, how we can minister to our husbands with our minds and with our emotions. Today we want to learn how we can minister to our husbands with our bodies. As we've been saying in these lessons, ministering is giving of ourselves to another or for another.

"First of all, then, we want to give our husbands a healthy body. There are probably many reasons why people suffer sickness, and I don't claim to understand all the reasons God allows us to be sick, but let me mention three: to learn a lesson, sickness unto death, and sickness for the glory of God. The first one is sometimes a physical lesson because we defile our bodies with things we know are destructive to them such as cigarettes, drugs, alcohol, adultery, gluttony, continued lack of sleep, laziness (which amounts to lack of exercise), and even eating junk food.

"If we continually abuse our bodies, we will merely be reaping what we sowed. Most of us took health in school and know that our bodies require proper cleanliness, sleep, exercise, and nutrition in order to maintain health. These are natural laws, just like the law of gravity. When we break these laws, we suffer the consequences—and so does our family.

"Most of you have heard my talks about nutrition at our Fellowship Day, but for the sake of you who haven't, I'll just run over a few basic things, and the rest of you can count it a review. If I seem in a hurry today, it's because I have so much material to cover, and I don't want to leave out any of it because I feel it's all important. Just bear with me while I gallop through it all, please.

"When we eat white flour or white sugar, we're robbing our bodies of the nutrients that were taken out and replaced by a few synthetic vitamins. When our bodies try to metabolize white sugar, they need B vitamins to do so. Refined sugar doesn't have any vitamins, just calories, so it robs them from our bodies in order to burn the sugar for energy. If we replace refined sugar with natural sweets like unrefined honey, maple syrup, or molasses, we'll feel much better. It's best to go very easy on any sweets; fruits, vegetables and grains supply all the sugar our bodies need.

"When you get all the nourishment and fiber from whole grains rather than refined grains, you'll feel much better too. Read the labels on the food you buy. When a loaf of bread says wheat bread and it has caramel coloring, it just means it's bread made from white flour and colored to look brown like whole wheat bread. Avoid bleached white flour, artificial colors, flavors, and preservatives. Harold says at his age he needs all the preservatives he can get, but he's only joking. The best way to avoid all the additives is to bake your own goodies. It takes more time, but sitting in a doctor's office is also time consuming, and if you have to go out to work because your husband dies of a heart attack, you'll have even less time. The increase of heart disease in our country is directly related to the increase in refined foods.

"Steer clear of hydrogenated fats and animal fats. Remember, God told the Israelites not to eat fat or blood. Use vegetable oils such as corn, safflower, or olive oil. The cold pressed kind are best. Most margarine is loaded with chemicals and hydrogenated fats.

"Take a pound of butter and add it to 2 1/2 cups of corn oil in your blender or mixer. Don't let the blender overwork. Stir it carefully with a rubber spatula as you blend it. If the blender is laboring, turn it off and let it rest for a little while. You can even add a quarter of a cup of water just before it's done. Abraham fed the three angelic visitors butter.

"Instead of red meat, eat mostly fish, chicken, turkey, and eggs. Nuts, seeds, beans and grains are rich in protein also. The Lord was not a vegetarian, but to butcher a large animal in His day was quite an undertaking. They didn't have a freezer, so when they did butcher, it was probably for a feast day or a sacrifice, where all the friends and relatives could get in on it. Doctors are telling us now that too much red meat is causing heart, colon, and circulatory problems.

"Get plenty of fiber in your diet. Making 80% of your food intake raw fruits, vegetables, seeds, and nuts is the ideal. You'll also lose weight without much effort on such a program. And you'll feel great!

"On a sound nutritional program, you'll find everyone in the family having a much better disposition, including yourself. Your children will not be nearly so hyperactive and cranky if they don't get refined sugar.

"Make the food attractive when you serve it. Fancy serving teases appetites. If you've been used to fried meat, potatoes, and gravy, you'll have to retrain your family. Discipline yourself to eat well first. When they see the difference in how you look and feel, they'll likely jump on your band wagon. If you make the nutritional changes slowly for your family, they might not even notice. Jane Kinderlehrer has written a book you'll enjoy called *Confessions of a Sneaky Organic Cook*. I'll give you a list of some helpful books on nutrition to help you get started.

"If you're not a member of the church co-op, I'd urge you to join so you can get nutritious foods at lower prices. Some of the things we order are hard to find in the grocery stores. If you belong to another church, you might consider starting a co-op in your own church.

"Use real, unsweetened fruit juices, herb teas sweetened with honey, and plain old water instead of soft drinks, coffee, teas, and sweetened drinks. Diet pop has chemicals which are under suspicion by researchers. Put six tablespoons of apple cider vinegar and six tablespoons of honey into a little hot water in a half gallon pitcher and mix well. Then add cold water and refrigerate. It's a lot like ginger ale. Some folks do add a little ginger. Harold likes it warm in the winter and cold in the summer. The potassium in the vinegar gives you a lot of energy. Runners use it a lot.

"Now after all that, I want to say here, as I've said about our minds and emotions, use common sense and balance. I Corinthians 3:16 and 17 says:

> Know ye not that ye are the temple of God, and that the Spirit of God dwelleth in you?
>
> If any man defile the temple of God, him shall God destroy; for the temple of God is holy, which temple ye are.

"There are people who put a constant supply of destructive food into their bodies and scoff when they're exhorted to eat more carefully. They tempt the Lord by their foolish self-indulgence and gluttony. These same people are often bitter when God doesn't heal them. On the other hand, some people go to the other extreme and make eating health foods a religion. For them I have some other Scripture. In Matthew 15, Jesus tells us what really defiles a man. The Pharisees were asking Jesus why He and his disciples did not ceremonially wash their hands before they ate. Read verse 11 to us, please, Claire."

> Not that which goeth into the mouth defileth a man; but that which cometh out of the mouth, this defileth a man.

Emily proceeded, "Now this response offended the Pharisees, which concerned the disciples, so Peter asked Jesus to explain this parable. Let's start again with His answer in verse 17. Pam, read 17-20 for us please."

> Do not ye yet understand, that whatsoever entereth in at the mouth goeth into the belly, and is cast out into the draught?
>
> But those things which proceed out of the mouth come forth from the heart; and they defile the man.
>
> For out of the heart proceed evil thoughts, murders, adulteries, fornications, thefts, false witness, blasphemies:
>
> These are the things which defile a man: but to eat with unwashen hands defileth not a man.

Emily continued, "We should eat carefully, with a view to nourishing our bodies, not just gratifying our lusts. On the other hand, it should not become so important to us that we become pharisaical and legalistic about food.

"Make yourself a little sideline study as you read through the Bible. Write down what God's people ate, especially Jesus. Write down what God told His people they could and could not eat. His point was to keep them healthy, and the same laws which the Creator provided for the Israelites will also keep us healthy. Jesus fulfilled the ceremonial law, and it is no longer necessary for us to offer sacrifices, but we are not told that he fulfilled the dietary law. We're not under the law to tithe, but most Christians tithe under grace because they know it's God's program and they're blessed in doing so. We should perform more under grace, by God's Spirit, not less. We should desire more of what God intends for us, not less.

"A good book to read concerning the dietary law is *God's Key to Health and Happiness*. It's on the list I'm giving you today. This author is the one who convinced Harold and me not to eat unclean meats. We're not in any bondage about it, nor do I want to put you in any bondage. I just feel that if God wanted His people Israel healthy and gave them a program for good health, we can, under God's grace, benefit from that program, and I'm recommending it to you for your consideration. Study it over and pray about it."

Emily acknowledged the lady sitting next to me who had raised her hand.

"Emily, since you've been teaching about nutrition, our family has made some slow but drastic changes in our eating habits. I just want to add an amen to what you're saying. We all feel much more energetic and the kids' grades in school have improved considerably. The teachers also say they're better behaved. I guess it's because they're not all hyped up on sugar. In addition, Joe and I have both lost a lot of weight.

"I'd like to add something further, too. In the book, Emily just recommended, *God's Key to Health and Happiness*, the author brought out the Scripture about wearing garments of mixed material. His wife switched to all-cotton underwear, and a lump in her breast went away. I switched to all cotton underpants, and an infection I had went away. Then I read in a magazine article that scientists are saying synthetic fabrics cause infection because they don't allow the skin to breathe properly. Synthetics hold moisture in rather than absorbing it, and fungus or bacteria can multiply easily."

"Thank you, Yvonne. That was a helpful addition. Our main thrust in this lesson today, of course, is our sexual ministry to our husbands, but if we are encumbered with a vaginal yeast infection, suffering from chronic fatigue, recurring headaches, or any other poor health problems, it will be difficult for us to minister to our husbands in this capacity—or any other capacity, for that matter.

"Now let me add here, Paul had some kind of infirmity in the flesh which the Scripture is not really clear about. That way we can identify with him, whatever our own infirmity may be. He sought the Lord three times to remove it, but the Lord did not do so and told him why. 'My grace is sufficient for thee, for my strength is made perfect in weakness' was God's answer in I Corinthians 12:9. Sometimes we may have to minister when we don't feel like it, claiming God's grace as we do. But notice also, Paul did ask that this thorn in the flesh—this 'messenger of Satan to buffet me'—be removed. We also need to request healing from God, and unless the Lord refuses us, expect Him to heal us.

"Be careful that you don't fall into the trap of having faith in your faith. Your healing depends on God's faithfulness to His Word, as you lay hold on it in faith, but there's a fine line of difference here that either makes you a humanist who is trusting in his own faith or a believer who is trusting in the promises of God. If your faith to be healed is what makes you well, what are you trusting in? It's a very subtle deception, but quite popular today. Those who are trusting in their ability to believe God, or speak something into existence, are usually disappointed and then disillusioned. God's methods and timing are sovereign. Let us not approach God as though He were a genie in a bottle.

"Next you need to give your husband a clean body—inside and out. A clean colon will usually mean your breath will be sweet, and you'll have little body odor. A magnesium deficiency, by the way, can cause us to have abnormal body odor. The best way to keep a clean colon is to keep a clean conscience and a sweet spirit. Hatred, guilt, resentment, unforgivingness, bitterness, jealousy, suspicion, anger, worry, or any of the other negative emotions can cause your colon to become constricted—knots in your stomach, as they say. Food can putrefy before it can be evacuated and cause many health problems indicated by a coated tongue and bad breath.

"Drinking sufficient water and, again, lots of fresh fruits and vegetables and whole grains, which includes the bran, will give the colon a good brushing down. Celery is excellent. If you can afford a juicer, fresh vegetable juices will cleanse your whole system. If you already have colon problems—you're often constipated—take a glass of prune juice every morning, eat chia or psyllium seeds with your breakfast cereal (you can get them in a health food store). It's still true that an apple a day keeps the doctor away. Some laxatives can be harmful and habit forming.

"This may sound like a strange thing to discuss in a Bible class, but Harold and I have talked the ears off a man trying to convince him not to divorce his wife. This man could no longer tolerate her bad breath, her body odor, and her dirty house. She had also gained about forty extra pounds. Obviously, her colon was clogged, and she smelled like a backed-up sewer. His rejection of her only added to her condition. I'm sorry to say the story had an unhappy ending; he left.

"Keep your body clean on the outside too—no perfume or deodorant cover-ups. By the way, a spray bottle of undiluted rubbing alcohol works great for a deodorant; it's cheaper, and it doesn't contain aluminum which can be harmful. We use the 91% because it evaporates more quickly. Wash your hair often enough so it smells nice and isn't greasy. Keep your fingernails filed and clean. A husband may go to work and come home grubby, but he doesn't want to come home to grubby kids and a grubby wife.

"Give him a trim body too. You may have a problem with the metabolism of your calories—you don't burn up as much as you eat. Then eat less calories! You don't need as much food as the slender lady next door to keep you going. You'll have to fight the 'battle of the bulge,' but be vigilant.

"If your husband is fat as well, that's probably your fault; you're the cook. He may stubbornly tell you he wants chocolate cake and he buys candy on the road, but you can approach him along the lines of 'I love you and I don't want to be a widow. I'm changing our diet so we both get thinner. We'll feel much better and last a lot longer. I want to look nice for you so you aren't ashamed of me when you take me someplace, so please cooperate with me so I'm not tempted if I fix something fattening for you while I'm trying to reduce.'

"Now I'm not recommending some fad reducing diet; just eat less food. Don't put food in bowls on the table. Put it on each family member's plate, and gauge your meals so there aren't any left overs. Fix enough so each person gets enough but isn't tempted to take a second helping. There won't be anything for a second helping. Gradually, so no one notices, cut down on the size of servings.

"Of course if you have company, you'll bring out the serving bowls, but don't fix enough food for the Fifth Army, just because you're having company. Don't use the excuse of having guests or eating out to be gluttonous. It might help you to do a careful Bible study on gluttony and its results.

"Fast one 24-hour-day a week. It cleanses the system and shrinks the stomach. It will help you spiritually and physically. Jesus said in Matthew 6:17: 'Moreover when ye fast. . . .' He didn't say 'if'. He expected people to fast regularly. Of course if you have a physical problem, you'll want to do this under the direction of your doctor. If you feel nauseous or develop a headache, it's probably a good indication that your colon is a mess. You need a good internal cleansing.

"If you want to reduce faster, fast twice a week. The Pharisees did, and Jesus didn't rebuke them for fasting, only that they did it for show. You don't always have to do a complete fast; you can drink fruit or vegetable juices. That may be the best way to start out if you've never fasted before. However, a plain water fast is the best cleanser. By the way, use distilled water if you have chlorine and fluoride in your water. These are toxins in themselves.

"Besides eating less, eat nonfattening foods. Red meats are more fattening than fish, turkey, or chicken. I understand pork is about 40% fat. We get a mindset about having to have roast, mashed potatoes and gravy, and then a sweet desert.

"Now if your hubby is a slim Jim, you'll have a tougher time, but it's more important than ever. He may view your obesity as letting yourself go because you don't care for him as much as you did when he was courting you. A man likes to be proud of his wife. She represents his taste. When he introduces his little missus, he's saying, 'This is the woman I chose over all the others.' If he's kept himself in good physical condition, and she hasn't, there's an element of embarrassment for some men. Some few men really like the looks of fat women, but most don't.

"Be careful of snacks and junk foods, like potato chips and other salty things. Salt causes your blood vessels to lose their elasticity and it holds water and fat in the tissues. Harold and I use one of the vegetable salt preparations that is low in sodium.

"Just having victory over a sugar addiction is going to pull off most of your pounds. Cut down your bread intake to no more than one or two slices a day. Make yourself carrot and celery sticks to munch, or a few raw nuts. You're better off to legislate no in-between snacks, but if you feel terribly hungry, eat something that will stick to your ribs a while, and you'll probably eat less in the long run.

"For having said all this about the overweight problem, don't develop a complex about being fat. If you make a big issue over it, you'll begin to hate yourself and develop an ugly personality. Don't go to the other extreme and open yourself for spirits of Anorexia Nervosa.

"Studies have shown that most women want to be thinner than what their husbands would like them to be. They want to look like a Barbie doll whereas their husbands want them to look a bit more cuddly. Also, recent studies have shown that being moderately overweight will give you a longer life expectancy than being the ideal weight as shown on the Metropolitan height and weight tables. In other words, when I'm talking about being fat, I mean 30% over the Metropolitan weight tables. Those who have diabetes, high blood pressure, or other physical problems will want to keep their weight lower than that. Just recognize that excess weight is unhealthy and detracts from your looks and work on temperance just as you would any other character development in your life.

"If you're not really active in sports or gardening, or some other strenuous activity, do some active exercises every day. They should be the huff and puff variety so your blood circulates well and your lungs get a good work out.

"Read some exercise books and settle on an exercise routine that you can do without fail and that doesn't depend on the weather. If you exercise in the same place at the same time every day, it will become a habit like brushing your teeth. Develop a routine that uses all of your muscles, toning the body well so your tummy is flat and you look svelte. Exercise will not only burn up calories, it will make you feel more energetic. Sedentary people feel sluggish in mind and body. Exercise gets the blood flowing and cleansed as it flows through the lungs. It also relieves tension and worry.

"Practice posture correction too. Slouchy posture will age you in looks and in how you feel. Stooped shoulders press on the lungs so they can't do their job. Sagging stomach muscles can't hold your reproductive organs or your colon properly. Lazy posture accounts for a good deal of the backaches about which we complain. Stand straight against a wall a few times a day. Tuck in your seat, pull in your stomach, point your feet straight ahead.

"Correct duck feet or pigeon toes. Your walk can detract from your general appearance. Ask a friend to watch you walk, or examine your footprints on soft earth or snow. If you walk with your feet straight ahead, your back and stomach muscles will be much better aligned, and you'll have fewer aches and pains to mumble about.

"Pretend someone is pulling you up by the top of your head towards the back a bit. Now this new posture may hurt a bit to begin with, because you've let some muscles shrink and others stretch, but bear with it a couple weeks, and you'll love the poised, younger looking, younger feeling, new you. Your husband will notice too. Let him know you're on an improvement program to please him because you love him.

"Give your husband a well-dressed body. Dress like a Christian, not a heathen, so his testimony is not hindered—nor yours. Dress modestly everywhere but in your bedroom. If you're too warm, avoid synthetic fabrics. As Yvonne just mentioned, they don't allow the skin to breath. Ask your husband or a close friend, 'Is this outfit provocative? immodest? sexy?' A woman's clothes can easily cause men to stumble."

The pastor's wife, Wanda, raised her hand and Emily acknowledged her.

"Ladies, last week, not one, but two of the men from the church approached me and asked if I wouldn't speak to the women about their clothes. They said they felt guilty and embarrassed because when visiting after church, they had to avoid looking at several of the sisters; their dress was so seductive. Please pray about each of the purchases you make and teach your daughters to dress modestly too. We should all set an example for our young women, and we shouldn't offend our brethren in this area either. Our men folks have enough trouble in the flesh out in the work place; they shouldn't have to flee youthful lust when they come to church. The Lord realized this when he spoke through the apostle Paul in I Timothy 2:9-10. Let me read that for us:

> In like manner also, that women adorn themselves in modest apparel, with shamefacedness and sobriety; not with broidered hair, or gold, or pearls or costly array,
>
> But (which becometh women professing godliness) with good works.

"When I say modest, I mean your clothes should call attention to your face, not your sexual parts. Don't point up your derriere, your breasts, or your legs. Writing on a T-shirt rivets attention on your breasts. I saw a skirt the other day with a pretty country scene and a child flying a kite. The kite was placed in the vicinity of the crotch. This will direct the eyes of men to look where they should not. It's the natural travel of the eye to take in the scene and follow the string to the kite. I can't help but believe that these clothes are designed to be sexy, and we should not be so naive that we purchase this type of outfit.

"A lot of bare flesh is more seductive than many women can imagine. Short shorts, halters, and tight-fitting clothes, especially stretch knits, are no-no's for a godly Christian woman. This type of clothing stumbles the men with whom we come in contact. It negates any opportunity we may have to witness to the unsaved or build up the believer.

"Another thing that is inappropriate is the wearing of men's clothes. Pants with a front fly and slouchy army-fatigue-style blouses are not feminine. Men love to see a women in ruffles, bows, and flowers—filmy, fluffy, and decidedly feminine attire. Even a simple cotton housedress can look that way. Husbands don't expect you to dress up to scrub the kitchen floor or grub in the garden, but they don't like to come home to someone who looks like their brother either."

"Thank you, Wanda. Yes, Millie."

"Emily, what about pants?"

"I was afraid someone would ask that. I've asked the Lord about this for years, and I'm still not sure how to answer that. Deuteronomy 22:5 says:

> The woman shall not wear that which pertaineth unto a man, neither shall a man put on a woman's garment: for all that do so are abomination unto the Lord thy God.

"In Bible days men and women both wore long tunics—dresses we'd call them. In fact there are some people still dressing like that in the East today. Years ago in China, the women wore pants and kimonos and the men wore robes (essentially a dress). But in every culture the people know that one type of clothing is for the man and another for the women.

"The women in America very seldom wore men's style pants until World War II when they worked in the defense plants, and the women's lib ideology began to take root. Most feminists want every one equal, and they want us to look alike. Before World War II, if a woman went biking, she wore bloomer-style pants in which no man would have been caught dead. Even then, the older women raised their eyebrows and questioned whether biking was proper for women. They believed if an activity required men's clothing, it was not an activity for women. When I was a girl in school, we were not allowed to wear pants to school except under our skirts in the cold weather.

"Today it's hard to tell who is a man and who is a woman, especially among the young people. Even pictures in the newspapers and magazines advertising clothes are often indistinguishable. Ladies' dresses and suits are tailored just like men's suits. Even the material is the same. This is a result of the feminist push, and personally I don't like that push. I have noticed, however, a swing back to more ruffles and lace and a lot more dresses and skirts. I think many women are returning to femininity again.

"You might ask yourself when you buy clothes, 'Would a normal man wear this?' If your answer is yes, maybe you should pass it up. Think: 'I'm glad God made me a woman and I'm looking for clothes that will demonstrate to God, and everyone else who sees me, that I appreciate His choice of sex for me. I want to dress so people will know I am a woman.'

"Some women wear pants in the winter to stay warm. You might consider knee socks, leg warmers, or the warmer style of panty hose. Some wear pants for sports activities or gardening. You might try culottes in that case.

"I don't want to be legalistic about clothes. Pray before you buy, but then be obedient to the Lord and His Word. Be honest with yourself. Don't try to justify what you feel in your conscience is wrong.

"Let's add another dimension here. Dress in clean clothes that fit your figure. If you're still plump, don't wear horizontal stripes. If you're long and lean, don't wear vertical stripes. Dark clothes will slenderize you and so will thin belts. Wide belts, especially in contrasting colors, will tend to make you look wider and shorter. There are books in the library that will help you pick up hints on how you can enhance your appearance. They will tell you what colors to wear to highlight your hair and eye and skin coloring, how to wear your hair to bring out the beauty of your shape of face.

"There's a balance needed here too. We shouldn't be looking like the world's people with a sinful emphasis on clothing and style, but, on the other hand, we shouldn't look like frumps either. We're wearing some fashion or style no matter what we put on, so to be ten or twenty years behind the style is not more spiritual than being in style. Don't feel you have to have the latest fad; it's a waste of money. Buy more conservative styles and they'll be 'in' a lot longer. If the styles are immodest, don't conform. I understand the Queen of England wore her skirts below the knees when the mini-skirts were in style. She set the pace; she didn't follow someone else's pace. We should be an example to the world, not them to us. We should be clean, very neat, and tasteful in our appearance. Dress as unto the Lord and unto your husband. Please them both.

"I'm not going to dwell too long on make-up. There are fine Christian women who definitely think women should wear make-up, and there are fine Christian women who think we should not. I happen to fall into the category that says do what you think God wants you to do, and don't judge the rest of the ladies. Leave them to their conscience. You might ask yourself, as I did when I was a new and young Christian, 'Why am I wearing make-up? Who am I wearing it for? Why? Examine your motives and be honest with yourself. If you do wear make-up, keep it moderate. Excess make-up associates you with harlots and fast women. It makes your features look hard and accentuates your flaws or wrinkles.

"I copied down what Wycliffe Bible Encyclopedia says about the painting of the eyes. Let me read what it says in the last paragraph:

> . . . In the Bible the use of eye paint always has evil associations. The Hebrew word Kahal, "to paint (eyes)," occurs only in Ezk. 23:40, in a description of the efforts of an adulteress to entice her victims. Eye paint (Heb. puk) is mentioned twice in connection with makeup. Jezebel painted her eyes before she went to confront Jehu (II Kgs.

> 9:30, RSV). Jer. 4:30 (RSV) compares Judah and Jerusalem to a woman who enlarges her eyes with paint in an attempt to secure deliverance by seduction. Here the verb is Qara, basically "to tear," also "to make large or wide," graphically fitting the appearance of painted eyes.[7]

"Under the word *eye*, Wycliffe's has more to say along the same line. Again, I'm just reading the last couple paragraphs:

> Painting around the eye was common for women in ancient Egypt and Babylonia, but among the Hebrews it is mentioned chiefly in connection with women of ill repute. The eye lids above and below the eyes were blackened with black powder of antimony or stibium. However the translators of the KJV sometimes translated the word "eyes" by "face." Thus Jezebel actually painted her eyes (II Kgs 9:30, ASV). Jeremiah says, "Though thou enlargest thine eyes with paint" (Jer.4:30, ASV; cf Ezk. 23:40). . . .[7]

"I think that speaks for itself. Our Heavenly Father is not too busy to be concerned about every small detail of our lives. Ask Him what you should do about make-up and abide by your own convictions, not what someone else tells you to do.

"One more point: when you're in good health, your skin glows and you naturally have more color in your face. If you have the joy of the Lord, you'll have a sparkle in your eyes that can't be manufactured by the make-up companies. Of course, one thing every woman must put on her face each morning is a radiant smile, and remember to touch it up a bit throughout the day. If you don't feel joyful, find some way to show forth love. John indicates in the 15th chapter that if we abide in Him and love one another, His joy will remain in us and our joy will be full. Even a homely person with a beautiful smile is attractive.

"Let me close this section with I Peter 3:3 and 4. Veronica, will you read that for us please?"

"Sure.

> Whose adorning let it not be that outward adorning of plaiting the hair, and of wearing of gold, or of putting on of apparel;

> But let it be the hidden man of the heart, in that which is not corruptible, even the ornament of a meek and quiet spirit, which is in the sight of God of great price.

"I think for all our pastor has preached about the occult, I shouldn't need to caution you about jewelry, but some of you are new and some have come from other churches. Be careful you do not buy, or even receive as a gift, anything connected with the occult. An ankh an Italian horn, the peace symbol, crosses, charms, signs of the Zodiac and the pentagram, the so-called star of David (which was not connected with David, but rather with Solomon after he became involved with heathen wives and allowed their witchcraft practices to enter his kingdom) are all associated with witchcraft. Many of the people involved in witchcraft are pushing occult jewelry and sending demonic spirits with these trinkets. When you bring occult items into your house, you give grounds for evil spirits to dwell there. We'll cover this in more detail in a few minutes when we discuss house cleaning. If you wear jewelry, be moderate. An excess of jewelry can also make you look like a hooker.

"Yes, Mary."

"Our good grooming (or lack of it) communicates to others, not only what we think of ourselves, but what we think of them. A wife who feels it's unnecessary to dress nicely for her husband says, in effect, 'I've got him now; he's in my clutches and I don't have to be concerned how I look anymore.' She says, by her actions, that she's lost respect for herself and for him. He will unconsciously lose the respect and admiration which he had for the nicely groomed lady he courted. He may also unconsciously let his own appearance slip, which in turn will lower his self-esteem and his wife's respect for him. If we are well groomed at home, it demonstrates to our husband, and our children too, that we have a godly acceptance of ourselves and think highly of them."

"Careless or careful," Emily added, "our grooming will rebound to us, and, going on to our next subject, so will our housekeeping. If we keep a clean, tidy house, the rest of the family will respect the house and help us keep it that way. If we don't care, neither will they."

"Let's move quickly through the housecleaning part of this lesson now. You've given your husband yourself—a healthy, clean, trim, well-toned, well-postured, and attractively dressed body. Now give him your hands to clean, to cook, to sew, and to launder. Last week I asked each of you to bring a tip for housekeeping. Raise your hand

and be brief and to the point so everyone gets a chance, please. Mary?"

"Keep house. Don't let your housework slide so you have to clean it all up when someone is coming. Organize your work so it's always all clean. In little bits, slowly but surely it takes less energy, and you can always be glad to see someone ring your doorbell."

"Excellent advice. And Mary's house is always all clean. Pam?"

"Don't collect stuff you don't need. Don't accumulate socks with holes or boxes of mending. Have a sew or throw day (or week). If you have a project you haven't touched for a year or two, give it away or throw it away. Don't collect old pictures and papers your kids did in school, or birthday cards from 1950. Keep all keepsakes in one small box or a scrapbook of outstanding work for each child. Work on it with them; they may love a picture you would toss. But don't be a pack rat. Have a garage sale once a year so you can get rid of what you don't need. Clean your closets of clothes you never wear; then go through the dressers and closets with your kids and weed out the things they've outgrown or don't wear. The church has a large room in the basement in which we keep used clothes for anyone who can use them. When someone in the area has a fire, our Helps Group finds out what sizes are needed and packs up several boxes for that family."

"Good, Pam. Sharon?"

"We've lost the art of spring cleaning. My mother used to put us through a white glove inspection every year during spring vacation. We had to wash or dust the bed springs, the woodwork, the underside of the dresser. Every inch in our room had to be free of dust and dirt. If she wiped it with her white glove and there was the least show of dirt, we cleaned again until no smudge could be found. Then we helped her do the same thing in every room of the house. Curtains were washed or dry cleaned. Furniture was shampooed, rugs shampooed, windows and walls were washed. That house was spotless. I try to do the same thing every year. I'm probably not as thorough as my mother, and I have only four children to help; she had eight. At the end of the week, I'm really worn out, but it makes me feel great to see it sparkle when we're done."

I breathed a sigh of inadequacy and I wasn't alone.

Emily smiled understandingly. "We could all stand to clean for a white glove inspection, couldn't we? Maybe those of us with grown children could do most of this in that boring, tail-end of winter instead of developing cabin fever. Fran?"

"Always stay ahead of regular chores like washing, ironing, dishes, and mending. When these things aren't done quickly, they pile up and become mountains that loom before you. It gives you a negative feeling about the chore that was neglected. And when you finally attack all that work, it takes you forever to get it done. The psychological reaction is to avoid it again because the remembrance of all those dishes or all that ironing is odious to you. If everything is always done, you have a feeling of accomplishment and contentment. How do I know about this? I plead the Fifth Amendment."

"I think I'll nominate Fran to receive the award for the most improved housekeeper of the year. Merry Lou?"

"A stitch in time saves nine. If we go through the dirty clothes and mend things before they go in the wash, we can usually save a lot of extra mending and sometimes save a garment from being totally ruined. I put everything that needs mending in a little basket by my chair in the living room. While Fred and I talk or he reads the Scripture or a Christian biography to us, I get all my hand mending done. I'm teaching the children to mend their things too—even the boys. The machine mending and sewing of new clothes I do every Wednesday. I've scheduled the entire day with nothing else so I have a big block of time and few interruptions. I can usually finish a whole outfit in that one day. In the summer I teach the girls how to make their clothes for school."

"A stitch in time can refer to other things as well," added Emily. "If we clean our drapes, carpets and furniture frequently, the dust won't deteriorate them as quickly. Dust rots fabric. Drapes and furniture should be vacuumed often between cleanings. Betty?"

"Keep refrigerators defrosted and clean. An overworked 'frig' adds dollars to the electric bill. No one needs hidden containers of green fuzzy science projects growing in there. I have a recipe called Must Goes. We get out all the good left overs—this must go and that must go and make a soup or casserole."

"That's cute, Betty. I have a suggestion of my own. Keep a projects list of all your storage space—cupboards, drawers, closets, shelves, etc. Routinely clean one or two a week. If you do this on a regular basis, all your storage areas will be clean and neat, and you can always put things away where they belong. Do food storage areas more often so you don't have spoilage or collect bugs. Sandy?"

"I've found it really helps to clean the walkways to your house. If you sweep the sidewalks by the front and back doors and inside the garage, you track in far less dirt. Also shake out the foot mats by these doors often. In the warmer weather, it helps to hose the walks down and in the winter keep them shoveled . I also make the kids wash their hands as soon as they come in from playing and immediately after meals. It certainly does cut down on fingerprints all over the walls and furniture."

"Good. Ann?"

"Keep papers sorted and filed. Ask your husband to sort through a little every evening. We get such an incredible amount of junk mail, mixed with important mail or items that are interesting things to read when we have a little more time, plus the kids' papers and newspapers. If I don't keep this stuff shuffled and sorted, some important insurance paper will disappear, and we'll spend hours hunting for it. I've learned to clear up these papers every day, but make sure Ray has a chance to look all these things over and make any important decisions necessary concerning them."

"It does make you feel like you run an office, doesn't it? Claire?"

When I tidy the house, I carry a big box around with me from room to room and pop all the clothes, toys, and other misplaced items in the box. As I pass where these things belong, I put them away. It sure saves a lot of steps. I'm working on teaching the children to pick up after themselves, but I like the house to be real nice when Jim comes home, so I pick it up myself and then charge the kids for maid service, which comes out of their allowance."

"Good strategy. Wanda?"

"Teach your children to clean the house and keep it clean, including your boys. They will appreciate what cleaning house means when they get married. Give each child a set of chores. Expect them to help clear the table and take turns with the dishes. Children should learn to dust, tidy, sweep or vacuum the floor, hang up their clothes, pick up their toys, and generally be responsible for the cleanliness of their rooms. This one bit of household management will save you untold time in the long run and make your children orderly, pleasant people with whom you can enjoy living. "

"Wanda's children are good examples of helpfulness and responsibility too. Let me add here, start them very young. If mother has a positive cheerful attitude toward work, the children will catch that. If she's negative with lots of murmuring and complaining, they'll catch that too. And if she puts all the nasty jobs she doesn't want to do on the kids, they will resent any cleaning jobs and try to skip out of them like she does.

"Any more tips?"

"Fran gave mine," said Dori.

"Claire gave mine," Shirley added.

"And some forgot?" asked Emily.

There were sheepish nods.

"That's O.K.; we have some good tips and we're pressed for time. Let's move on. Women need to clean house of more than dust and grime. There are evil spirits that take up residence in our houses too. We don't have to allow that. They cannot come in or stay there if we remove their grounds for being there. Harold and I have noticed some houses that seemed to have spirits of strife in them. Everyone who lived in that house got a divorce within a short period of time—even Christians who lived there. The house should have been cleansed of those spirits. Throw out all occult-related items. These things give grounds for evil spirits to dwell in our houses. We invite trouble when we ignore the Scripture. Turn to Numbers 33:52, please. Shirley, will you read that, please?"

> Then ye shall drive out all the inhabitants of the land from before you, and destroy all their pictures, and destroy all their molten images, and quite pluck down all their high places.

"Now in Deuteronomy 7:25 and 26. Sheila, will you read it please?"

> The graven images of their gods shall ye burn with fire: thou shalt not desire the silver or gold that is on them, nor take it unto thee, lest thou be snared therein: for it is an abomination to the Lord thy God.
>
> Neither shalt thou bring an abomination into thine house, lest thou be a cursed thing like it: but thou shalt utterly detest it, and thou shalt utterly abhor it; for it is a cursed thing.

"The majority of rock records and tapes," admonished Emily, "are full of witchcraft, and the disco and country western music is loaded with spirits of Melancholy, Divorce, and Adultery. Sensual books and pictures are unclean items that are an offense to God. Let your teenagers know that if they bring that junk in the house, they'll find it in the trash burner. Watch what you allow in your house; remember the meaning of keepers at home includes being a guardian of that home. Teach your kids to detest and abhor what God detests and abhors. Watch out for little knickknacks, many of which are associated with heathen religions. The New Age movement is striving to put the symbol of the rainbow everywhere they can. Though God said the rainbow was a sign that He would never again destroy the whole world by water, the New Agers have made it an occult symbol, just like 666.

"Just as God doesn't want us to be spiritually unfaithful to our husbands, dabbling in witchcraft is spiritual adultery. If you were to come home and say, 'Well, I was down the street kissing and petting with John Doe this evening. I wasn't at all serious about it—just curious. I don't believe in that sort of thing. I don't want to go all the way, you understand; just checking it out,' That he would be jealous is an understatement. 'Not to worry,' you could say. But he would be rightly upset. Yet people today ignore God's Word and fool around with Ouija boards, Dungeons and Dragons, check out their horoscope, visit a fortune teller for a lark, or play levitation at a party. All of these are spiritual adultery, and God is jealous for his Bride because He knows His Bride's lovers are demon spirits who will steal from her, kill her, and destroy her. To draw the Bride back, He will allow her to be plundered by the 'Midianites.' Whenever your family suffers financial loss, ask yourself if you have any idols. Are we seeking information, direction, comfort, or power from a source other than God? Or are we giving our time, adoration, or attention to another god? How about the god of sports? The god of money? Our house? Our husbands? Our kids? Remember, for our own good, God removes our idols. Flee anything that even hints of the occult, and keep your loved ones and the things God has given you in their proper relationship to Him.

"Replace all occult, or suspect things, with Scripture plaques on your walls, good Christian music, books, and magazines. Ask the Holy Spirit to guide you into all truth about the items in your home. If you feel a real strange attachment to something, keep praying about it. If your husband is an unbeliever, you may not be able to throw away his things, or if some of you single girls live at home with unsaved parents, you can't pitch their belongings, nor can you dictate what kind of music they listen to or what they watch on TV. However, you can bind up the spirits that may be in these abominable things, and you can anoint the house with oil and dedicate it to the Lord. We all should dedicate and anoint our homes. Look at Deuteronomy 20:5. Merry Lou, will you please read that?"

> And the officers shall speak unto the people, saying, What man is there that hath built a new house, and hath

> not dedicated it? let him go and return to his house, lest he die in the battle and another man dedicate it.

"Enlist your husband, if he's willing, to lead you all in a dedication of your home. Anoint each room and then anoint each one in the family and dedicate or rededicate all of you unto the Lord. In Jesus' name, command spirits of strife and contention to leave your house.

"Now let's all turn to Proverbs 3l. This is the famous passage on the virtuous woman. Each of us would do well to memorize it and meditate on it frequently, especially when we get a little self-satisfied. It would probably be refreshing to read it in a different version from time to time also. Margie, will you read verses l0-3l for us, please?"

> Who can find a virtuous woman? for her price is far above rubies.
>
> The heart of her husband doth safely trust in her, so that he shall have no need of spoil.
>
> She will do him good and not evil all the days of her life.
>
> She seeketh wool, and flax, and worketh willingly with her hands.
>
> She is like the merchants' ships; she bringeth her food from afar.
>
> She riseth also while it is yet night and giveth meat to her household, and a portion to her maidens.
>
> She considereth a field, and buyeth it: with the fruit of her hands she planteth a vineyard.
>
> She girdeth her loins with strength, and strengtheneth her arms.
>
> She perceiveth that her merchandise is good: her candle goeth not out by night. She layeth her hands to the spindle, and her hands hold the distaff.
>
> She stretcheth out her hand to the poor; yea, she reacheth forth her hands to the needy.
>
> She is not afraid of the snow for her household: for all her household are clothed with scarlet.
>
> She maketh herself coverings of tapestry; her clothing is silk and purple.
>
> Her husband is known in the gates, when he sitteth among the elders of the land.
>
> She maketh fine linen, and selleth it; and delivereth girdles unto the merchant.

> Strength and honour are her clothing; and she shall rejoice in time to come.
>
> She openeth her mouth with wisdom; and in her tongue is the law of kindness.
>
> She looketh well to the ways of her household, and eateth not the bread of idleness.
>
> Her children arise up, and call her blessed; her husband also, and he praiseth her.
>
> Many daughters have done virtuously, but thou excellest them all.
>
> Favour is deceitful, and beauty is vain: but a woman that feareth the Lord, she shall be praised.
>
> Give her of the fruit of her hands; and let her own works praise her in the gates.

Emily continued, "*Virtuous* actually means strength or ability. The dictionary speaks of virtue as excellence, strength, courage, valor, worth, moral excellence or goodness, justice, temperance, prudence, fortitude, and chastity. The Moffatt translation reads: 'A rare find is an able wife. She's worth far more than rubies.' So it is a good thing for us to have physical strength. In verse 17 that strength is reemphasized and again in verse 25. That's all the more reason to give attention to our health.

"Her price is far above rubies. She is valuable. She is a precious treasure. Part of Satan's lie today is that women aren't as important as men. Some Christian women feel they have little value because they're supposed to be in submission to their husbands. This lie is linked to the pride of Satan. He wanted to be like the Most High and was not satisfied with his position or his ministry. His pride destroyed everything for him and his lies are still linked to that pride. Watch for it. Many women feel that because they are in a support position as wives, they're not worth anything. Humility, as we've said before, is not that we think of ourselves as worthless; it's not thinking of ourselves at all. It's being God-centered rather than self-centered. From God's perspective, women have a high value. It is in heathen countries, where people don't have God's perspective, that women are not treated with honor, respect, and protection. Incidentally, it's the pagan core of the women's liberation movement that is responsible for destroying a good measure of the honor, respect, and protection which women have enjoyed in America.

"Let us go on to verse eleven: 'The heart of her husband doth safely trust in her, so that he shall have no need of spoil.' This is a very broad area; it includes sexual faithfulness, which I would like to emphasize here for a moment. A big program has been fostered in the kingdom of darkness to ensnare the children of light into sexual sin. Paul told Timothy to flee youthful lusts. We need to cleanse our minds and hearts so we're not one of today's fatalities. How many of you have heard, in the last five years, of a preacher going off with the church secretary or the preacher's wife running off with another man?"

Every hand was up.

"We're all sadly aware of a church about thirty miles from here that has never fully revived since the pastor went off with another woman. Thirty miles in the other direction, a whole church and school have never recovered from a similar occurrence. In both these cases it was the man who left. But we might ask why. Of course we don't know the answers; we only know the rack and ruin we see after the damage has been done.

"These were folks with lust spirits that were never dealt with. The Devil laid his plans very skillfully over a period of many years to destroy the relationship between the husband and wife, even before they were married, and then he crowded in relationships that were wrong until the lust spirits manifested like a time bomb.

"It isn't always the man; sometimes it's his wife. Keep your feet at home and your eye contact loyal. One shouldn't need to mention faithfulness to Christian women, but the enemy of the Church seeks to destroy a man by taking away his helper. Nothing breaks the heart of a man of God like the loss of his partner—it's literally like tearing him in two. Nothing ruins his testimony as the break-up of his home. Guard your mind against fantasy, self-pity, and loneliness. Don't let the Adversary get a foot in the door of your mind with thoughts or emotions toward someone besides your husband. These are forerunner spirits to unfaithfulness. Watch and pray.

"Ask yourself, 'Have I inherited or picked up spirits of Harlotry, Lust, Seduction? Or do I have the characteristics of a strange woman? Am I loud? Silly? Do I feel rejected by my father? Do I hate men and want to get even with them?' If you sense that you have lust spirits, get them cast out before they destroy you and your home, and encourage your husband to do the same, if he's troubled.

"As I said before, verse eleven is broader than sexual faithfulness. There's an economic trust here that's probably more in context with the passage than sexual faithfulness; though what we've just said was necessary to consider. Our husbands need to trust us with the family money. Wives must learn to be wise and frugal when they shop.

"Look at this little jewel; she's definitely not lazy. She goes a good distance to get the best bargains. She's up early and late, working hard. She's ready for the winter with plenty of warm clothes. She manages the servants. She's well dressed. Notice also that her husband can trust her enough that she selects a field and buys it. She doesn't buy impulsively; she considers a field. She buys quality. She also adds to the family earnings by making things at home and selling them.

"When we buy quality, we actually spend less money in the long run. An exception would be clothes and shoes for small children. They grow out of them so fast that unless you can hand them down to the next youngster, it's not important that they last for a long time. Do be careful, however, that you buy good enough shoes that the child's foot is properly fitted. A well-fitted shoe is necessary for a well-formed foot.

"Garage sales are still the best buys for clothes and many household goods. Often, you can find clothes that you could never afford to buy in the stores. Teens are a bit more touchy because of the peer pressure, but if they go with you, they'll pick what suits them. Yes, Martha?"

"Our children never felt neglected or self-conscious about their clothes. We had a well-structured budget, which included only a moderate amount for clothing. It was to be equally divided between the five of us. We made it a challenge to make, or find at garage sales, all we needed, and at the end of the year put all we had left in our clothing fund into the offering at the Missionary Conference. We made our clothes a matter of prayer. The kids and I often sold crafts or vegetables and bought clothes or shoes with the proceeds, rather than touch the fund. Our own yearly garage sale netted us enough to buy at other garage sales. One year we spent nothing from the fund. All three boys had paper routes and Mary baby-sat as often as she could. She and I made a whole lot of our clothes that year. She make such cute little outfits that we soon had half-a-dozen of her girlfriends at the house on Saturdays making their own clothes."

"That's an excellent idea, Martha. It sounds like your candle did not go out by night either. Yes, Mrs. Watsen."

"There's another kind of faithfulness I think should be mentioned here—the faithfulness of our being there when the husband and children need us. Feet can run all over town doing nothing, like coffee klatches, window shopping, and other time wasters. Even good constructive activities such as P.T.A. and volunteer work for charities need to be scheduled so we're home when our family needs us. I've tried getting hold of some girls for a week at a time. It didn't seem to matter what time of day or night I called, there was no one home, or a lonely husband or child would reply that she was not home. Sometimes they didn't even know where she was. Don't divide yourself between your husband and friends, relatives, or adult children. He comes first. There may be exceptions, such as aged or sick parents, daughters having babies, or a friend who has just lost a loved one; but if you are gone all the time, you're not taking good care of your hubby."

"Thank you, Mrs. Watsen. There's also a trust that involves loyalty. Don't talk bad behind your husband's back. It will boomerang, damaging your relationship. Say all the good things you want; that will boomerang even faster, and he will experience such happiness, you will be well rewarded. Sheila?"

"Don't share your sex life. That's totally private. When that door is closed, it's closed for privacy's sake. Your husband does not want to feel he's sleeping with a reporter."

"Well said, Sheila. Trust includes faithfulness, it includes his reputation, it includes his children, and it includes his money.

"Verse 23 seems to be out of context, but its place here indicates there's a connection between her fine character, industriousness, and good appearance and the fact that her husband is known in the gates when he sitteth among the elders of the land. The respected elders of the city would sit at the gates. When the people had a question to be judged, they would bring it before these wise men. You might say it was the local court. A man's wisdom and respectability were judged, not only on the basis of his own character, but by his wife and family. This is still true today. A sloppily dressed wife, disorderly children, and a shabby house always have dishonored and always will dishonor a man and so will poverty. A lazy or gluttonous wife can make a man poor and so can a wasteful wife. At this point let's open up the discussion for ten very brief exhortations which represent the principles of Biblical finances. Betty?"

"Whenever you do anything with money, think in terms of being his helper—you're helping him by not being extravagant, by buying wisely, by training the children in the use of money."

"Good. Merry?"

"Never use money to manipulate your husband or children. And don't use bedroom blackmail when he won't buy you or the kids what you want. That's a Jezebel spirit in operation."

"Amen. Fran?"

"Obey your husband in spirit as well as definite spoken requests concerning the use of money."

"Very perceptive and very important. Marlene?"

"Don't have his and her money. This policy divides the marriage. It says to one another, 'I don't trust you!' Jesus trusted one purse to Judas and he knew he was a thief. It's probably wise to have a certain amount allocated to the wife to handle groceries, household goods, and clothing as well as a personal fund so she can buy a present for her husband without having to ask him for the money, but separate managing of each partner's funds is sure to separate their relationship."

"I agree. Wanda?"

"Don't buy on credit. Don't use credit cards. Many of our Christian leaders, after years of seeing their sheep with the wolf constantly at their doors, are advising young people to save, with concerted effort, to buy a house outright with cash. One wise pastor, whose church was paid for and whose people were financially free of debt, for the most part, exhorted the congregation to give a large Sunday offering (not their tithe money) for a couple whose wedding was to be in three months. This offering, together with what the couple had saved and their parents had given them, enabled them to buy a small older home outright. By the time they needed a larger home, they were able to save the money and buy a newer, larger home outright again. My husband is seriously considering doing the same thing here. Getting people financially free is the biggest help in putting broken marriages back together again."

"What a blessing a young couple can be when they're not bound with a load of debt. Ann?"

"We need to watch out for the hiss of the serpent when we buy. The virtuous woman considered her purchase. The world is full of fast talking salesmen who put pressure on you to buy today or you will have to pay much more tomorrow or next week. Sometimes they'll tell you that your name will be put on the computer and if you don't buy this product, or join this buying club, you can never have the opportunity again. Never buy under pressure. If a product is of good quality and it is a good buy, they don't have to promote it with high pressure.

"Sometimes an item on sale is not really any less than it normally is. The 'sale' sign is there to psychologically induce you to buy it now, because you think you're saving money. Study prices so you know what the going price is for items you need and check with consumer-guide-type magazines to determine the best quality for the money."

"Good advice. Sandy?"

"Be content. Be willing to do without, and in the long run you will have more. Hardship can draw you very close together, if you respond to it in the right way. Greed is insatiable, and the pride of life will soon bring you to ruin."

"That sounds like a proverb, doesn't it? Mrs. Watsen?"

"Pay your bills before you buy groceries and other things. You'll be surprised how much you can do without and how creative you can be when you work with what's left after essential bills are paid."

"Sage advice. Jan?"

"Give the kids an allowance; otherwise they'll nickel and dime you into the poor house. It will also teach them that they have to manage their own money or do without. They also have to earn what they get so they learn the concept of reward for labor."

"How true. Yvonne?

"Tithe. It's a must if we want God's blessing. And we'll be even more blessed if we add offerings and alms to that tithe. Let's not be gullible geese either, that respond to everything we hear on the electronic church. Some of those preachers live in posh condominiums and drive the most expensive cars, and they do it with money they coax out of naive listeners who feel they're giving to spread the Gospel.

"Tithes belong to the Lord," Yvonne continued. "We don't actually give them. We're bringing a portion—only one tenth—back to the One Who gives us power to get wealth. In doing so we enrich the church where we are fed spiritually. We give our alms and offerings cheerfully to the storehouse or beyond to the poor or wherever God directs us. Giving in every area of life will always rebound unless our motive is to receive for ourselves. Offerings are not to be given as an investment. Self-interest is seldom rewarding."

"Yvonne is referring to Malachi 3:10:

> Bring ye all the tithes into the storehouse, that there may be meat in mine house, and prove me now herewith, saith the Lord of hosts, if I will not open you the windows of heaven, and pour you out a blessing, that there shall not be room enough to receive it.

"Let's be careful we don't go overboard in withdrawing our giving to Christian organizations outside the Church. Just because some preachers have been unwise or even crooked in handling money sent to them, there are still valid works that are ministering to believers and to people the churches don't reach. Many are a blessing to the churches. However, these gifts should be in addition to our tithe. Tithe should go to the church where we fellowship. Sharon?"

"Keep careful records of all your expenditures so you know where your money is going. That way you can give a good account to your husband. My sister was horrified to realize how much she actually spent on groceries each week. She only spent $60.00 when she shopped on Saturday, but she'd send the kids to the corner store for little items all through the week which really added up."

"Excellent point. One more, please. Margie?"

"If at all possible, sacrifice and save one tenth of the weekly earnings and invest it wisely in more than one place. I realize this has to be a joint effort, but sometimes the wife is so eager to spend that the husband finds it hard to save. If you save, you'll not need to get into financial bondage in an emergency, and you can pay cash for whatever you need. But never deplete your savings for luxury items."

"Those are all excellent suggestions. I'm sure if we all follow that advice our own works will follow us in the gates, and our children and our husbands will arise up and call us blessed. Dori?"

"It seems to me that this gal is going night and day, working her socks off, and all it says about her husband is that he sits."

Emily enjoyed a hearty laugh with the rest of us.

"Well, it looks that way, doesn't it? I'm sure some of you who have husbands who work in an office or do selling, feel that you work harder than he does, but leadership and brainwork do require a lot of energy—ask any student during exam time. The stress of decision making and handling business or dealing with the public can be hard work too. Jesus was not working in the carpenter shop after He began His public ministry, but we're told that He was exhausted and wanted to get away for a bit just to rest. Strength does go out of you when you are giving out of yourself to other people all day, especially spiritually.

"One more note about the husband in this chapter, and then we need to move on. The husband of the virtuous woman is known in the gates when he sitteth among the elders of the land. Today he would be an elder in the church, perhaps a pastor.

"Now I can almost hear someone say, 'You don't know my husband; he's not leadership material. He has soooooo many problems.' That's not ours to judge. God used some very imperfect men to do some very important leadership jobs. Moses was an imperfect leader, but God used him. We know he was imperfect because he wasn't allowed to enter the Promised Land. Besides, it took God eighty years to prepare Moses before He could send him off to Egypt to lead His people. James tells us that Elijah was a man of like passions as we are, but God answered his prayers.

"We just need to do what God asks us to do. Obey God! We won't have to answer to God for our husbands' imperfections, but if we do not do the things which will qualify our husbands to be in a leadership position, God will hold us responsible. I would surely hate to stand before God and try to explain my behavior if I was the reason my husband could not be an elder or a deacon. We need to be sure it's not our rebellion which keeps our husbands from ruling his own house well. If we're rebellious, the children will learn that lesson well without any special effort on our part. Please turn to I Timothy 3. Read verses 1-7 for us please, Sandy."

> This is a true saying, If a man desire the office of a bishop, he desireth a good work.
>
> A bishop then must be blameless, the husband of one wife, vigilant, sober, of good behavior, given to hospitality, apt to teach;
>
> Not given to wine, no striker, not greedy of filthy lucre; but patient, not a brawler, not covetous;
>
> One that ruleth well his own house, having his children in subjection with all gravity;
>
> (For if a man know not how to rule his own house, how shall he take care of the church of God?)
>
> Not a novice, lest being lifted up with pride he fall into the condemnation of the devil.
>
> Moreover he must have a good report of them which are without; lest he fall into reproach and the snare of the devil.

"We've mentioned laziness as a drain on the family budget, but it can also have a terrible effect on the order and cleanliness of the home. Maureen is on vacation this week, but she wanted to share her testimony with us about how she has overcome slothfulness so I asked her to write it down. I'll just read it to you:

> I was set free from the bondage of slothfulness at a home schooling convention in Indianapolis where Mr. J. Richard Fugate spoke. In one of his four messages that day, Mr. Fugate spoke so strongly about "lazy mothers" that I came under heavy conviction, finally realizing that

slothfulness was my problem and the reason I was having such difficulty with home schooling this year. I had attributed my distress to "burn out" and hadn't recognized the true source of the interrelated "symptoms" I had been experiencing. These symptoms included fatigue, depression, lethargy, inability to concentrate, confusion, procrastination, aversion to work, sleepiness, insomnia, etc. My house was dirty and full of clutter and disorganization. To cook a simple meal for my family was a monumental task. Home-school materials piled up in boxes and envelopes and led to time-consuming searches for needed items. I experienced difficulty planning the teaching because I couldn't think creatively or clearly.

My second year of home-schooling became an increasingly frustrating experience, much more difficult than the first year had been. Even so, my children (ages 18 and 15 ) did well in their studies. My 15-year-old's standardized test scores went up more than two grade levels to "post high school" in all tested areas. My children had truly been taught by the Lord (Isaiah 54:13), and their spiritual growth was even more impressive than their academic growth.

As Bill Gothard points out in his booklet, *How to Conquer Slothfulness*, most slothful people do not believe they are slothful. I was no exception. Slothfulness comes on gradually, the result of making little "soft choices" in daily decisions. Sluggards rationalize. They would be more diligent if there were but fewer obstacles in their path or if working conditions were just more favorable. "The sluggard will not plow by reason of the cold . . ." (Prov. 20:4). Meanwhile, they rehearse the reasons why they are unable to begin the projects they know must be done. "The sluggard is wiser in his own conceit than seven men that can render a reason." (Prov. 26:16). They always have an excuse, no matter how farfetched. "The slothful man saith, There is a lion without, I shall be slain in the streets" (Prov. 22:13). Everything is difficult for the sluggard. "The way of the slothful man is as an hedge of thorns . . ." (Prov. 15:19). Even eating is too much work sometimes. "A slothful man hideth his hand in his bosom, and will not so much as bring it to his mouth again" (Prov. 19:24). The slothful live in a world of wishful thinking. The tension between their restless minds and inactive bodies produces destructive frustrations. "The desire of the slothful killeth him; for his hands refuse to labour. He coveteth greedily all the day long..." (Prov. 21:25-26). They blame the alarm clock when they do not get up in the morning, not realizing that "slothfulness casteth into a deep sleep" (Prov. 19:15), so deep they don't even hear the alarm, having conditioned themselves to ignore it through repeatedly staying in bed after it rings, or pushing the snooze alarm three times. They can't understand why they live so shabbily, having failed to heed the Lord's admonition about sleep. "Love not sleep, lest thou come to poverty..." (Prov. 20:13). "... Drowsiness shall clothe a man with rags" (Prov. 23:21). "I went by the field of the slothful, and by the vineyard of the man void of understanding; and lo, it was all grown over with thorns, and nettles had covered the face thereof, and the stone wall thereof was broken down. Then I saw, and considered it well: I looked upon it, and received instruction. Yet a little sleep, a little slumber, a little folding of the hands to sleep: So shall thy poverty come as one that travelleth; and thy want as an armed man" (Prov. 24:30-34).

I had gone up for prayer many times at church but experienced only temporary relief. I would have more energy for a few days but soon realized there was really no difference in my life. "No difference, no deliverance."

But on May 30, when Mr. Fugate preached so strongly about lazy mothers, I came under such conviction that I was able to recognize and acknowledge my sin before God and truly repent. I am so grateful to him for having the courage to say the things he said. He was blunt, but what he said was the truth. Most of the women in the meeting didn't seem to like him; he was stepping on our toes! His words cut to the quick. There was very little applause when he was finished. But I left that meeting rejoicing—exhilarated—because the Lord had done something in my heart in an instant. He had cleansed it of the unrighteousness of slothfulness according to His promise that if we confess our sins (not our symptoms or complaints) He is faithful and just to forgive us our sins and to cleanse us from all unrighteousness (I John 1:9). From that moment my domestic life began to spiral in a healthy direction instead of the downward spiral of interrelated aspects of slothfulness that had plunged me into a mire of despair.

I can't even remember what Mr. Fugate said that brought me under such conviction, but what seems to stick with me now is that whenever I'm tempted to make those little "surrenders" to myself, those little "soft choices" in daily decisions (such as stay in bed a little longer, wait a few more minutes before starting a project, etc.) I find myself dealing very firmly with myself. The moment an "I don't feel like doing that now" thought develops, I immediately say, "Too bad; you're going to do it anyway." The essence of Mr. Fugate's message was that the permissive "Dr. Spock" upbringing that most of us have had has turned us into self-centered, undisciplined, self-indulgent, lazy mothers.

It is interesting that I find myself enjoying being strict with myself. Before my repentance, I was so bound in slothfulness and self-indulgence that I could not be strict with myself. I lost the battle every time I mustered up the energy to even try.

It has been nearly three months since my deliverance, and I am a different person in so many ways. The progress I have made in organizing my home, organizing, planning, and teaching school, getting things done, creative thinking, etc., since that day has been significant. All the symptoms that accompanied slothfulness have vanished (fatigue, lethargy, confusion, procrastination, frustration, sleepiness, insomnia, aversion to work, depression, etc.). I am getting more accomplished in a day than I used to accomplish in a week—and enjoying my work. I am eager to learn more about how to cook and clean and garden and teach and to do all the things that I used to try to avoid doing, erroneously thinking I was overloaded with responsibilities and burned out. The more I do and the more organized I get, the more hours there seem to be in the day. Disorganization and clutter cause a very stressful, tiring, unproductive state of affairs.

I enjoy being helpful and doing useful things. Instead of despising work, I like it now. I can't think of anything more fun to do than to work—at ANYTHING!—at whatever the Lord wants me to do with my day, for I have

> learned to give each day to Him. Sometimes He wants me to play tennis or rest, or spend several hours in His Word. There is a healthy mix and balance of spiritual, mental, and physical activity and rest in the days we give to God.
>
> For several days the Lord had me weeding mint and bean fields with my son and daughter and a teenage friend. I walked and hoed 5-7 hours a day in the hot sun, got tanned, conditioned, and paid a good wage. Some days I even pedaled a bicycle 5 miles to get to the fields. I felt wonderful. The sleep that comes well deserved after a hard day's physical labor is so blessed.
>
> I am still reaping the benefits of that physical conditioning; my legs have strength they haven't had for years. I had spent so much time sitting and sleeping that my legs would hardly support me when I stood or walked. Much of the fatigue I had experienced was due to weak muscles. The Lord continues to show me the interrelatedness of the symptoms caused by the spiraling effect of the SIN of slothfulness.
>
> Scripture tells us that the truth will make us free (John 8:32). When God's holy standards for Christian conduct are communicated in plain language with no apology, beating around the bush, or compromise, the Holy Spirit can do His work of convicting hearts, bringing about godly sorrow that worketh repentance, . . . and setting the captive free!

We could have heard a pin drop. I was deeply convicted myself, and I'm sure most of the others in the room felt the same. "I'm selectively slothful," I thought to myself. "I go like a house-a-fire in the things I want to do and procrastinate on the things I dislike doing. That's why everything isn't always all done."

Emily continued, "I'm glad Maureen shared that with us. You'll note that she was freed from an evil spirit after conviction and repentance. Some people try to evict spirits without repentance and wonder why they never seem to get free or stay free. The spirits have grounds to stay or to come back because these people have not turned away from the sinful activity which allowed these spirits to enter in the first place. I call this revolving-door deliverance. It doesn't go anywhere.

"The booklet Maureen was referring to, by Bill Gothard, is put out by the Institute in Basic Youth Conflicts. If you haven't attended one of these seminars, you have missed a tremendous spiritual growth experience. These seminars are held annually all over the country in major cities. A group from our church goes every year to the basic and the advanced seminars. I'll give you the address in the book list I hand out next week. Maureen has attended both the basic and the advanced seminars but the meeting in which Maureen heard Mr. Fugate was the Indiana State Convention of Home Educators which is not connected with the Institute in Basic Youth Conflicts.

"This is a good place to break for lunch. When we come back, we'll cover the area of ministering to our husbands sexually. Veronica, will you please close this part of lesson five in prayer and also give thanks for the food."

"Father, we want to minister to our husbands with our bodies. Enable us to give our husbands a healthy, clean, trim, well-dressed body. Help us to be like the virtuous woman in strength, industry, and every area of faithfulness. Forgive us for the sin of laziness and cleanse us. Deliver us from justifying ourselves. We thank you now for this food and ask that you will bless it for our bodies. Bless also our fellowship with one another. In Jesus' name. Amen."

# 9. THE MINISTRY OF OUR BODIES (CONTINUED)

The luncheon gave me an opportunity to meet many of the ladies in Emily's class. I tuned in the spectrum of conversations around the large table. The consensus of opinion was that these lessons were great, but not as easy to implement as they were to learn. I was glad to find that I wasn't the only one who felt that way. Dori and Shirley were quiet and somewhat preoccupied with their thoughts.

The lunch break was relaxing, but no one wanted to linger. We were all eager to get back upstairs for the rest of lesson five.

Emily went to the platform and resumed the lesson. "Now that you have ministered to your husband with your mind, your heart, and your industrious hands, it is time to minister to him sexually. All these other capabilities could be ministered by his mother, his grandmother, his sister, or his favorite aunt, and he could remain single; but the sexual ministry is that which really makes the relationship a marriage. The Bible language is 'to know' one another. It is the act which makes a man and woman one flesh.

"It was in this area particularly, that the Creator, in His infinite wisdom, knew man needed a helper suitable for him. The animals wouldn't do. It was God's opinion that it was not good for man to be alone, so He made an help meet (or fit) for him. Incidentally, it may help us in our ministry to our husbands when we clearly understand that God's purpose in creating a woman was so she could be a help to her husband and he wouldn't have to be alone. In I Corinthians 11:9 it says very clearly, 'Neither was the man created for the woman; but the woman for the man.' If a married woman is a hindrance rather than a help and she's not there when he needs her companionship, I firmly believe she's missing God's purpose for her life.

"It is in this physical sexual union that we have a picture of the Church's spiritual union with Christ. The Spirit of the Lord is within us, yet we reach out for fellowship with our Lord until we have 'met' Him—'know' Him, as it were. Then, from this relationship with our Lord, we bring forth fruit. Spiritual babes are 'born again' because of our spiritual relationship with the Heavenly Bridegroom. Just so, physical children are born from our physical relationship with our husbands. The physical union is an immensely important part of the type we are to portray of the Church's relationship to Christ.

"The sexual union is sacred and just as God calls His Bride into the prayer closet for private fellowship, so the married couple must consider their sexual relationship a sacred private encounter not to be discussed in detail with others or to be viewed by others as though it were something of little value—profane, as it were.

"Hebrews 13:4 says:

> Marriage is honorable in all, and the bed undefiled: but whoremongers and adulterers God will judge.

"Let me read that for us in the *Amplified New Testament*:

> Let marriage be held in honor—esteemed worthy, precious, [that is], of great price and especially dear—in all things. And thus let the marriage bed be (kept undishonored,) undefiled; for God will judge and punish the unchaste (all guilty of sexual vice) and adulterous.[4]

"As the Bride of Christ is sanctified *unto* Christ, so we are sanctified *unto* our husbands. *Sanctified* simply means set apart. But a sanctified person or thing is set apart unto something or someone. So we are set apart unto our husbands in the marriage act. We must call our minds apart from all the duties of the house, the children, the unpaid bills, from the ministry of the church, from all our hurts and disappointments, from all our problems, from all his failures and from every foolish fantasy.

"Modern psychologists are recommending that women fantasize that they are with another more exciting man during the sex act—a movie star or sports hero. Nonsense! That's adultery during the very act of love! How hypocritical and how destructive to the very fiber of the marriage relationship. On the contrary, we need to concentrate on the person of our husbands. If you are having difficulties accepting him, then handle this in your quiet time with the Lord before you come to this situation.

"The Devil's snare is to fill the wife's mind all day with negative things about her husband, or at least just before bedtime. He hasn't fixed the faucet washer for three months. The dryer has been down all winter, but he sits and reads or watches TV all evening. Worthless creep!"

There was an identifying ripple of laughter.

"Just keep in mind where these thoughts are coming from and why. I think every wife could grumble about a lot of undone things and rehash old (or new) hurts and disappointments, but what does it accomplish? A victory for marriage-breaking spirits! State your disappointments to clear the air and then forgive and forget. When you find yourself berating your husband, turn the Devil's station off, and tune the dial in your head to Philippians 4:8; it's much better listening.

"Write a list of his good qualities—those things you admired when you wanted to marry him, the things he's done for you, the things the children like about him, the things his mom and dad are pleased about, the things for which the neighbors compliment him. Sometimes, if you're the critical type, you can see him better through the eyes of others. If you are critical or judgmental, no other man could please you either. I hate to be so blunt and harsh, but critical spirits love to hover in bedrooms where they can destroy our sexual ministry to our husbands.

"When your list is started, keep adding to it. Then start thanking the Lord for everything good you find. Next, begin to thank and praise your husband. Be grateful. Verbalize your gratefulness and your love. Look for every little thing he does that is considerate and thoughtful and compliment him. Be sincere, not phony, but watch and you'll find more and more for which you can admire him. And here's a little secret; when you notice the good things instead of the bad, he'll do a lot more of the right things because we all like to be commended for good behavior.

"Now, back to the bedroom. You've forgiven him for hurts and disappointments, and you've stirred up your love for him before you ever opened the door to the bedroom. Now, your part of the act of marriage is to concentrate on the situation at hand—no mind-wandering. This in an act of love. This man is expressing his love to you in a deep communion, and you are expressing your love to him in a deep communion. You're alive with expectation. You're receptive. You've set yourself apart from everything else unto him. You are verbalizing your love.

"It is a picture, if you will, of your spiritual communion with your Heavenly Bridegroom. Consider a moment this communion with the Lord. You put everything else out of your mind. You pray, verbalizing your appreciation, your gratefulness, your adoration, and your love. You reiterate your commitment and then you actively wait on the Lord to receive from Him. You reach out to Him with your spirit to hear what He says to you in His Word and in that still small voice in your spirit. You don't just wait with an empty head—you're not passive—that's transcendental meditation (the fast lane to the asylum). You're tuned in to Him and expressing your delight in how much He loves and cares for you.

"We demonstrate Christ's love, in type, in the bedroom. It too is a communion which involves not only our spirit, but our mind, our emotions, and our body. And we need to put our whole selves into it too. We don't lie there like a piece of meat. We enter into the experience. We caress, touch, stroke, and pet as we are being caressed, touched, stroked, and petted. We respond to his kisses with passion and demonstrated pleasure. We express enjoyment in words, hums, actions or gestures. We communicate to him what pleases us and discover what pleases him.

"I asked Harold, from a man's viewpoint, what I should say about sex to the ladies. He said that men like to think that their wives like them sexually too. They'd like to think that their wives are turned on by their manliness, that they're admired physically, not just the fellow who pays the bills, but that they're appreciated and desired sexually as well. A wife need not feel out of place to occasionally 'attack' her husband. He feels like he's succeeded in his manliness if she's interested in him sexually. He said 'I don't know how many men have complained to me, "She just lies there like a dead fish." They 'allow' their husbands to proceed with a sigh of resignation or exasperation.' Harold said to tell you, 'Let your husband know you like his attention even to the point of soliciting it.'

"I would add this, however; the husband is by nature the leader and the aggressor. If you are usually the one soliciting a romantic situation, something is definitely wrong. Perhaps you have been such a shrew that he's lost all his romantic inclinations toward you. Perhaps you've turned him down so many times he's afraid to ask anymore."

A very pretty woman in the front row raised her hand.

"Yes, Veronica?"

"How can you turn down your husband when you just don't feel up to it, without making him feel rejected or hurt?"

"You can just say, 'I don't feel like it tonight.' If he knows you usually do want him and if you always communicate it with love and an affectionate response, indicating that it's not that I don't want you or I'm mad at you, but that I'm just not capable of performing, most men will understand. Explain why—physically or emotionally. It is more loving to say no with kindness than 'All right, if you insist'—a yes that really means no. A yes of resignation beams out rejection more than simply saying, 'I'm just not capable of responding tonight. I can't put myself into it.' However, denial should be a *very* rare occasion. If it's frequent, check your health, your schedule, your attitudes, whatever reason, and conform yourself to the Word of God. Perhaps you need a nap when the children take theirs. A couple of my neighbors take turns watching the children every afternoon for an hour so each one of them gets an hour's break each day.

"This is the most important area of your ministry to your husband, and it's a godly ministration. This lack of ministry has been the ruination of many good men of God. Because they were denied sex at home, they fell prey to temptations outside of the home. I think we mentioned before that if a man has a dynamic, outgoing, leadership type personality—a lot of drive, he is also likely to have a strong sex drive. If you married that kind of person, it is your responsibility to meet those needs. If you'll think of it as a ministry, you can enjoy it as much as he does.

"Another thing that will dampen your husband's ardor is rebellion. He asked you to pay an electric bill and you found a sale on coats, so you bought one and the bill went unpaid. He asked you not to go to a certain part of town alone, but you went anyway. Disobedience to our husbands means they can't trust us. How can they believe that we're submissive in the bed if we're not submissive when they're out of sight?

"I know I'm overworking the type of the Church and the Bridegroom, but I make no apology. When we disobey the Lord, our intimate fellowship is broken, and we cease to bring forth fruit. As Christians, when we disobey God, our own guilt causes us to hide from God until we are so miserable that we come in repentance and get things squared away with the Lord. We need to do the same thing with our husbands. 'He [or she] that covereth his sin shall not prosper, but whoso confesseth and forsaketh it shall be blessed' (Prov. 28:13). We need to confess our disobedience to our husbands and also to God who tells us to obey our husbands.

"Back to what Harold was saying—I guess he hasn't heard any blues being sung by husbands whose wives pounce on them. Those men probably wouldn't say anything anyway because no one would believe them."

Emily had to wait a moment for the laughter to cease.

"Harold said, 'Though a woman is not usually the aggressor, sometimes she should say, "I want you and I need you." And other times she should indicate that she's available by more subtle means like a special candlelight dinner, soft music, perfume, a special nightgown that says I'm 'wantable.' Husbands want to feel they please their wives so much that their wives enjoy sexual relations. The husband feels fulfilled when he knows his wife has a fulfilling sexual experience. If she doesn't, he feels he has not been successful. It's kind of like giving one another gifts. The wife gives her husband a sweater, which he really likes and he wears it often. But he gives her a sweater which she doesn't like and seldom wears. She thanks him and says it's nice, but it's written all over her face that she doesn't really like it. Some women seem to have that attitude about sex. They don't really seem to enjoy it and it's written all over their faces.'

"Now that's a message straight from the men through my husband. Please take it to heart. Essentially what Harold is saying is put yourself into it. You get out of something what you put into it. On the other hand, you're not 'investing' in sex either. If it's self-gratification you're after, you'll always lose. It's the same principle in every area of life; Mark 8:35:

> For whosoever will save his life shall lose it; but whosoever shall lose his life for my sake and the gospel's, the same shall save it.

"If we give ourselves exuberantly in the sex act, and we experience orgasm, it brings our husbands pleasure to see our pleasure, and it brings us pleasure too. It's like tithing; we give cheerfully out of a heart of love, but we can't outgive God. We keep on receiving blessings. When we give, we always receive. When we give with the motive of getting—when we grasp after something for our own selfish ends—we usually lose. It's difficult to separate this in the act of love. We desire to experience orgasm because we know our husbands want us to. Society has told him that he's less than a man if he doesn't achieve this every time and simultaneously as well. And society has told us that we have it coming. Modern women expect this. We're 'entitled' to it, and if we don't, we're at least supposed to be disappointed.

"Most of our grandmothers didn't even know the word orgasm or expect anything more than the affection, the romance, and the joy of fulfilling their husbands. When they did experience it, I'm sure they were thrilled, and if they didn't, they enjoyed making their husbands happy. Their pleasure was in giving, and I'll bet they experienced it more than they were telling because they were relaxed about it—that is those who were really ministering to their husbands in love.

"Many women, just a little over fifty years ago, were taught that sexual pleasure was sin. If a woman experienced orgasm, she was considered immoral. Her husband would definitely have suspected her morals or her sanity, and she would have felt guilt and shame. Many women who were taught this way denied themselves any interest or enjoyment of sex. It was considered a duty which they performed because it was expected of them. This asceticism was probably a hold-over from the Roman Catholic Church. These ascetic, so-called Victorian ideas, which came down through our 'foremothers,' were not Biblical, they were unbiblical, and even the Catholic Church appears to be changing its view in this area.

"In the past fifty years, the pendulum has swung in the opposite direction toward hedonism. That too is totally unbiblical. We, as Christians, need to set the pace by bringing sexual balance into our own lives and by opposing hedonism and asceticism wherever we can. I think I see a move back, on the part of common-sense people, to a moral, Biblical view of sex. God's laws are based on God's love for us. He has our blessing in mind when He issues directives. As the Creator, He made us with a complementary sexual anatomy and physical, emotional, and mental sexual drives. He did this, not only so we could reproduce, and He'd have more people to love, but also for our absolute pleasure. Read Song of Solomon if you doubt me.

"By the way, when we choose not to reproduce, we rob ourselves and God of having more people to love. The over-population propaganda is a myth propagated by the New Age Movement, of which Zero Population Growth is a part. To avoid an increase in the earth's population they push abortion, homosexuality, euthanasia, and suicide. They're planning to eliminate all the Christians and those who don't agree with their plans for a New World Order. We'll touch on that in the next lesson when we talk about the attack against our ministry.

"Let's go back to the supposition that sex is evil. This is definitely not God's opinion, as we said before. Unfortunately, we are still plagued by traces of this notion in many people's minds—that sex is dirty. Fornication and adultery *are* unclean, but the marriage bed is precious in God's sight, as we read a few minutes ago in Hebrews 13:4. We should be able to sense God's presence and approval during the act of love, and be able to pray and praise Him for this union and for one another.

"In Song of Solomon 5:1, the Bridegroom has entered his garden. At the end of the verse it appears that an observer, the Creator of this beautiful experience, is adding His encouragement 'Eat, O friends;

drink, yea drink abundantly, O beloved.' The Moffatt translation puts it in a separate parenthesis '(Eat away, dear ones, drink your fill of love!)' My attention was called to this by a book called *A Song For Lovers,* by S. Craig Glickman."

Emily held up the book with her finger holding a page.

"Let me read to you from a couple of paragraphs:

> Nevertheless, the words of the lovers are not the last words of the night. A mysterious voice is the last to speak. "Eat, O loved ones; drink and be drunk, O lovers."
> Who is speaking to the lovers here?[18]

"Mr Glickman concludes it is God himself. I'm skipping to the bottom of the page:

> He lifts his voice and gives hearty approval to the entire night. He vigorously endorses and affirms the love of this couple. He takes pleasure in what has taken place. He is glad they have drunk deeply of the fountain of love. Two of his own have experienced love in all the beauty and fervor and purity that he intended for them. In fact, he urges them on to more. "Eat, O loved ones; drink and be drunk, O lovers." Eat together from the feast I have prepared for you. That is his attitude toward the giving of their love to each other.[18]

"I think Mr. Glickman expresses God's viewpoint beautifully. You're welcome to borrow this book from me if you like.

"Satan has attacked the marriage bed from Genesis until now. I think we can safely say that if a couple's sexual relationship is poor, the marriage is poor. A bad sexual relationship will either be the cause of a failing marriage, or the result of it. We cannot compartmentalize it. We cannot say, 'The only good thing we have going in our marriage is our sex life.' Nor can we say, 'Our marriage is perfect but for our sex life.' It's just not so. The way we respond to one another sexually is intertwined with our mental, emotional, and spiritual responses concerning the in-laws, the finances, the children, our work, our health, and every other aspect of the life we share. The wife who gives her husband a tongue-lashing at the supper table will not expect a tender embrace as they slip into bed that night.

"We've discussed in other lessons how Satan attacks our marriage through our minds and emotions. Now let's see how he lays his snares in the sexual area. In the world's understanding of sex, the man uses love to get sex, and the woman uses sex to get love. But love is a misnomer here. It's really lust—the kissing and petting that stirs up passions. This often goes on in the courtship, perhaps even in casual dating with several different fellows before a girl sets her heart on a particular young man and they get married. Statistics tell us that few people get married today who have not experienced the sex act prior to marriage. I don't believe all the statistics I hear, but that is the Devil's plan—promiscuity before marriage and frigidity after marriage. It's really a clever ploy Satan uses to draw young people into his net. He plots to destroy our marriages before we ever walk down the aisle.

"We have been hearing reports for several years now that witches throughout the world fast and pray for the destruction of Christian marriages. Each solid Christian home is a vertebrae in the backbone of the Church, and each solid Church is a vertebrae in the backbone of a nation. If Satan can weaken our marriages before we ever say 'I do,' he can cripple that marriage and maybe destroy it.

"Let's examine how Satan lays his snares. When a girl does not feel loved and treasured by her father, she often looks for acceptance from the boys. However, if she feels worthless, her behavior will often be promiscuous. She will do anything to get a boy to accept her. She'll use sex to get love. In doing this, she heaps up guilt and condemnation upon herself and feels even more worthless. Meanwhile she's drawing a great deal more rejection from her dad, and if she gets pregnant, it's a huge dose.

"Let's say a young girl—Susie, we'll call her—feels rejection by her father. He may justify his attitude because Susie was the fourth child and he was already feeling the burden of a growing family. She may have been the fourth girl and the fourth disappointment of a daddy who had been waiting for some while for a little roughhouser with whom he could play football. She may have caused this rejection by being rebellious, or she may have been rebellious because she felt rejected. The two work in a vicious circle.

"When my boys were teens, I warned them to be cautious of any girl who had a poor relationship with either her father or her mother. 'How she responds to her father is probably how she'll respond to you, and she'll be a lot like her mother.'

"Now our young friend Susie has a poor relationship with her dad, and she seeks acceptance with the boys. She becomes promiscuous, experiences guilt, and subsequently more rejection from her dad. All of this negative emotional upheaval which she experiences is related to the sex act.

"Let's say Susie gets saved and marries a Christian man. Unless she gets some help, she's very likely going to find herself with a negative attitude toward sex. She may consciously or unconsciously think of it as dirty or disgusting because she associates her past experience of guilt and shame with her present experience, which should be one of joy and delight. She may become totally frigid and not understand why.

"The husband will react in a number of ways. He may step up his efforts to satisfy her. Satan will undoubtedly twist his actions around in her mind so she imagines that he only cares about sex—that he thinks she's only a cheap 'in-house prostitute'. Again she feels unworthy and rejected. The harder she may try to be a sexual companion, the more tense she becomes, and the frequency of his attempts only solidify the iceburg.

"Of course, talking over frigidity or impotency is very difficult, so they have a communication barrier, and walls are constructed in this area too. If he felt rejection from his father, he will have walls built up as well, and find it difficult, if not impossible, to give and receive love. His own feelings of rejection will make him interpret her frigidity as rejection of him.

"The husband may busy himself in sports or business to take his mind off of his incompetence as a lover. He may, if he is unstable spiritually, seek affairs with other women. This reinforces his wife's notion that he only thinks of sex and doesn't really love her for herself.

"He may approach her with perversion—oral or anal sex, wife-swapping, masochism, or sadism. The adult book stores are loaded with weird sex right out of the pit of Hell. This will totally assure her that sex is the worst sin a woman could commit, and she'll freeze their water bed on contact.

"Now Susie's plight is repeated by many others who may have been virgins when they were wed, but they have never been content that God chose to make them a woman instead of a man. They pray 'Thy will be done,' but they don't accept the body God picked for them to serve in—the vessel the potter made into which He pours His life and from which he pours out His life to others. If He made it a female vessel, He saw that it was good. God deems the capable woman much more valuable than rubies—He *treasures* us.

"It is necessary for a wife to feel she is a precious jewel—a ruby. Your husband may not be adept at expressing his appreciation of you, and all of us could stand improvement—polishing the jewel—but many women place such a low value on themselves that they cannot feel they have anything to offer their husbands physically. They don't accept themselves, and they assume their husbands couldn't possibly accept them either. This self-rejection projects out to their husbands and others as well. (Usually the in-laws). When someone keeps saying, 'I'm not good enough for you; you don't like me, do you?' the idea finally does take hold in the other person's mind. Self-rejection is an evil spirit. If you feel that way, get it thrown out.

"Now we don't want to leave Susie a pillar of ice with walls around her. Let's put our heads together here. What can we tell Susie to help her get out of Satan's net? Fran?"

"Susie needs to go to her father and be reconciled. She must forgive him and ask his forgiveness for disobedience, rebellion or dishonoring him. She can also ask her heavenly Father to tear down the walls she's built between her father and herself. If her father is dead, she can still forgive him and ask God to forgive him and her."

"Mary?"

"As you said, Susie probably needs deliverance from Self-rejection but she also needs deliverance from spirits of Rejection, Rejection from the womb, Rejection from men, Fear of rejection, Rebellion, and probably a whole bunch more."

"No doubt. Sheila?"

"Susie will also need to open a gentle and meek communication line with her husband, asking for his help, but also letting him know she doesn't blame him and she wants to try because she loves him."

"Good. Merry?"

"If Susie was promiscuous, she needs to break ungodly soul ties with her former boyfriends. And she needs to forgive herself and her husband, too, concerning rejection."

"Even if he didn't reject her?"

"She thinks he has. She's feeling the hurt. Even if it's only in her imagination, probably the only way she'll erase those hurts is if she forgives. What harm can it do?"

"Hanging on to the offense is what does the damage, isn't it? For those of you who may not understand what Merry meant by a soul tie, turn to I Samuel l8:l. We discussed this in one of the other lessons, but we'd better explain again here so it's clear. We see in this passage that Jonathan's and David's souls were knit together and Jonathan loved him as his own soul. That word *knit* means tied or bound together. The word *cleave* can mean the same thing. Genesis 2:24

says, 'Therefore shall a man leave his father and his mother and shall cleave unto his wife: and they shall be one flesh.'

"When we consummate the act of love, we make a soul tie. We cleave or bind ourselves to this man. If it is in the bounds of marriage, it is a good, godly soul tie. We give something of our life to that person and he gives something of his life to us. It binds us together as one physically, mentally, spiritually, and emotionally. Ephesians 5:32 says: 'This is a great mystery: but I speak concerning Christ and the church.' There is probably a spiritual dimension here that we won't fully understand until we get to heaven.

"However, if a woman has premarital, or extra marital relations, or she was married before, she also has given that person a part of her soul, as it were, and something of him is still part of her. Turn to I Corinthians 6, please. Read that for us please, Betty—verses 15-20."

> Know ye not that your bodies are the members of Christ? shall I then take the members of Christ, and make them the members of an harlot? God forbid.
>
> What? know ye not that he which is joined to an harlot is one body? for two, saith he, shall be one flesh.
>
> But he that is joined unto the Lord is one spirit.
>
> Flee fornication. Every sin that a man doeth is without the body; but he that commiteth fornication sinneth against his own body.
>
> What? know ye not that your body is the temple of the Holy Ghost which is in you, which ye have of God, and ye are not your own?
>
> For ye are bought with a price: therefore glorify God in your body, and in your spirit, which are God's.

"We see here that it's the sex act which makes us one flesh. A woman with soul ties to others will need to break those past soul ties. She can pray something like this: In the Name of Jesus Christ, I break every ungodly soul tie I have with (and then name the person or persons). Fully restore my soul, Lord. In Jesus' name. Amen.

"What are some other things we can recommend for Susie? June?"

"If Susie has rejected her womanhood, she needs to get her will in line with God's will, and perhaps get deliverance from Rejection of womanhood. Perhaps surrender is the word I should use."

"Yes. for some it's definitely giving up a struggle. Wanda?"

"I've read three excellent books in the last couple of months by Elizabeth Elliot, *Let Me Be a Woman*, *The Mark of a Man*, and *Love Has a Price Tag*. They are all excellent concerning the difference between men and women and the role God has given each sex. I'll be glad to loan them to anyone interested."

"Thank you, Wanda. I have *Let Me Be a Woman*, so any of you can borrow my copy too.

"We've been overdosed with magazine articles, newspaper columns, and books on the subject of sex. Many of these writers have profaned the marriage bed, making the act of love a performance—spectator sport or recreational sex. There's more keeping up with the Joneses in the bedroom than there is in the market place. Remember, the love act is two people loving one another physically. If you're totally caught up with techniques, you'll miss the whole beauty of the experience. Relax and enjoy it. Women have become obsessed with techniques and expect their husbands to be some kind of sexual technique expert. It's a physical union of love not an olympic game. The sex act is not something your husband does *to* you. It's not even something he does *for* you. It's something he does *with* you.

"Some women get really depressed about a lack of orgasm. They feel cheated because they seldom or never experience it. This reminds me of a happy little community in the Ozarks that I heard about some years ago. The people were poor, but they grew enough to eat, and their basic needs were met. They lived life just fine. They were for the most part contented, cheerful folks—until the Sears Catalog came. They began poring over those big books chocked full of goodies they didn't have and couldn't afford to buy. Soon they felt deprived and very discontented. Covetousness moved in like a heavy fog over the little mountain valley. Young people began trekking out to the big city so they could buy all those wonderful things. What had been a peaceful community became a place of complaining, bitterness, and anger.

"America has also been engulfed in a fog of sexual covetousness. Don't be swayed by the world's propaganda from the true sexual communion God intends for His people. There is a sweet mystery surrounding the act of love. The world's sexual revolution marches right on by the emotional and spiritual depths of the marriage act to conquer physical feats which in themselves never bring a deep and lasting satisfaction. We are whole persons and sexual communion involves our whole being—body, soul, and spirit.

"Sex is not the glue which holds a marriage together, either. I just finished reading a book called *The Way Home* by Mary Pride. She says so well, and so logically, that marriage is not for companionship, nor for intimacy, nor is it a social contract, but to produce fruit for God. He said to Adam, 'Be fruitful, and multiply, and replenish the earth, and subdue it.' Since God made Eve to be Adam's helper, she was to help him fulfill this command.[19] I can't do justice to what Mrs. Pride says in this book. This is must reading for all of us. She's saying what a lot of modern Christian writers are failing to tell us—we need God-centered marriages not me-centered or us-centered marriages. When our shared interest is to bring forth children and raise this family together, there will be commitment and self-sacrifice, a binding that will not easily be broken.

"Since America has entered the 'sexual revolution,' sex has become revolting to many. Since the emphasis has been placed on self-gratification, fewer people are ever satisfied. Divorce is rampant because some people think they can get more out of sex with a new partner. The grass always seems greener on the other side of the fence.

"We have sex education in the schools, and almost every magazine or newspaper has some article about sexual 'know-how.' However, it appears that concerning this subject we are ever learning and never able to come to a knowledge of the truth. Because modern women know about orgasm, and many experience it, does not necessarily mean that these women have a richer more enjoyable sex life. The climax is not the whole experience. The sex act has become goal-oriented toward orgasm. As such it sometimes produces striving rather than loving. Yes, we do want this to happen, but if it doesn't, don't affix blame on your husband or yourself. Enjoy the sweetness of the experience and look forward to the next opportunity. Orgasm every time is an ideal to reach for. If you have an ideal situation, rejoice, and if you don't, rejoice anyway, and keep reaching for the ideal. The pathway to your destination can be just as enjoyable as the point of destination. Women often overlook the trip there because everyone talks so much about the place for which they're headed.

"Have you every played a game of tennis? Volleyball? Baseball? Do you always win? Do you still play? Still try to win? It's still fun to play even when you don't win, isn't it? Have you ever tried to share your faith with someone? Did you have the joy of winning that soul to Christ? Every time you tried? Did you quit trying? Expecting? Looking for the opportunity? I hope not. None of us are always successful in what we attempt to do, but we try again and enjoy ourselves while we try. The same is true of our sexual relationship. Let us not make orgasm an idol. Let it be a by-product of an obedient relationship with our husbands.

"We've been sold such a bill of goods concerning this whole thing that we can't just relax and enjoy ourselves. The world fails to point out that sex is meant to be a physical expression of love which includes, as we've said before, a psychological, emotional, and spiritual involvement. Sex can demonstrate lust, which is taking; or it can demonstrate love, which is giving. Lust is selfish and self-centered. Love is unselfish and centers on the loved one. Lust is disappointing; love is beautiful. Lust can never wait; love is patient and kind. Attitudes are involved. Character is involved. The total personality is involved. We cannot compartmentalize sex. Love cannot function without a commitment to one another—a trust in our spouse. We surrender ourselves with abandon to the one whom we trust. We allow ourselves to be vulnerable when we become one flesh with another. I honestly wonder if people outside of the body of Christ can really experience this total dimension of love because it includes a spiritual quality which is absent in their inner man.

"A woman can be so caught up striving for a physical sensation that she forgets she's loving this man who is loving her. She can become so tense and so nervous, because she's not achieving, that she *can't* reach orgasm. Relax, respond, and reach out to him. Those are the three R's of romance.

"Now don't misunderstand me; know-how can be a help. Just keep in mind that your attitude and your husband's attitude are more important than the physical techniques. Tim and Beverly LaHaye have written an excellent book entitled *The Act of Love.* Harold and I often give it as a wedding gift—a little early. Wanda has a copy which I'm sure she'll be glad to loan you, and I also have a copy you're welcome to borrow. Another book which is excellent concerning know-how is *The Key to Feminine Response In Marriage* by Ronald M. Deutch.

"A few of you are still single. Wait until about two weeks before your wedding day before you read this type of book; otherwise you could have some trouble in the flesh. That's why I'm not being more specific in what I'm saying today. Single women should know before they get married what is involved in the physical ministry to their husbands. However, the specific details are best read later on.

"The main thing with which each of you single girls need to be concerned is to keep yourselves pure for the one for whom God is preparing you. Groom yourself to be a godly woman, and God will be able to give you to a godly man. Learn as much as you can about housekeeping and child care. Keep your mind off sex and concentrate on building your character and being a servant. Responsible self-control now will bring you a future of blessing from God whether you marry or stay single. You'll see, as we continue here, that it is usually during your teens and early twenties that Satan lays his snares for your future marriage.

"You also need to be prepared for the possibility that God may have a different calling for your life than that of the ministry of a wife. Read I Corinthians 7 very carefully and rest your future in God's hands. Getting married whether God wants you to or not, could result in a very unhappy marriage. And perhaps I should add, in this day and age, rejecting marriage because you want to do your own thing rather than serve as a ministering wife could bring you a life of frustration and disappointment also.

"Now then, what are some other things that Satan uses in our lives to destroy the enjoyment God planned for the marriage bed? Fern?"

"What you taught us about the Jezebel spirit would definitely affect the couple's love-making. If she's continually trying to maneuver him to carry out her plans, she will surely emasculate him, and her lack of respect for him when she's accomplished her purpose, will make her repel any of his advances. I saw this spirit in myself. I was always arguing with my husband and demanding or threatening to get my own way, but I got deliverance from that spirit and my husband can't get over the difference. 'You're not going to argue with me?' he'll ask. 'No.' I tell him, 'I got rid of that Jezebel spirit.' When he asks me to do something, I say 'O.K.' I can testify to this: it has really made a difference in our relationship."

"Thank you, Fern. Sheila?"

"Another aspect of the Jezebel spirit is bedroom blackmail. I've known a couple of women who used to brag about getting their own way by using sex, but it has destroyed their marriages. The husband of one of these women was too proud to beg for sex. He finally became impotent, and they both lost out. They're still together, but his resentment of her is very obvious—and she's not bragging anymore. The husband of the other woman told my husband he felt like he was sleeping with a prostitute because he had to pay in some way for any sex he got. (Reminded me of that Jezebel tract you read to us a few weeks ago.) Eventually he divorced her and married a woman who didn't 'charge' him."

"While we're discussing the damages of withholding sex," said Emily, "let's cover the Scripture about this. Some women, especially Christian women, still think that sex is something to be tolerated only for the propagation of children. They believe that when you're pregnant or you already have four or five children, then there's no need for sex. Phooey! That idea came from the father of lies. That's not God's idea, as we've already pointed out from Song of Solomon. Here's another couple of verses from Proverbs 5:18 and 19. I'll read them:

> Let thy fountain be blessed: and rejoice with the wife of thy youth.
>
> Let her be as the loving hind and pleasant roe; let her breasts satisfy thee at all times; and be thou ravished always with her love.

"It sounds to me like this is instruction to a man who is no longer young because the writer refers to the wife of his youth. They may have already done a good job of replenishing the earth, but he's still instructed to be ravished with her love. This is how the dictionary defines ravish: '. . . to transport with strong emotion, esp. joy; affect with rapture; fill with ecstatic delight.'[17] Children or no children, we still have an important ministry to fulfill.

"Some women also have a dreadful fear of pregnancy. Where do you suppose that fear came from? The same place all other fears come from. I know a healthy, lively woman who has had nine caesarean sections. I know the daughter of a woman who had five children, though she had an RH negative problem. None of the five had complications. And just recently I met a woman with eleven children with an RH problem. Now I'm not suggesting you ignore your doctor's warnings not to get pregnant again. It may be best, for a time, to use protective measures, but don't withhold sex. Turn to I Corinthians 7, please. Dori, you read verses 1-5 for us, please."

> Now concerning the things whereof ye wrote unto me: It is good for a man not to touch a woman.
>
> Nevertheless to avoid fornication, let every man have his own wife, and let every woman have her own husband.
>
> Let the husband render unto the wife due benevolence: and likewise also the wife unto the husband.

> The wife hath not power of her own body, but the husband: and likewise also the husband hath not power of his own body, but the wife.
>
> Defraud not one the other, except it be with consent for a time, that ye may give yourselves to fasting and prayer; and come together again, that Satan tempt you not for your incontinency.

"Thank you Dori. I think that passage is self-explanatory. Defraud means to deprive, to hold or keep back, withhold, or cheat. Defrauding our husbands is not godly. The godly woman ministers sexually to her husband. It is wrong to deny him. Now there are certain circumstances where it's unwise to partake of sex, such as during certain stages of pregnancy. The Scripture is very precise about certain times of abstinence in connection with the menstrual cycle and after the baby is born. These are for our health and well being. The following passages refer to these times of abstinence. I'll repeat them for you slowly so you can write them down. Leviticus 15:19,28; 18:19; 20:18; Ecclesiastes 3:5; Proverbs 5:15-20; I Corinthians 9:25-27.

"O.K., let's continue exposing the snares Satan sets for the destruction of our marriages. Yvonne?"

"I read a testimony of a woman who was molested when she was a young person. She loved her husband very deeply, but was repelled by his love-making advances. She would grit her teeth and try to respond to him, but she could not really give herself whole-heartedly. It was not until she went for deliverance prayer to get rid of frigidity that she remembered the man who had molested her. She realized that she needed to forgive him. When she did, all the spirits connected with frigidity came out. Fear of giving and receiving love was one. She said her whole marriage has turned around. She now thoroughly enjoys the physical love experience."

"Doesn't it make you angry to see how Satan starts so early. We need to teach our children to guard themselves. We can't be with them every minute. Wanda?"

"Incest is being exposed more and more throughout the country. I'm appalled that a father could devastate his own child in this way. However, it is more often a stepfather or an uncle. It infuriates me even more to realize that the girl's mother was knowledgeable of the situation but allowed it for fear of losing her husband. The same holds true for incest as it does for a stranger. If you have been sexually abused, you will need to forgive the man responsible and your mother if she was involved. It is also important to forgive yourself. Often a child who is the victim of incest has strong guilt feelings and many deep hurts. She feels worthless. Many prostitutes were victims of abuse. But God doesn't have any scrap people; there's cleansing and deliverance and restoration available for everyone. Mary, who washed Jesus feet with her tears and dried them with her hair, had been a woman of ill repute. She who was forgiven much, loved much. Rahab, the harlot, is found in Jesus' family lineage."

"I'm glad you brought that up, Wanda. I'm sure if there's no one here who has had such an unfortunate experience, one of us will no doubt cross paths with someone who carries this burden. Merry?"

"Another snare is lesbianism. I have a friend in another town who had some homosexual experiences in college. She's married to a Christian man, but she can't seem to shake the guilt of her past. She associates her present experience with the past unconsciously and has a strong negative reaction. She's repelled by the very thought of sex. She's confessed her sin, but it still clouds her marriage. She adores her husband."

Emily threw this one into the lap of the class: "What could we say to help that girl? Jan?"

"She probably needs to forgive the girl with whom she had this relationship and break ungodly soul ties with her. Then she needs to forgive herself as well. She no doubt opened herself up to unclean spirits from which she needs deliverance. Sin—our sins or our parents' sins—is what opens the door to demons. Take her back a little further. Why did she get into this unnatural relationship in the first place? I would guess there was a spirit of rejection there. She probably has suffered some deep hurts and needs to forgive some other people too—possibly her father or her mother.

"We're seeing a terrific increase in our nation in homosexuality for a number of reasons," Jan continued, "but mainly, I believe, because the order of the home is all mixed up. The God-given distinction between men and women is blurred beyond recognition. The proper roles of husband and wife are confused, and the leadership authority vested by God in the husband is abdicated by the man and usurped by the wife. The men become effeminate and passive. Check most of the pictures of Jesus, especially from the seventeen and eighteen hundreds. He looks like a milk-toast. Any man who worked as a carpenter—no power tools, mind you—walked mile upon mile, stood teaching for days on end, and camped outdoors a great deal is not going to look that emaciated."

"Amen! The Church is pictured as the Bride of Christ, but this doesn't mean that the men of the Church should be effeminate. Yes, Veronica"

"I think we should mention the aspect that our ministry is a lifetime job. We should encourage the Susies we meet to hang in there and work it out until it works. Marriage does not end until the death of one or the other. The feminists have preached that the family is obsolete so loudly and so frequently that even women in the Church are believing it and acting on it. Women are running away from their husbands to find fulfillment in life. Some even leave their children with the husband. Others are so caught up with material things that they're divorcing their husbands for someone who can buy them the finer things of life. I heard just last month of a woman who divorced her husband to go look for a man who could do a better job of satisfying her sexually.

"Marriage is for keeps. A vow is a promise and when we say those marriage vows before God, we'd better realize how seriously God takes those vows. He said it's better not to vow than to vow and not pay."

"That's right, Veronica, marriage is not a try-it-and-see-if-you-like-it situation. If we didn't realize all our husband's faults until we walked out of the church, that's too bad. We're here now and we must make the marriage succeed. Everyone has problems; another husband will only have a different set of faults. And a woman who isn't fulfilled in her home is not going to be any more fulfilled outside of it."

There were several hearty amens to that one.

Emily gestured toward me. "June, will you read Malachi 2:14-16 for us please? This is addressed to a man, but it's God's viewpoint on the permanence of marriage we're after here."

> Yet ye say, Wherefore? Because the Lord hath been witness between thee and the wife of thy youth, against whom thou hast dealt treacherously: yet is she thy companion, and the wife of thy covenant.
>
> And did not he make one? Yet had he the residue of the spirit. And wherefore one? That he might seek a godly seed. Therefore take heed to your spirit, and let none deal treacherously against the wife of his youth.
>
> For the Lord, the God of Israel, saith that he hateth putting away; for one covereth violence with his garment,

> saith the Lord of hosts: therefore take heed to your spirit, that ye deal not treacherously.

"Thank you, June. Let's cover the passages in the Gospels about divorce. Someone find those for us please, and let's read those."

Betty spoke up, "Luke 16 is one of them."

"Read that for us, Betty."

"It starts in the eighteenth verse:

> Whosoever putteth away his wife, and marrieth another, committeth adultery: and whosoever marrieth her that is put away from her husband committeth adultery.

"There's another passage in Matthew 5:31 and 32, Emily," volunteered Sharon.

"Good. Read that for us, Sharon."

> "It hath been said, Whosoever shall put away his wife, let him give her a bill of divorcement:
>
> But I say unto you, That whosoever shall put away his wife, saving for the cause of fornication, causeth her to commit adultery: and whosoever shall marry her that is divorced committeth adultery.

"Matthew 19 is another place," said Wanda.

"Usually when God thinks something is important," said Emily, "He inspires several writers in the Scripture to repeat the issue often from a different perspective. Go ahead, Wanda."

"I'll start with verse 3:

> The Pharisees also came unto him, tempting him, and saying unto him, Is it lawful for a man to put away his wife for every cause?
>
> And he answered and said unto them, Have ye not read, that he which made them at the beginning made them male and female,
>
> And said, For this cause shall a man leave father and mother, and shall cleave to his wife: and they twain shall be one flesh?
>
> Wherefore they are no more twain, but one flesh. What therefore God hath joined together, let not man put asunder.

> They say unto him, Why did Moses then command to give a writing of divorcement, and to put her away?
>
> He saith unto them, Moses because of the hardness of your hearts suffered you to put away your wives: but from the beginning it was not so.
>
> And I say unto you, Whosoever shall put away his wife, except it be for fornication, and shall marry another, committeth adultery: and whosoever marrieth her which is put away doth commit adultery.

Emily picked it up from there, "Look at Mark 10. This is a similar passage to the one we just read, but verse 12 adds something the other passages don't have. Read that verse, please, Sandy."

> And if a woman shall put away her husband and be married to another, she committeth adultery.

"Romans 7 is another place we should look at, Emily," Sandy added.

"Thank you, Sandy. We'll let Ann read that for us. O.K., Ann? Start with verse 1 please, and read through verse 3."

> Know ye not, brethren, (for I speak to them that know the law,) how that the law hath dominion over a man as long as he liveth?
>
> For the woman which hath an husband is bound by the law to her husband so long as he liveth; but if the husband be dead, she is loosed from the law of her husband.
>
> So then if, while her husband liveth, she be married to another man, she shall be called an adulteress: but if her husband be dead, she is free from that law; so that she is no adulteress, though she be married to another man.

Emily continued, "What does marrying and remarrying do to the personality? I'm sure we don't understand the full implications of the one flesh mystery. That's why we need to just obey God. Turn with me to James 4:4.

> Ye adulterers and adulteresses, know ye not that the friendship of the world is enmity with God? Whosoever therefore will be a friend of the world is the enemy of God.

"I think these Scriptures are self-explanatory. Marriage is a permanent bond. If you consider it a bondage, that's your problem. It's all in the way you look at it. God's viewpoint, as we've just seen, is that He hates divorce, and remarriage is adultery, fornication being the single exception. And the idea in James, since that verse is addressed to those living in adultery, is that adopting the world's viewpoint on marriage makes us the enemy of God. I surely wouldn't care to put myself in that position, would you?"

Fran raised her hand and Emily acknowledged her.

"What about the woman whose husband is violent, Emily. My neighbor left her husband after years of beatings. When he started to abuse the children, she left."

"She probably did the right thing. He might come to his senses and get himself together once his prop is gone. Many men do. Separation is not divorce. However, I do think it should be for a desperate reason such as your neighbor's and not just because the wife finds the husband difficult to live with. A woman can't expect a man to remain celibate during a long separation, whether she separates herself by sleeping in another room or runs home to mama or a neighbor. I can fully appreciate a woman getting away from violence, but I have seen women separate or divorce because they couldn't get their own way or because they thought they had been wronged.

"These women are punishing their husbands. They're making them do penance. When they think they have suffered enough, they will condescend to let them grovel and plead for forgiveness and then march triumphantly back into their palace as Queen—Queen Jezebel. They prey on their husbands' consciences like vultures and heap guilt and condemnation on them. That's witchcraft and mind-control. Punishment is God's business. He says, 'Vengeance is mine, I will repay.' He tells us to forgive one another as He has forgiven us. These women surely wouldn't want God to forgive them the same way they forgive their husbands."

"Even adultery?" asked Veronica. "I have a friend who is struggling with this question."

"Yes, you can even forgive adultery. It may be very difficult to trust him again, but I have seen or heard about many a situation where the marriage was held together because the wife was willing to forgive—really forgive—not hold it over his head like a hammer; not recall it every time he did something to displease her.

"My theory is that when a man's wife ministers to him as we've been discussing in these lessons, if she makes him feel loved, needed, understood, and if he feels he's fulfilling his manhood by satisfying her sexually, he'll be content to stay home. If she emasculates him, he may go find someone who will make him feel like a man.

"Some women take advantage of the fact that their husbands are Christians to put pressure on them sexually as a form of punishment. They force their husbands to burn in the flesh by denying them sex for a week, a month, even several months. Then if they fall into sin, they attack them for their sin. Whose is the greater sin, I ask you? That of the tortured or the torturer?

"Paul says in I Corinthians 5 that a man or woman would do best to remain single so he can serve the Lord and not be caught up with the affairs of married life. But if a person's going to burn, then let him marry. It's not wrong to do so. Now a man (or a woman) *can* contain himself. I am not making excuses for adultery or fornication. However, if John Doe marries Susie, and she denies him, what can he do but burn. The Lord tells him not to commit adultery and not to divorce, but his wife won't fulfill her ministry to him, so he yearns and burns and climbs the walls with frustration. It's a good thing I'm not God; I might help the situation out real quick by a funeral so this poor man could remarry an unselfish woman with a proper understanding of a ministering wife.

"I've seen some of these sweet Susies here and there across the country. They are ever so lovely at church and PTA. They appear as the very epitome of righteousness and piety. But the sin of failure to minister in the sexual area is as odious to God as the behavior of a prostitute; perhaps more so because it is so hypocritical. Just as a seductive man impregnates a woman and leaves her to bear her shame alone, this woman drives her husband to adultery and lets him bear the blame alone. I often wonder if there isn't some deeper motive, conscious or unconscious, which causes these women to devastate someone sexually. Is it possible that they have never forgiven some man who injured them as a child, and they're vindicating their hurts on their husband?

"I used to wonder what Paul meant when he told the husbands to love their wives and not be bitter against them. After hearing about one after another sexually frustrated husband, I can understand why a man would develop bitterness toward his wife. Sexual torture or squandering his hard-earned money can definitely encourage a husband to develop an attitude of bitterness.

"Now let me add this: not every man who cheats on his wife has been denied at home. Some rascals have lust spirits and no matter what their wives do to minister to them, they'll never be satisfied until they get saved and get those demons cast out. If a woman has done all she can do and she checks her behavior with the Lord and His Word, she should not let anyone throw guilt on her. Some men, to justify their own sin, will try to point the finger of blame at their wives. She can keep sweet and still reject that blame.

"A woman is free to divorce the man who insists on living unfaithfully, especially with the likelihood that he will bring home A.I.D.S. or some other venereal disease, and wipe out the whole family. Jesus did insert a 'save for fornication' clause when he spoke of divorce. However, He didn't say she *had* to divorce him. I've known of some awful creeps whose wives believed God to save them,and they came out of that mess. The families are still intact, the children never had to be torn apart, and the marriages are restored. God can give grace to go through it and come out blessed in the end. Women in this situation need a lot of prayer so they make the right decision. Yes, Fern."

"I heard a tape by Rob Ireland about marriage and divorce. He mentioned that people can have spirits of Divorce which work in the marriage to separate the couple. Once those spirits are cast out, the marriage gets on a much more solid footing."

"I'm glad you brought that up, Fern. Divorce spirits can move down the family line from generation to generation. Sociologists tell us that children of divorced parents are more likely to divorce than the children of parents who have a good marriage. This can be Divorce or Marriage-Breaking spirits that have transferred to the children from the parents or it can be that the children have picked up patterns of selfish behavior from their parents which cause trouble in any relationship. The fact that their parents were not willing to make the marriage work has a definite influence on the children when they grow up and get married.

"It's also important that both the husband and the wife get Divorce and Marriage-Breaking spirits cast out. If only one gets help, it will only do half as much good. Half is better than none, but it would surely work better toward solving the problem if both of them were to get help. They should also get free of Strife, Contention, Argumentation, Pride, Rejection, Rebellion, and Childish Self-Will. They may also need to deal with Ahab and Jezebel. Divorce and marriage problems are much more indicative of a spiritual deficiency than a social, physical, or emotional difficulty.

"Before we finish talking about the snares which Satan lays, I'd like to mention again the effect of the Babylon Box on the marriage. Impressionable children who view the attitudes of lust beaming out of almost every program, are bound to pick up spirits of lust over a period of years. My generation grew up without TV. I can compare the three generations I've watched grow up as far as lust is concerned. TV is a tool which Satan uses to attach spirits of lust to people. Yes, Wanda."

"Emily, I was saved when I was fifteen. I had been a movie-goer and also partied and danced with my worldly friends. But when I became a Christian, I was taught that these things were worldly and that if any man loved the world, the love of the Father is not in him. It took a little while, but I soon turned my back on those things, and the Lord put better things in my life to take their place. My church taught that nominal Christians did worldly things because they did not believe the Bible was the Word of God, and they weren't really born again.

"Television was just coming out when I got saved. The parents of my girlfriend, who took me to the church where I found the Lord, had a TV. They would have devotions during the commercials and then go back to watching the movie on TV. Somehow, in my head, it did not add up. If movies were wrong in the theater, they were wrong in the living room. As I look back, I can see how Satan could not get the Christians to go to the theater. True believers had convictions against going to the movies or going to any worldly amusement place, so the Devil brought it all into the home with all the attendant lust spirits.

"The Church's standards have been lowered. The standards of Christian colleges and Bible schools have been lowered too. It was unheard of for students in Christian schools to go to the movies, and Christian kids who went to public schools were concerned about damaging their testimony if they were seen coming out of the show. Christians didn't want the Lord to return and find them sitting in such an ungodly place. They felt terrible giving the money, which God gave them to steward, to producers of films which promoted lust, adultery, and violence. Today movie attendance is a commonplace thing in many Christian circles. The flick has afflicted us.

"It is also commonplace, not only in the world but in many Christian circles, to hear of fornication and adultery. This was a rare occurrence in my young days, and a grief to all who heard about it. I remember a young couple who were married about the same time my husband and I were married. They were disciplined by the church because their baby was born too soon after the wedding. The elder who read the disciplinary statement wept like a baby, and there wasn't a dry eye in the church. I agree with Emily that the TV has had an adverse affect on the Church. The Church has now been conditioned to accept immoral behavior. We've come a long way, baby—a long way down."

There were a few "Amens" and a few "Oh, dears."

"Thank you, Wanda. I think the thing that bothers me most is watching children soaking up a steady diet of worldly entertainment loaded with lust and realize their parents are insensitive to what's taking place right under their noses. These youngsters are open windows for spirits of Lust, and their parents are condoning it by allowing them to watch it. If you turn off the picture tube, most of the music by itself is loaded with lust. I fear for the next generation of marriages. Ladies, it's time we entreat our husbands to leave Babylon and head back to Zion.

"Now I've got that off my chest," sighed Emily. "We are a bit over our usual time. I'm sure there are many more snares we could discuss that work to destroy our marriages, but some of you need to get home to get dinner started. Forgive me for galloping through so fast. There was a lot here that I felt should be covered. Let us remember to watch for the roaring lion's tactics and pray. Bind Marriage-breaking spirits in your home, especially in the bedroom, and anywhere else you spot them. Let us pray for one another. None of us is immune.

"Colossians 3:23 says: 'And whatsoever ye do, do it heartily, as to the Lord, and not unto men.' This applies to our sexual ministry as well."

Emily asked Sheila to close in prayer, and we were soon on our way out. The ladies seemed very quiet.

"There's an awful lot to think about," I thought to myself. "She dropped a lot of heavy stuff on these ladies today. I wonder how they're handling it."

I was handling my own thoughts as we headed home, until Emily broke the silence, "Well, what do you think of my lovely ladies? Aren't they a fine group?"

"I could tell who your two antagonists were—Dori and Shirley. They sat right behind me, right?"

"They're not too hard to spot, are they? They're not bad girls at heart. They've just been led astray by the 'liberation lie.' You expect to see it out there in the world, but it's painful to see members of the body of Christ sucked up in Satan's vacuum sweeper."

"Aunt Emily, they didn't have a whole lot of argument with this lesson, except for a couple of whispered exchanges between them."

"Well, the feminists push sex. Their thrust is that the woman should be the sexual aggressor. Ask for a date, pay for the date, be promiscuous if you like. Be unfaithful if you like. The men have been doing it for years; now it's our turn. In fact, don't bother to marry; have a career and just be a play girl. Marriage should be eliminated; it's outmoded. If you happen to get pregnant, you should have the choice of abortion. If you want a child, you don't have to be married; you can provide for the child yourself. That's why they're clamoring for government daycare centers; they want the taxpayers to provide for their child. You don't even have to be bothered with a man at all; you can have artificial insemination like a cow and live by yourself, or with a lesbian lover. June, it's sick; it's totally self-centered, selfish, irresponsible, and it is SIN. Their whole philosophy is taking rather than giving."

"Aunt Emily, to say men have been doing this for years is wacky reasoning. It's like saying that men have been robbing banks for years; now it's our turn."

"Some feminists are saying that too. I read all the time about women beating up people, women committing armed robbery and violent homicides. I'm telling you, when people believe a lie, they're not thinking rationally. The lie appeals to their selfishness, not their common sense. Whether you're a man or a woman, when you're always taking, you lose, and when you're always giving, you gain. It's that same biblical principle: 'For whosoever will save his life shall lose it: and whosoever will lose his life for my sake shall find it' (Mt. 16:25)."

"Aunt Emily, if women thought they were being exploited by men and that it was wrong, why are they trying to copy what the men have been doing. What they're saying is 'Now we want to be irresponsible and evil too.' "

"That's right. That's just what they are saying without a twinge of conscience. That's our corner up ahead."

Snappy roused from his cool spot in the shade to welcome us. Uncle Harold waved from behind the lawn mower.

"Can I help you with anything, Aunt Emily?"

"Not right now, June. I believe I'll lie down and take a little nap. My get up and go has got up and went."

"Well, please call me when you start supper. I'm going up and check my notes and pray for a bit."

Ruth's room was becoming a cherished sanctuary to me. "I've made some deep commitments to God in this place," I thought to myself. I sat down on the bed with my notebook and put together an outline.

1. Give your husband a healthy body.
2. Give your husband a clean body inside and out.
3. Give your husband a trim body that is well toned and exhibits good posture.
4. Dress for God and your husband with modesty, femininity and good taste.
5. Give your husband your hands to clean, to cook, to sew, and to launder.
6. Clean your house of occult and unclean items and entreat your husband to dedicate it to the Lord.
7. Use as a pattern the virtuous woman in Proverbs 31.
    a. She's strong, healthy and industrious.
    b. She's trustworthy sexually, financially, and with her time and her tongue.
    c. Her hard work and fine character contribute to her husband's eligibility to sit in the gate.
8. Minister to your husband sexually.
    a. The sexual union is a type of the Church's communion with her Bridegroom.
    b. Get rid of negative attitudes and concentrate on the act of love.
    c. Communicate to your husband that you appreciate and enjoy him sexually.
    d. Don't be caught up with the world's fixation on orgasm and techniques.
    e. Relax, respond, reach out to your husband. (The three R's of romance)
    f. God is pleased with the sexual union of a married couple.
    g. We must free ourselves and others from the many snares Satan lays for our marriages.
    h. To withhold sex is to fail in our ministry to our husbands.
    i. God hates divorce. Adopting the world's viewpoint on divorce makes us the enemies of God.
    j. A woman is free to divorce an unfaithful husband.
    k. TV is an avenue through which Satan can fill us with spirits of Lust.

My notes were difficult to arrange in an outline. There were so many helpful testimonies, suggestions, questions, and answers. I realized afresh how important the sexual aspect was to the total ministry of a wife and how much all the other facets of ministry meant to the sexual aspect.

I knelt and began to pray. (Perhaps you'd like to pray something similar.) Lord, I prayed in my heart along with Veronica for a healthy, clean, trim, well-dressed body. Help me to be self-discipled enough to achieve that. Help me also to be like the woman in Proverbs 31.

Lord, I know I've done a lot of the right things in my sexual ministry to my husband, but I also see that I've done a lot of wrong things. I want to please you in this area of ministry to my husband. Help me to direct my thoughts away from his shortcomings and dwell on the many fine qualities I see in him. Let your love flow through me in this ministry to him and through him to me as well. The desire of my heart is that our love relationship in every area will portray the union of love between the Church and her Bridegroom. Please grant me the desire of my heart, Lord. In Jesus' Name. Amen.

# 10. THE ATTACK AGAINST OUR MINISTRY

The remaining week with Harold and Emily was filled with pleasant activities including a family cook-out with Pete and Ruth and her family. I could see the fruit of Emily's ministry as a wife in my cousins and that godly heritage repeated again in Ruth's family.

We enjoyed church activities (where Harold "sat in the gate"). We canned and froze and dried enormous amounts of fruits and vegetables from their bountiful garden and orchard. Somehow, in the midst of it all, Emily managed to plant me in a lawn chair under a shade tree with a tall glass of lemonade to read the huge stack of books she had recommended to me. Before I knew it, the Friday of Emily's last lesson on The Ministry of a Wife had arrived, and we were on our way back to the church.

"Aunt Emily, this has been one very full vacation—full of learning, heart searching, decisions, and blessings I can't count. Some of this has been pretty heavy, too; I'm not sure I can possibly implement everything you've said we should do in these lessons. I feel discouraged because I fall so far short of this ideal wife that you've been describing."

"Would you like God to lower the standards so you could feel more comfortable with the requirements?" Emily responded with her usual sweet smile.

"No, no. I just feel inadequate."

"You're not alone. I feel the same way myself. We're talking about what God wants us to be. His standards are high. Yet our goal should be to live up to His standards, not ours. The ministering wife of the Scripture is an ideal which we should seek to emulate. Why should we be satisfied with less when God isn't?"

"That's just it; I'm not satisfied with what I see in myself because I'm sure God is not satisfied. But there's so much. . . ."

"Take a look at Isaiah 53:11. This verse has been a mainstay for me over many years:

> He shall see of the travail of his soul, and be satisfied: by his knowledge shall my righteous servant justify many; for he shall bear their iniquities.

"My Saviour suffered spiritual pains of childbirth to bring me forth as a born-again child of God. That's what travail is—labor pains. You know how you felt when you brought your children into the world. Following all the pain, there was a deep satisfaction in the enjoyment of your babies. The pain was soon forgotten because it was crowded out with joy.

"However, if parents have a child who is stubborn and rebellious, that joy is forgotten because it's crowded out by sorrow. Now if a parent knows the child is trying to obey, that parent will not be grieved like the parent of the child who willfully disobeys. When our children are trying to obey, we move to help them. God does the same thing. He leads us into all truth by His Holy Spirit; then when we take steps to obey, He helps us. Jesus Christ wants to live His life through us, as He says in Galatians 2:20:

> I am crucified with Christ: nevertheless I live; yet not I, but Christ liveth in me: and the life which I now live in the flesh I live by the faith of the Son of God, who loved me, and gave himself for me.

"Philippians 2:13 says: 'For it is God which worketh in you both to will and to do of his good pleasure.' As long as we're attempting to obey the Lord, we can count on His help. However, we do need to ask for it."

"Lord, help!"

"That's it. I'd worry more about you if you thought you had arrived. We turn at the next street.

"Just remember, June, when the Holy Spirit convicts us of sin, He pinpoints a specific item, and it is something which we can correct with the help of God. Satan doesn't convict; he condemns. It's a blanket of heaviness that is not specific—just that we're wicked and God doesn't want us. That kind of heaviness we must rebuke in the name of Jesus because it's demonic. There's no way to correct ourselves in a demonic depression. The Holy Spirit points the way out of conviction with obedience to God's Word. ('. . . Godly sorrow worketh repentance.') When we change, we go forth rejoicing (II Cor. 7:10)."

We were the first ones in the building this time, so I had an opportunity to observe the ladies as they came in. Dori and Shirley sat behind me again.

Wanda led us in prayer, and Emily took her place behind the podium. She pulled a sheaf of papers out of a large brown envelope and waved it in the air.

"I'd like to call your attention to a new packet on the market. It's published by a feminist organization called Tongue-in-Cheek Publisher. It's entitled 'The Great Putdown.' Included in the packet are the following plans; I'll read them to you:

> Plan 1. How to make your husband feel entirely inadequate because he isn't a master plumber, electrician, mechanic, landscaper, painter, etc.
>
> Plan 2. How to make him feel that his means of earning a living is unimportant, beneath your dignity, or your social standing, and, most of all, insufficient for the needs of the family.
>
> Plan 3. How to make him recognize that if you weren't providing the major portion of the family earnings or scrimping so hard your knuckles are red and you've lost 40 pounds, the family would be in the poor house.
>
> Plan 4. How to make him feel like an ogre if he corrects the children, and worse if he doesn't.
>
> Plan 5. How to thoroughly embarrass him in front of friends, relatives, and fellow employees, as well as the children, by pointing out to them all his foolish mistakes and shortcomings. Cleverly devised humor is included in this plan so you'll never appear in a bad light yourself.
>
> Plan 6. How to make him feel entirely inadequate as your lover, so that you can rest assured he will never make romantic advances more than once a month.
>
> Plan 7. How to make everyone know the divorce was all his fault because he was an absolute failure as a husband.

"You can order all seven plans in this one large packet, or one at a time. Is anyone interested?"

Marge was shaking her head sadly. "I don't think I'll need any, Emily, I believe my neighbor has the whole packet. I could borrow her plans—that is, if I were crazy enough to want them."

"Well, I can see you ladies are not into this sort of thing, but from what I've observed, they must be selling like hot cakes.

"Now, with my tongue out of my cheek, I would like to seriously present to you the ways in which our ministry is being attacked and what we can do about it.

"If you read your Bible, and if you are at all knowledgeable about world affairs, you are aware that we are in the last days and likely to see the disclosure of the Antichrist very shortly. Let us turn to I John 2:18-29. Merry, read that for us, please."

> Little children, it is the last time: and as ye have heard that antichrist shall come, even now are there many antichrists; whereby we know that it is the last time.
>
> They went out from us, but they were not of us; for if they had been of us, they would no doubt have continued with us: but they went out, that they might be made manifest that they were not all of us.
>
> But ye have an unction from the Holy One, and ye know all things.
>
> I have not written unto you because ye know not the truth, but because ye know it, and that no lie is of the truth.
>
> Who is a liar but he that denieth that Jesus is the Christ? He is antichrist, that denieth the Father and the Son.
>
> Whosoever denieth the Son, the same hath not the Father: *[but] he that acknowledgeth the Son hath the Father also.*
>
> Let that therefore abide in you, which ye have heard from the beginning. If that which ye have heard from the beginning shall remain in you, ye also shall continue in the Son, and in the Father.
>
> And this is the promise that he hath promised us, even eternal life.
>
> These things have I written unto you concerning them that seduce you.
>
> But the anointing which ye have received of him abideth in you, and ye need not that any man teach you: but as the same anointing teacheth you of all things, and is truth, and is no lie, and even as it hath taught you, ye shall abide in him.
>
> And now, little children, abide in him; that, when he shall appear, we may have confidence, and not be ashamed before him at his coming.
>
> If ye know that he is righteous, ye know that every one that doeth righteousness is born of him.

"In this passage we see that the one who denies that Jesus is the Christ is the Antichrist. He's a liar. We're going to examine further what the Scripture says about 'The Lie.' We'll be looking at quite a lot of Scripture today, so please be patient, gird up the loins of your mind, and pay close attention to each verse. I'm laying a careful foundation from the Word for what I have to say today. Turn to John 8:43-47. Yvonne, please read that for us."

> Why do ye not understand my speech? even because ye cannot hear my word.
>
> Ye are of your father the devil, and the lusts of your father ye will do. He was a murderer from the beginning, and abode not in the truth, because there is no truth in him. When he speaketh a lie, he speaketh of his own: for he is a liar, and the father of it.
>
> And because I tell you the truth, ye believe me not.
>
> Which of you convinceth me of sin? And if I say the truth, why do ye not believe me?
>
> He that is of God heareth God's words: ye therefore hear them not, because ye are not of God.

"Jesus is speaking here about the Devil being the father of lies. Let's look at some of the consequences of trusting in these lies. June, please read Jeremiah 13:24-25."

> Therefore will I scatter them as the stubble that passeth away by the wind of the wilderness.
>
> This is thy lot, the portion of thy measures from me, saith the Lord; because thou hast forgotten me, and trusted in falsehood.

"Now turn to Revelation 22:15. This describes those outside the gates of heaven. Dori, please."

> For without are dogs, and sorcerers, and whoremongers, and murderers, and idolaters, and whosoever loveth and maketh a lie.

"Turn to Romans 1:23-25. I'll read this one:

And changed the glory of the uncorruptible God into an image made like to corruptible man, and to birds, and fourfooted beasts, and creeping things.

Wherefore God also gave them up to uncleanness through the lusts of their own hearts, to dishonour their own bodies between themselves:

Who changed the truth of God into a lie, and worshipped and served the creature more than the Creator, who is blessed forever. Amen.

"Turn now to I Timothy 4:1 and 2. Fran, please."

Now the Spirit speaketh expressly, that in the latter times some shall depart from the faith, giving heed to seducing spirits, and doctrines of devils;

Speaking lies in hypocrisy; having their conscience seared with a hot iron;

"Let's look at the two major passages that describe the Antichrist. II Thessalonians 2. Betty, read that for us please—the whole chapter."

Now we beseech you, brethren, by the coming of our Lord Jesus Christ, and by our gathering together unto him,

That ye be not soon shaken in mind, or be troubled, neither by spirit, nor by word, nor by letter as from us, as that the day of Christ is at hand.

Let no man deceive you by any means: for that day shall not come, except there come a falling away first, and that man of sin be revealed, the son of perdition;

Who opposeth and exalteth himself above all that is called God, or that is worshipped; so that he as God sitteth in the temple of God, shewing himself that he is God.

Remember ye not, that, when I was yet with you, I told you these things?

And now ye know what withholdeth that he might be revealed in his time.

For the mystery of iniquity doth already work: only he who now letteth will let, until he be taken out of the way.

And then shall that Wicked be revealed, whom the Lord shall consume with the spirit of his mouth, and shall destroy with the brightness of his coming:

> Even him, whose coming is after the working of Satan with all power and signs and lying wonders.
>
> And with all deceivableness of unrighteousness in them that perish; because they received not the love of the truth, that they might be saved.
>
> And for this cause God shall send them strong delusion, that they should believe a lie.
>
> That they all might be damned who believed not the truth, but had pleasure in unrighteousness.
>
> But we are bound to give thanks alway to God for you, brethren beloved of the Lord, because God hath from the beginning chosen you to salvation through sanctification of the Spirit and belief of the truth:
>
> Whereunto he called you by our gospel, to the obtaining of the glory of our Lord Jesus Christ.
>
> Therefore, brethren, stand fast, and hold the traditions which ye have been taught, whether by word, or our epistle.
>
> Now our Lord Jesus Christ himself, and God, even our Father, which hath loved us, and hath given us everlasting consolation and good hope through grace,
>
> Comfort your hearts, and stablish you in every good word and work.

"I know these are long passages, but God's Word is the truth which combats 'The Lie,' so this is where we must build our foundation. Revelation 13 is another Scripture describing the Antichrist and his 'lie.' We'll read this whole chapter as well. Shirley, please."

> And I stood upon the sand of the sea, and saw a beast rise up out of the sea, having seven heads and ten horns, and upon his horns ten crowns, and upon his heads the name of blasphemy.
>
> And the beast which I saw was like unto a leopard, and his feet were as the feet of a bear, and his mouth as the mouth of a lion: and the dragon gave him his power, and his seat, and great authority.
>
> And I saw one of his heads as it were wounded to death; and his deadly wound was healed: and all the world wondered after the beast.

And they worshipped the dragon which gave power unto the beast: and they worshipped the beast, saying Who is like unto the beast? who is able to make war with him?

And there was given unto him a mouth speaking great things and blasphemies; and power was given unto him to continue forty and two months.

And he opened his mouth in blasphemy against God, to blaspheme his name, and his tabernacle, and them that dwell in heaven.

And it was given unto him to make war with the saints, and to overcome them: and power was given him over all kindreds, and tongues, and nations.

And all that dwell upon the earth shall worship him, whose names are not written in the book of life of the Lamb slain from the foundation of the world.

If any man have an ear, let him hear.

He that leadeth into captivity shall go into captivity: he that killeth with the sword must be killed with the sword. Here is the patience and the faith of the saints.

And I beheld another beast coming up out of the earth; and he had two horns like a lamb, and he spake as a dragon.

And he exerciseth all the power of the first beast before him, and causeth the earth and them which dwell therein to worship the first beast, whose deadly wound was healed.

And he doeth great wonders, so that he maketh fire come down from heaven on the earth in the sight of men,

And deceiveth them that dwell on the earth by the means of those miracles which he had power to do in the sight of the beast; saying to them that dwell on the earth, that they should make an image to the beast, which had the wound by a sword, and did live.

And he had power to give life unto the image of the beast, that the image of the beast should both speak, and cause that as many as would not worship the image of the beast should be killed.

And he causeth all, both small and great, rich and poor, free and bond, to receive a mark in their right hand, or in their foreheads:

> And that no man might buy or sell, save he that had the mark, or the name of the beast, or the number of his name.
>
> Here is wisdom. Let him that hath understanding count the number of the beast: for it is the number of a man; and his number is Six hundred threescore and six.

"You will also want to read the entire book of Daniel to add to what we've read here today about the Antichrist.

"Jesus said in Matthew 24:24:

> For there shall arise false Christs, and false prophets, and shall show great signs and wonders; insomuch that, if it were possible, they shall deceive the very elect.

"Now I would like to read to you from *Wycliffe Bible Encyclopedia*. This is what they have to say about 'The Lie.' I'll read it without the Scripture references and the Greek so it will flow together a little better. We've just read a good share of the verses.

> LIE. A false statement or piece of information deliberately given as being true; anything meant to deceive.
>
> Satan authored "the lie" in his original apostasy. Man in his apostasy likewise preferred "the lie" to God's truth. In the final apostasy, just before the second advent, the world will receive "the lie" of the Antichrist. False prophets (q.v.) readily become Satan's dupes by deceiving people with lies against God's truth. Unregenerate men, like their spiritual father, speak lies from their birth making them their refuge until they settle among liars forever. The lot of liars of every kind, along with other incorrigible sinners, will be in the lake of fire.
>
> God, of course, cannot lie. His truth is incompatible with a lie.[7]

"I'll stop there. 'The Lie' began in the garden of Eden when Satan told Eve, 'Ye shall be as gods.' This lie has taken many forms throughout history, but the basic premise has always been the same as it is today—man is god, or becomes a god. On the other hand, they also insist that Jesus was just a good man; that He had a human nature only. The corollary is 'Ye shall not surely die.' This makes man immortal like God. It is from this lie that reincarnation is being touted today.

"You may wonder, as I have, why anyone with a lick of common sense would believe such nonsense. I think I understand it now. If a person lives in sin and knows that a holy God has pronounced judgment upon that sin and upon the sinner who persists in that sin, that person must do something to quiet his conscience. As Adam hid in the garden, this person will hide under unbelief. He will eventually say there is no God or that we cannot know God. He will elaborate, with profound rhetoric, about human potential and self-realization. You see, if he dethrones God in his mind, then he eliminates the finger pointed at his sin. When he places man on that throne, he can blank out the laws which he is transgressing and make up his own laws. It stands to reason, then, that he must also get rid of the Scripture because it is the means by which God points the finger of judgment at his sin. Jesus said, 'The word that I have spoken, the same shall judge him in the last day.'

"By the same token, if a sinner can reason away the aspect of life after death, the resurrection of the dead, and the judgment of God, the sinner may think he can face death without fear. He may believe he will be reincarnated or some other facet of 'The lie.' He can hush his conscience and eventually sear it, which means cauterizing all the nerve endings so they are insensitive.

"People who love their sin cling to 'The Lie' as a child to a security blanket. This may help you understand why the world is so eager to be deceived. They love their sin. The remedy, of course, is repentance.

"In lesson 2 we touched briefly on the two spiritual kingdoms operating on our physical planet—the kingdom of darkness and the kingdom of light. The two rulers of these kingdoms are in constant conflict and as subjects of one or the other, we enter that conflict whether or not we choose to do so. The 'prince of the power of the air,' also known as the 'god of this world,' is Satan. He is called our adversary if we belong to Jesus Christ.

"The goal of Lucifer, in Isaiah 14:14, was to ascend above the heights of the clouds; to be like the most High. His subjects appear to have this same goal. They are also arrogant and proud. They exalt themselves as gods, and as gods, they work to gain control of the world's government, religion, education, social structure, and economy. Led by the spirit of Antichrist, they desire to set up a one world government over which the Antichrist will rule. This is the Beast, of which we just read in II Thessalonians 2 and Revelation 13.

"Contrary to this goal, the goal of the subjects of Jesus Christ is to humbly exalt Him. As John the Baptist said, 'He must increase but I must decrease' (John 3:30). They look forward to the time when Jesus Christ shall reign for ever and ever as King of Kings and Lord of Lords.

"The philosophy of those who walk in darkness is that man is god or becomes a god. That philosophy is humanism. Humanism is a religion. Even the Supreme Court decided that humanism is a religion. The humanists wrote their 'theology' in the Humanist Manifesto I and II. It is also found in the Communist Manifesto and in occult literature written from the early days of mankind until now.

"The philosophy of God's kingdom is that God is God and His subjects are His bond slaves, His friends, His sheep, His children and His Church.

"The religion of the humanists is ultimately paganism, heathenism or atheism. Their prophets teach the 'doctrines of devils.' They propagate 'The Lie.' The Babylonian-mystery-religion (witchcraft) is their foundation (though many would deny any religious inclinations whatever). The New Age Movement is just the age-old Babylonian paganism in sophisticated new wrappings. Many people in high government positions are promoting the New Age goals. Whether they really understand what is behind those goals, or are just being used by those who do, the results are the same. They are implementing the plan to establish a one-world religious system which will worship the Antichrist as god. No other religion will be tolerated by the New Agers.

"The religion of those who are God's subjects is Christianity. 'The disciples were called Christians first in Antioch' (Acts 11:26). God's teachers teach the doctrines of the Scripture. They propagate the truth.

"You may wonder why I'm comparing these two kingdoms so carefully. I want to make it very clear to all of you that we're in a war and we are being attacked. As I pointed out in lesson 2, if you read the end of the Book, you know that we win in the end. However, in the meantime, the fight can get pretty rough.

"We're going to discuss here today the attack against our ministry, but I want you to see that our particular battle is only one part of a major war in a conflict that began in the garden of Eden and will finish when the Devil, his angels, and all those who are his subjects will be cast into the Lake of Fire. How we handle our defensive and offensive maneuvers in this battle is very important, for there are souls who will be lost for eternity if we do not obey the Captain of our Salvation, Jesus Christ, and the orders He gives in the Scriptures.

"Let's examine carefully II Timothy 2:3 and 4. Please read that for us, Margie."

> Thou therefore endure hardness, as a good soldier of Jesus Christ.
>
> No man that warreth entangleth himself with the affairs of this life; that he may please him who hath chosen him to be a soldier.

"We need to get rid of the entanglements that hinder our walk with God and our testimony before men. Habits that keep us in bondage and lifestyles that are frivolous must be laid aside. We're at war! We need to put on the armor of God described in Ephesians 6. Let's look at verse 12. Maureen, will you read that for us, please?"

> For we wrestle not against flesh and blood, but against principalities, against powers, against the rulers of the darkness of this world, against spiritual wickedness in high places.

"Paul is speaking here of the spiritual realm. This is where the real warfare takes place. We tend to regard flesh and blood people as the enemy against whom we are fighting. The man who opens the pornographic adult book store, the legislator who passes laws which destroy the family or the feminist who marches for a woman's right to abortion are not the primary enemy. The demonic powers operating through these people are our real, though unseen, enemy. Turn over to Ephesians 1:19. I'll read through 21:

> And what is the exceeding greatness of his power to usward who believe, according to the working of his mighty power.
>
> Which he wrought in Christ, when he raised him from the dead, and set him at his own right hand in the heavenly places,
>
> Far above all principality, and power, and might, and dominion, and every name that is named, not only in this world, but also in that which is to come.

"Now look at verse 6 in chapter 2. Ann, please read that for us."

> And hath raised us up together, and made us sit together in heavenly places in Christ Jesus.

"Our spiritual position is in heavenly places with Christ. As we said, it's in this realm that the real warfare takes place.

"Now from our vantage point in the heavenlies, let us observe the flesh and blood enemies of God at work on the earth. They are marching against us from several fronts. We can see the 'Conspiracy' surrounding us from every quarter. Webster defines a conspiracy as a 'combination of people, working in secret, for an evil or unlawful purpose.'

"The conspiracy to which I am referring has been known as the Illuminati, the Capitalist Conspiracy, the Eastern Establishment, and a number of other descriptive names. They are merely people who are implementing the plans of the Devil. What is the plan? To prepare the world for the Antichrist who will be worshipped as God. It appears from Scripture that this man will be totally possessed of the Devil, which is an imitation of Jesus Christ, who was God manifest in the flesh.

"The Illuminati was founded on May 1, 1776 by Adam Weishaupt in Bavaria. (Though more recent research alleges that Ignatius Loyola was actually the initiator). This organization has, since its inception, infiltrated secret societies, governments, churches, schools, and every facet of society to overthrow all traditional institutions and replace them with a new world order.

"The core of the Illuminati is made up of international financiers. They have taken control of the economy of almost every country in the world, including our United States. In our country they sap the wealth of the people through the Federal Reserve System, a private corporation. With this economic power, they can finance wars, instigate revolutions, and determine the direction governments will take.

"They manipulate the government in the United States through the Council on Foreign Relations and the Trilateral Commission. They even control, in a great measure, the *type* of government a country will have. Their scheme has been to have two militarily balanced major powers at odds with one another so that they can hold the threat of war over the heads of the people in both nations. They loan money to governments; and by this stranglehold of debt and threat, they are often able to manipulate the governments of the world in order to accomplish their plans.

"For example, members of this conspiracy, sent money from the United States, to finance the Bolshevik Revolution and then later the Nazis in World War II. The conspirators are internationalists; they have no allegiance to any nation.

"It appears, however, that they are about to implement the final stages of their plan. Using the leverage of economic collapse and impending nuclear holocaust, they are moving quickly to combine the nations in the world into a one-world government. Many feel that this will be a Communist-type of government, but others feel it will be Socialism. Communism is just a radical form of Socialism. It will be whatever gives them total control. They have tried for years to do this, but have met with strenuous opposition.

"The conspirators own or control the major newspapers, magazines, TV, and radio networks and by this means control what they want the people to know. They have used the media to fill Americans with a terror of nuclear war. "Better red than dead" is the theme of their propaganda.

"Remember what it says in II Thessalonians 2? It is because the people receive not the love of the truth that God Himself sends them strong delusion that they should believe a lie. As we said before, people want to be deceived because they love their sin.

"These conspirators already have all the money they want. What they want now is power—absolute control. What is ironic is that they don't realize that *they* are being controlled by demonic forces because they themselves are taken captive by him [Satan] at his will, as it says in II Timothy 2:26.

"Dave Hunt points out in his book, *Peace Prosperity and the Coming Holocaust*, that even the Internationalists have lost control of what is now happening throughout the world. A grass-roots movement has sprung up which is working toward a New Age planetary society. According to Constance Cumbey in her book entitled *The Hidden Dangers of the Rainbow,* their common denominator is a mystical psychic experience. 'Transformation' is the New Age terminology for what we would call becoming demonized. This global or planetary consciousness has mystical dimensions which go beyond the carefully calculated maneuvers of the Illuminati.

"The alarming thing is that the New Age Movement is not limited to a few lunatic preachers, psychedelic drug users, and spirit mediums; it has also drawn well-known intellectuals in government, science, education, journalism, and other influential positions throughout the world. They are just demonized by more intellectual demons. It involves thousands of groups throughout the world which are informally linked together by 'networks.' As Satan imitates everything else that God does, he has sought to imitate the organic union of the body of Christ. It is a significant foe with whom we are reckoning.

"To complicate matters, they do not all wear uniforms and wave a flag. They are often subversive. In fact, a great many of these folks don't even know they are involved in a conflict, that they are part of a diabolical plan, or even that they are on Satan's side. Many do not even know that Lucifer, Satan, and the Devil are one and the same person. They have already believed 'The Lie.' They are thoroughly deluded. Some of these souls are beyond hope. Others can still be rescued. Many of them are in church on Sunday.

"The people on the inside of the conspiracy, who *do* know what's going on, hate God, His Word, and His people. In movies, TV, books, and magazines, they picture Christians as hypocrites, ignorant, intolerant and prejudiced. Of late we are depicted as crazies who are trying to take away their freedoms merely because we're trying to restore some decency to this country. They have labeled us as dangerous. They believe Christians stand in the way of progress—*their* progress.

"As they implement the Aquarian Conspiracy, known also as the New Age Movement or the New World Order, we Christians are their major resistance.

"Psalm 2:2-4 says:

> The kings of the earth set themselves, and the rulers take counsel together, against the Lord, and against his anointed, saying,
>
> Let us break their bands asunder, and cast away their cords from us.
>
> He that sitteth in the heavens shall laugh: the Lord shall have them in derision.

"Their ultimate plan is to eliminate orthodox Jews, Christians and uncooperative Moslems. Those who do not receive the Luciferic initiation will experience what the New Agers call a 'cleansing action.' Researchers of the New Age Movement say that they want to eliminate a couple billion people anyway (yes, half the population), so it stands to reason that the folks resisting 'The Plan' would be the first to go. They speak of Global 2000. By then they hope to have a one world government in which all 'planetary citizens' will have taken a Luciferic initiation.

"Numbers of Christian writers are expecting a cashless society in the very near future. They predict that everyone will have an international credit card and then, essentially, an international number for every person on the earth, marked on the right hand or the forehead so there will be no problem with identification. Without that mark one will not be able to buy or sell. The Luciferic initiation may very well be the 666 'mark.' Revelation 13:17 indicates that there will be a mark, a name, and a number. Any one of these, or a combination of them, will lead to eternal damnation.

"For some of you, this is not new information, but there may be others here today who have never heard these things. I wanted to sketch the entire scene for you, so you get a panoramic view. I'm just skimming the top of the waves. I'll be giving you a bibliography after class. You will want to read these books so you can really grasp what we're talking about here today. I urge you to do so. I don't have time today to document what I'm saying, but if you will investigate the books on this list, you will find plenty of documentation.

"We're moving into an era of polarization. God is allowing the adversary to put pressure on mankind to force each one of us to declare our choice clearly. God is separating the sheep from the goats. We're being given small choices and then bigger ones to progressively confirm our loyalty to Jesus Christ or our denial of Him. In the future our choices could mean life or death. We will need God's grace and God's courage. Some wise person once said that courage is not a lack of fear but rather the mastery over it.

"God is still on the throne, and Satan and His hosts cannot do anything to us which our Father does not allow. He only allows what is for our eternal good and His glory. While we're going through these trials, we may not think the events are very good, but He's refining us and will bring us forth as pure gold. God's perspective is eternal, and we need to see things from His perspective.

"God's prophets foretold a one-world government, a one-world religion, an Antichrist, and the mark of the Beast. In *His* time all these things will come to pass, and not until then. In 1982 the New Agers put over $500,000 in advertisements that said Lord Maitreya, the Christ, would speak to humanity on TV and radio within the next two months. But he didn't; it wasn't God's time. The Pharisees wanted to kill Christ several times, but 'no man laid hands on him; for his hour was not yet come' (John 8:20). When the time came for Him to lay down his life, He said, 'Father, the hour is come' (John 17:l).

"To the disciples, it was a tragedy; their hopes were dashed until the resurrected Lord opened their eyes and they understood that Christ had accomplished their salvation on the cross. As usual, the hosts of Hell meant it for evil, but God used it for good. Our concern must be that when God's hour for the Antichrist arrives, *we'll* be ready. The Lord said to occupy till He comes. We just need to ask God what we should be doing to occupy.

"We're not quite ready to discuss what we will do to occupy. Let's return to our panoramic view of our 'attackers.' This army marches to a rhythm of humanism, hedonism, atheism, socialism, mysticism, and occultism.

"Now enters the feminist movement into the picture. I want you to see its part in this drama as an important arm of the conspiracy. Some feminists are unaware that they are dupes being used by those who foster the women's movement to accomplish their devilish goals. These women think they are fighting for equal rights and equal pay and all those other things they've been told they're being denied. In the New World Order, *no* one will have any rights except those in control. Feminists are participating in the very destruction of the things for which they're striving.

"Other feminists are knowingly flowing with the Antichrist's scheme and are doing their best to bring about the destruction of the family, the church, and the sovereignty of our nation."

Dori could hold her peace no longer. "Emily, are you saying that the feminist movement is part of the New Age Movement?"

"Yes, indeed. A very important part."

"But the New Age Movement is a recent development. The women's movement has been going on for over a hundred years."

"The seeds for both of these movements were planted centuries ago. All of Satan's plans go back to the Garden of Eden. Let me read to you a few things Dave Hunt says about the connection between these two movements: I'm reading from *Peace, Prosperity and the Coming Holocaust*, p.68 and 69:

> The ERA campaign failed to reach its 1982 goal of an amendment to the United States Constitution, but the major force behind the movement was spiritual, not political, and is still gaining momentum. The Women's Movement is one of the most important parts of the New Age Movement. It is at the heart of the consciousness revolution that is sweeping the Western world....
>
> ..................................................

> Many of those involved in the Feminist Movement may sincerely believe it is a political crusade to gain equality with men. In fact it is more than that: it is also a spiritual movement based partly upon a reawakening of "goddess consciousness," and its real goal is matriarchy, not equality. One major spiritual force behind some aspects of the feminist movement is witchcraft, which is based upon the power of female sexuality derived from a mystical relationship with "Mother Nature" and "Mother Earth."
>
> Take, for example the Women's Conference held in Southern California during April 24-25, 1982. Its title was "Women: The Leading Edge of the New Age."[13]

"Mr. Hunt proceeds to quote from the literature distributed at this conference. The brochure from which he quotes was handed out from the Universal Goddess Center, Inc. and makes very clear their emphasis on witchcraft. You're welcome to borrow Dave Hunt's book, if you like."

Emily held up a small leaflet. "This little tract was sent to me by Concerned Women For America (CWA). It's entitled 'Do These Women Speak For You?' Beverly LaHaye has compiled here a number of quotes from feminists to show what they believe. Let me read a few of these so you can see the connection of feminism with humanism, socialism, and hedonism:

> By the year 2000 we will, I hope, raise our children to believe in human potential, not God.
>
> —Gloria Steinem (Editor of Ms. Magazine), *Saturday Review of Education*, March 1973.

> Feminism is an essential stage of humanism. We must keep evolving.
>
> —Betty Friedan (called "The mother of the Women's Liberation Movement"), *Kansas City Times*, April 6, 1981.

> It is as absurd to say one is for women's rights but not for the ERA as it is to say . . . one is a humanist but not a feminist. . . . For feminism is the last evolutionary development of humanism. Feminism is humanism on its most advanced level.

—Riana Eisler, "Women's Rights and Human Rights." *Humanist Magazine*. November/December, 1980, p.6.

No deity will save us; we must save ourselves. Promises of immortal salvation or fear of eternal damnation are both illusory and harmful.

—"Humanist Manifesto II" (signed by Betty Friedan, founder of National Organization for Women): *Humanist Manifesto I & II*, Prometheus Books, 1973, p. 16.

Feminism rests on the belief that it is up to women to rescue the planet from the deeds of patriarchy and that women will join hands to build a feminist/socialist revolution.

—Karen Clark (co-author and currently a Minnesota State Representative, avowed lesbian, member of the Rules Committee of the 1984 Democratic National Convention which adopted a gay rights platform). The Document: Declaration of Feminism, 1971. p. 2.[14]

"But Emily, the women's movement does have other *good* goals as well," pleaded Dori.

"Like?"

"Well, for example they've worked for women's suffrage. We now have the right to vote."

"I'm not real sure that's good. Women are easily deceived because they are made by God to be trustful. Unscrupulous politicians use that trust to get into power and stay there. Some of the most treacherous traitors this country has ever known were elected to power, in part, by deceived women voters.

"The big gun-control push is being rammed through because of a propaganda campaign aimed at the fearfulness of women. The conspiracy must disarm the general public before they can gain total control. The same thing is true concerning the peace and disarmament deception. Suave politicians are very covetous of the women's vote. Harold had a lady tell him, 'Oh, I'm voting for so and so; he's so handsome.' I'm surely not saying men can't be deceived, they can be and often are. I'm also not saying all women are deceived. I am saying there's a greater tendency for women to be deceived because of their very trustful and dependent nature.

"I believe the saddest part of women's suffrage is that it tends to divide the home. A close friend of my father never went out to vote, though he was a very patriotic man. He said his wife would always vote contrary to whatever he voted, so she just cancelled his vote. That marriage ended in separation. Voting was not the only wedge that divided that home, but an important one."

"Feminist groups have pressured congressmen to vote for issues that are destructive to the family, the Church and the nation. I don't see women in the Old and New Testament running the government of the country, except maybe Jezebel and Athaliah."

"Are you saying we shouldn't vote?" asked Shirley.

"No. Now that the women have the vote, I think we, as Christian women must use our vote and also our lobbying power to influence our congressmen for godly legislation. If we don't, the women in Satan's camp will surely push our legislators until they write the Devil's laws on the books. In fact, I think it's because many Christian women (and Christian men alike) have left the governing of this country to the ungodly, that we have such outrageous laws on the books now. What I am saying is that it would have been a whole lot better if godly men had taken their responsibility for overseeing the nation's government and left the women out of the picture altogether. I also think we should seek the counsel of our husbands and our pastor concerning what we do in the area of politics."

"Did you lobby against the ERA Amendment?" asked Shirley.

"I did indeed. I wrote to my state senator and representative, urging them to vote against it and gave them a long list of reasons why it would be detrimental to women and men as well."

"Why? Shouldn't we have the same rights as men?"

Emily replied gently and slowly, "If you mean that we should have the same 'right' to be drafted and sent into combat on the front lines without the privacy to change our clothes or go to the bathroom, and without protection from lecherous men on both sides of the battle, NO.

"If you mean that working women should have the 'right' to do heavy physical labor or lose their jobs, NO.

"If you mean that we would have the 'right' as homemakers to pay social security as a self-employed person through our husbands' paychecks, NO.

"If you mean that homosexuals would have the 'right' to marry one another and adopt children, NO.

"If you mean that women who are working, going to school, attending conventions, or even entertaining overnight guests would be entitled to free or subsidized day-care centers for their children at the expense of the American people to the tune of several billion dollars a year, NO.

"Think of what will happen to the next generation of children growing up from infancy to adulthood with the 'values clarification' (in other words, new world brainwashing) dispensed by socialist/humanist teachers. The government will not be paying for any day-care centers with the taint of religion. If ERA were passed, these centers would follow naturally because women would have a right to the same freedom as men to work without the burden of children .

"To continue our hypothetical situations, if you mean that women would be given the 'right' to minister as pastors, priests and rabbis, NO.

If you mean that women's right to be supported by their husbands be relinquished for equality, NO.

"Let me say here that I am aware that ERA was turned down. I also am aware that the feminists and the media are being relatively quiet about ERA, but don't let that fool you. They have not given up and we must not give up our efforts to block them at every turn. Watch your state legislature. This is where they're pushing ERA now. Write to your state congressmen and let them know how you feel about ERA. It can do almost the same damage on the state level as it would on the federal level. In those states which already have ERA, women have lost a great many of the protections they once had. Check it out.

"Let me read to you Section 2 of the ERA Amendment: 'The Congress shall have the power to enforce, by appropriate legislation, the provisions of this article.' That sounds harmless enough doesn't it. However, this is the Trojan horse of the whole ERA Amendment. This 'harmless' section gives the federal government unlimited dictatorial power because all laws involve men and women. State laws protecting women would be superseded by federal law which, according to this constitutional amendment, could no longer discriminate against men in such things as alimony, child support, and awarding the children to the mother in divorce situations.

"For example, in our state of Indiana, the law says that a husband who deserts his wife or children without reasonable means of support is guilty of a felony. ERA would automatically erase that law from the books because it discriminates against men.

"This amendment is not intended to better our lives as women; it is intended to put much greater control in the hands of the federal government and the federal courts and to virtually destroy the powers of the states.

"The conspiracy wants to eliminate the states altogether and replace them with regional government—10 regions controlled by the Federal Government. Now do you see why I lobbied against ERA, Shirley?"

"Yes, but how else can we women obtain our rights?"

"ERA would not gain for women any new rights. We already have federal and state laws on the books that protect women's rights, but women must see that the laws are enforced. The Equal Employment Opportunity Act guarantees equal pay for equal work. If I work in a factory inspecting spark plugs as they come off an assembly line and a man with the same seniority on the next assembly line does the same job for $1.00 an hour more pay than me, I will have to appeal to some enforcement commission, the court or whomever, to be sure the law is enforced. The same would be true of a constitutional amendment.

"Let me throw this in for good measure. The Scripture doesn't tell us to demand our rights. It tells us to look out for the rights of others such as the poor. The Lord tells us to take up our cross daily and follow Him. He tells us to be crucified with Him, to lose our lives for His sake and the Gospel's. Dead people don't have any rights. If we've reckoned ourselves dead indeed with Christ according to Romans 6, why should we be concerned with our rights? However, He says that if we lose our lives, we'll find them.

"We have all noticed, I'm sure, that since the feminist movement has made big waves, women are not held in respect as they once were. Men are afraid to hold open a door for us for fear we'll scowl at them and hiss, 'Male chauvinist pig, don't you think I can open a door by myself?' We often have to change our own tires if our husbands are not with us. We're seldom offered a seat if a meeting room is crowded. Some men think nothing of swearing and speaking or acting crudely in front of us. This is not universally the case, but after observing this whole thing for twenty years or more, I have seen the respect for women decline drastically. Women have demanded their rights and lost a great many of the advantages that they did have. I would say that women have far less now than when this whole feminist push started. More women have higher education, many more women are working outside the home, a larger percentage of women are in executive positions and in the professions. But they are not shouting about how fulfilled they are, because they're not. They ran after a pot of gold at the end of the rainbow and when they got there, the gold wasn't there.

"Betty Friedan wrote *The Feminine Mystique* in 1963. According to Mrs. Friedan, the American woman was sold a bill of goods by opinion makers who worked for those who would profit from the sale of goods used by women who stayed home. The magazines, TV, and advertising influenced women to marry younger, have many children and make homemaking their only career.

"She tells in great detail how the suburban housewife is not content because, as a homemaker, she isn't using her education, intelligence and talents. She should be able to have a husband and children, (if she so desires) and still work outside the home developing her talents, using her education and doing what is really important to her. The assumption is that this will bring her fulfillment.

"Mrs. Friedan held interviews with psychologists, doctors, and child-guidance authorities who informed her that these women (and their children) would be better off if they did not center their entire attention on being a sexual partner, housekeeper and mother, but found outside interests.

"So, American women listened to Mrs. Friedan, who is also an opinion maker for those with a different vested interest. Women fled the 'feminine mystique' for the 'feminine mistake.' Now, Betty Friedan, like Dr. Spock, has a whole generation of people who followed her advice and who are reaping a crop of weeds from the bad seeds they have sown.

"Are marriages more solid now that women have left the home? NO. More than half of all marriages end in divorce.

"Are America's children better adjusted now that their mothers are not doting over them? NO. The second highest cause of death involving children, especially teenagers, is suicide.

"Are women better adjusted psychologically? Check the statistics of the mental hospitals. I think you will find that they are overcrowded.

"Are women fulfilled sexually now that they have interests outside the home? According to an article I read last year, many people have lost interest in sex because they are too busy and too tired from being busy. Besides that, they have been so preoccupied with sex that they're bored with it. Just perusing an assortment of women's magazines will show us that women are still not sexually fulfilled. The LaHayes, in their family seminars, found that the most sexually fulfilled couples were Spirit-filled Christians.

"If one of us were to go to the same suburban neighborhoods that Mrs. Friedan visited, and we interviewed the women who have 'escaped' the feminine mystique, I believe we would discover that these women are no more fulfilled and no more content than the women Betty Friedan interviewed.

"Fulfillment does not come from being a homemaker nor does it come from being a career woman. It doesn't even come from trying to juggle the two. Fulfillment comes when we are complete in Christ. When we open our hearts and receive His life, we become the children of God. As we walk in His Spirit in obedience to His Word, He fills our lives with purpose that no career can possibly give us, inside the home or outside the home.

"If a woman has only the goal of self-fulfillment, she is only thinking of herself. This is the essence of humanistic philosophy. The problem is not the woman in the home, but the humanistic 'self-centered' thinking of modern America which has caused the self-pity and discontentment of the American housewife.

"Whenever a man or woman is looking for happiness, they won't find it no matter where they look. However, if we are determined to fellowship with the Lord and from that fellowship reach out in love to other people beginning with our husbands and then our children and further to those outside the family, we will find fulfillment and happiness as a by-product. It's that same Bible principle that I keep repeating, '...whosoever shall save his life shall lose it; but whosoever shall lose his life for my sake and the gospel's, the same shall save it' (Mark 8:35).

"When I read Mrs. Friedan's *The Feminine Mystique*, I kept saying to myself, 'This sounds so logical, so true. Women do seem discontented.' I could understand women outside of the body of Christ being miserable, but why should women who know the Lord be that way?

"It also sounded just like the snake in the garden of Eden: 'Can't you have what you want?' I was aware that Mrs. Friedan was trained in psychology. She was trained to use words for the purpose of changing the way people think. Humanism shifts a person's focus from God to man—self. If we listen to the humanists long enough, we become self-centered instead of God-centered.

"An attack makes you think. First, it makes you defensive. Then when you see that your defense is weak, you examine the weakness. The weakness of the Church is that humanism has spilled from the world's system right into the doors of the Church. The Church didn't put her finger in the hole where the sea of humanism was dribbling through the dike. Now the sea has broken the dike and flooded not only the country but the Church. It will be very hard to build the dike again and pump the water out, but if we don't try, our country will not survive the flood.

"One thing we need to think through is this: what is my purpose in life? What are my goals? What is my philosophy of life? Who am I? Why am I here? If we are just mindless, purposeless blobs attending the daily chores with passive, empty stares, then we are missing what God has for us in life, and we are very likely to be discontented. God did not intend for the home to be a concentration camp for women. Write out your philosophy of life. Use the Scripture. You don't want to build a life's philosophy outside of God.

"I believe if Mrs. Friedan were to be totally objective and open her heart to Jesus Christ, she would find the fulfillment she has missed all these years. She actually is not as radical as some of those who have filled her shoes in the National Organization for Women. Let's not hesitate to pray for these women. They've swallowed 'The Lie,' but Jesus loves them.

"The woman's movement is essentially dead. Watch out, though. They may just be playing 'possum. Eventually they will totally fail. Anything based on humanism will fail because God always pulls down idols. When people put themselves—mankind—on the throne, God will depose them. Usually He merely lifts off His protective hand and lets them destroy themselves. If a person won't be *drawn* to God by His love, failure will often *drive* them to Him. God has no pleasure in the death of the wicked.

"We need to move along. How is this conspiracy in particular attacking our ministry as wives and mothers?

"The most desperate attack is the push to get the wife out of the home. She's being told that she's wicked for doing what God said: 'Be fruitful and multiply.' Tax regulations increasingly making it difficult for the wife to stay home and mother her children. The government is taking so much of the family earnings away in taxes of one form or another that many families do not have enough left to pay their bills. Don't give in to them. Find something that you can do at home that will either help the family save money or earn money or both. We don't need to buy everything everyone else has.

"One of the conspiracy's main thrusts is through education. We need to inform ourselves about what is happening in the government schools. Are you all aware of the power of the National Educational Association—the NEA? Let me read to you a quote from Barbara M. Morris' book, *Change Agents In the Schools*. This is page 17:

> . . . But specifically, change from what to what? Change from a Christian, sovereign nation to a Humanist/Socialist *inter*dependent nation-state in a dictatorship euphemistically called a "global community", with "world citizens" content with enslavement.
>
> In particular, government schools are striving to destroy the status, structure and stability of the family. Strong families make a strong nation and they must be eliminated if the proposed dictatorship is to be established and maintained. Look at your family and the families you know. How stable are they? The breakdown you see is not "just happening"—the chaos is planned.
>
> Public schools? They don't exist. But there *are* government schools and that's what this book is all about: the incredible hoax and ultimate tragedy—goverment schools that serve as change agents for the destruction of Christian Western civilization and to establish instead, a Humanist/Socialist "new world order".[15]

"The NEA is a large organization which pressures legislators to pass many of our socialist/humanist bills. It is the teacher's union whose publications and resolutions sound like a rewritten Humanist Manifesto I and II. It is through NEA teachers in our government schools that America's children are becoming secular humanists. They deny that they promote secular humanism because they realize that the Supreme Court has categorized it as a religion. If Christian teachers cannot teach Christianity in the schools, neither can the NEA teachers teach secular humanism.

"However, they *do* teach secular humanism. The NEA pushes for gay rights, abortion, sexual freedom, moral relativism, and has openly expressed hostility to Christianity, especially if Christian parents question the text books their children are required to read. The change agents are training the next generation to be global citizens of the new age and they are determined that every child in America will be forced to attend the government schools so they can indoctrinate every single child in the country. This is the reason they are so distressed with Christian schools and even more so with home schooling. The change they wish to effect is to rid the child of the values which they have learned from their home and church. They can't do this when the child is carefully protected by both of these institutions. Guard that right; they're endeavoring to take it away.

"Pornography has become big business in America. The craze in the last few years has been kiddie porn. Many young lives have been wrecked by the involvement in this abomination. Any man or woman who would ensnare a child in such an evil, will one day suffer the wrath of God. Yes, Wanda."

"It appears that lust spirits enter men much more readily through the eye and women through the ear. This is also true of legitimate sexual arousal."

"That's an interesting observation. I think I would agree. Men are much more taken up with pornography than women. I'm not going to dwell on this subject; I just wanted to mention it as one of the attacks on the family. It devastates marriages.

"Incidentally, *Playboy* and *Penthouse* backed ERA, according to Phyllis Schlafly. That tells us something right there. Why would publications that depict women as degraded playthings for men want women to have their 'rights?' Because they are attacking the family unit just as the feminists are. If women walk away from their responsibilities as wives and mothers, men can 'have' them without providing for them, protecting them, and cherishing them, and children can become nigh unto obsolete. Or they can be raised in government day-care centers and schools so they will be socialist/humanist products who are glad to be slaves of the conspiracy.

"America has, in the past, been a moral country in a large measure because America's women expected morality and fought against immorality. A major reason for the increase in immorality is that it is being taught, both intentionally and unintentionally, through the government school system and the communications media. As a keeper of the home, we must guard what comes into it.

"America's women have become so accustomed to living in and around moral garbage and manure piles that they have become inured to the smell. Twenty or thirty years ago, the women of America, overcome with a slight whiff, would have handed their husband a shovel and 'expected' a speedy removal of the smallest mound of immorality anywhere near their home. They would have followed with hose and disinfectant to clean up until every trace of the stench was gone.

"As women we need to get very intolerant of immorality. Silence condones immorality. God punishes a whole nation when sin runs rampant. Why should America be destroyed because a handful of people are bent on polluting her and recruiting our children to help them?

"Boycott the products of the companies who sponsor immoral and violent TV programs. Send a letter to the company and also to the broadcasting network explaining why you are displeased. Be courteous and kind but firm.

"Petition your city council to get rid of adult book stores, abortion clinics, and other seedbeds of immorality.

"I'm sure some of you have other good ideas. Yes, Fran?"

"I read about a group that organized to clean up the pornography in the stores within their county. They had decals made which stated, 'This store does not sell pornographic material.' They inspected the book racks in the stores and asked the manager if he would like to display the decal on his door so people in the community would be aware that his store was cooperating in an effort to improve the moral climate of the community.

"The members of the group were gracious and polite, not overbearing and demanding. They talked softly and carried a big stick. We do have the clout of buying power. If they found a store with obscene material, they were just as pleasant as they informed the management that they had found objectionable material in the store and were unable to place their decal on his door. They left their phone number, informing him that as soon as he stopped carrying this type of merchandise, he could give them a call and they would be glad to reinspect the store.

"They were also able to get an interview with the local paper explaining their program and asking the cooperation of the citizenry in avoiding the stores which refused to cooperate. During the interview they pointed out the correlation between pornography and rape, incest, child molestation, and even murder."

"That's a great idea, Fran. We could do the same thing in our county, couldn't we? If you haven't read it yet, I would recommend *The Mind Polluters* by Jerry R. Kirk. He tells how to rid your community of pornography.

"Turn with me to Jeremiah 2, please. I'm starting with verse 11:

> Hath a nation changed their gods, which are yet no gods? but my people have changed their glory for that which doth not profit.
>
> Be astonished, O ye heavens, at this, and be horribly afraid, be ye very desolate, saith the Lord.
>
> For my people have committed two evils; they have forsaken me the fountain of living waters, and hewed them out cisterns, broken cisterns, that can hold no water.

"Now skip down to verse 19:

> Thine own wickedness shall correct thee, and thy backslidings shall reprove thee: know therefore and see that it is an evil thing and bitter, that thou hast forsaken the Lord thy God, and that my fear is not in thee, saith the Lord God of hosts.

"When Harold and I read this chapter last week, I commented that it sounded like something a modern-day prophet could say. America has traded in the glory of God for gods which don't profit. We have to get rid of the things that don't profit, the broken cisterns that take the place of living water in our lives. I John 5:21 says, 'Little children, keep yourselves from idols.' We need to ask God to search our lives and cast out any idols.

"We need to ask God to forgive our forefathers for changing their glory for gods which don't profit. We need to ask God to forgive our government leaders and our teachers for leading us away from the living water to broken cisterns. Americans are parched and dry.

"Because the people of our nation have committed spiritual fornication by running after other gods, they have also been taken captive by a spirit of Fornication in the physical realm. Many are searching for a religion which will give them peace without repentance, but the Prince of Peace does not capitulate to our sin. His righteous, holy nature demands repentance. As John the Baptist prepared people for the coming of Christ with a message of repentance, so we must also prepare people for the second coming of Christ with a message of repentance.

"Now, what can we do to occupy until Jesus comes? What can we do in this battle? America has become so wicked that I cannot believe that God in His righteousness and justice could spare her from destruction—unless there was a widespread revival. My opinion is that we won't see that, though Harold and I pray for it. God would have spared Sodom and Gomorrah for ten righteous people, but there weren't even that many in those cities.

"God said in II Chronicles 7:14:

> If my people, which are called by my name, shall humble themselves, and pray, and seek my face, and turn from their wicked ways; then will I hear from heaven, and will forgive their sin, and will heal their land.

"He's not addressing the sinners; He's talking to *His* people. He's saying if His people will repent and turn from *their* wicked ways, He will turn things around.

"Is it hopeless? Are we over the brink? Has God already decided to destroy America? Is there no turning back His hand of judgment? I don't know. David fasted and prayed for his child until the child died. I think we must do the same for America. God's mercies are new every morning.

"Some think they are going to take over the world for God and present it to Christ when He returns. That contradicts II Thessalonians 2:3:

> Let no man deceive you by any means: for that day shall not come, except there come a falling away first, and that man of sin be revealed, the son of perdition.

"To throw up our hands in defeat and say all these terrible things are going to happen anyway is not an adequate excuse for side-stepping our responsibility to be salt and light.

"During the Civil War a dear southern lady saw soldiers fighting in the orchard. She grabbed up a broom and headed toward the door. A faithful slave stood in her way.

" 'Lawsy, Missy, you caint do no good out there with no broom.'

" 'Well,' she replied, 'at least I can show them whose side I'm on.'

"We may not win every battle in this war, but God requires us to show whose side we're on. The worst thing that can happen is that we'll have a martyr's death. Then, praise God, we'll have a martyr's crown.

"One of the things we should be very concerned about is the Constitutional Convention (Con Con). Urge your federal congressmen to pass a balanced budget amendment without a convention. Urge your state congressmen to restate their request for a balanced budget amendment without a convention. There is mischief afoot in a Con Con. The Conspiracy already has another constitution drawn up which will destroy the freedoms we now possess. This is where our greatest efforts should be spent. Right now, though our government does not always abide by this highest law of the land, we can still claim its protection. The promoters of the New World Order want to change our Constitution so it will be easier to make us part of a socialist/humanist world government. Send for Phoebe Courtney's pamphlet in the bibliography, *Beware a Con Con!*

"Now let's talk a bit more about how we can be salt and light. There are some who *will* come out of Babylon. We must do everything we can to reach those who do not know the Lord as Saviour. The night cometh when no man can work. We must be stewards of our time, organize our work so we get it done efficiently and can go to our friends, neighbors and relatives, even strangers.

"We need to learn how to explain the way of salvation to people. We need to know several Scriptures by memory which show them how to be saved from sin.

"Our lives are the means by which the Holy Spirit can convict people of their sin. Speaking of the coming of the Holy Spirit, Jesus said in John 16:8-11:

> And when he is come, he will reprove the world of sin, and of righteousness, and of judgment:
>
> Of sin, because they believe not on me;
>
> Of righteousness, because I go to my Father, and ye see me no more;
>
> Of judgment, because the prince of this world is judged.

"When Jesus went to the Father, He sent the Holy Spirit who lives in the believer and enables him to walk in the Spirit rather than the flesh. People don't see Jesus anymore; they see His life in us by the power of the Holy Spirit. Our righteous life convicts them of sin.

"If they can lure us into sin, they can get rid of the conviction. Many of the unsaved who taunt us and try to pull us off the path are actually relieved when we don't budge. They have lost respect for other Christians who have compromised, including pastors. We may hold out their only hope that Jesus can change lives. Our lives bring about revival or hinder it. It is essential for the battle that we keep ourselves close to God through prayer, Bible reading, memorization and meditation, fellowship with the local church, deliverance, and obedience. Keep short accounts with God; don't let unconfessed sin keep adding up. Sin cuts off our communication lines with the Captain of our salvation. If we follow afar off, we'll find ourselves out of the battle. Soldiers who are AWOL (absent without leave) never win any campaigns. Besides, stragglers make an easy target for the enemy.

"I'm not talking only about the sins of robbing banks and killing people. I'm also talking about lust, gossip, gluttony, bitterness, jealousy, indifference unkindness, anger, laziness, fear, and worry. These are sins the Church has often labeled problems or needs.

"Often when a church believes in deliverance, we tend to blame everything on evil spirits instead of dealing with sin as sin. Deliverance does not take the place of repentance and indeed will not last without repentance.

"On the other hand, nothing will take the place of deliverance from demons either. Because many churches have spurned the ministry of deliverance, we have seen good men of God fail morally and disgrace the Church and God's name. Had they been able to go to the men of their church and say, 'I have this besetting sin, which I've confessed and of which I've repented, but I am still overwhelmed by it. I have this compulsive behavior which drives me.' Had the ministry of deliverance been available, these men could have gotten the help they needed and spared themselves and the rest of the body of Christ from deep heartache and shame.

"How we spend our time shows the world what's important to us. We're to be a peculiar people. If there's no difference in our lives, why would the sinner feel any need for a change? Conversion means change.

"Alexis de Tocqueville, a French statesman and writer, visited America in 1831. He said then that America is great because she is good, and that when she ceases to be good, she'll cease to be great. It has happened, friends.

"Balaam could not get God to curse Israel because they were obeying God, so he told the enemies of Israel to teach them to sin. That same spirit that was in Balaam has worked through America's enemies to teach America to sin. One of the communist's stated goals has been to get America's young people away from religion and interested in sex. One reason they could get away with this is because the mothers of America were not guarding the home. Indeed, being keepers at home is a very important part of this battle! After all, we're training the next recruits—the replacements.

"The Devil hates the godly seed. His hirelings push abortion, suicide, euthanasia, oral sex, sterilization, and homosexuality. And now they want to get rid of the handicapped. Their underlying goal is zero population growth, which is a New Age teaching.

"Now, I'm sure that the rest of you want to share something. Sheila?"

"We need to lead our children to the Lord before Satan's people lead them down the path that leads to destruction. The world's folks are not waiting until our offspring reach the age of accountability.

We need to pray with them, ground them in the Scripture, see that they are in the house of the Lord, and, if at all possible, either teach them at home or send them to a good Christian school. I qualified that by the word 'good' because there are some Christian schools that are just as detrimental to our children as some government schools."

"Excellent point. There's no way we can undo all the humanistic/socialistic instruction our children get for six hours a day with fifteen minutes of devotions after supper. Even if we had two hours of devotions (which I wouldn't recommend), we have no idea what to counter when we aren't in that classroom with them. I know a couple of you have unsaved husbands who insist that the children go to the government school. If we're in a situation where we have no choice but to send them to the government schools, we will have to try our best and trust God for the rest. Betty?"

"I'm a bit on the shy side, but I've found that I can leave tracts in places where people will read them, such as waiting rooms or the student lounges at the local college. I've found that people are much more open to spiritual things than I thought. There's a hungry and thirsty world out there. Some folks just need to be fed."

"Yes, tracts have reached many people. Make sure you read them through yourself. Some are poorly written and some have bad theology. Those could do more harm than good. Yvonne?"

"We can have a neighborhood Bible class. I have a ladies' class once a week, and once a month my husband teaches both the men and the women in the evening. We've seen a few turn to the Lord. I make fancy little sandwiches and something unique to drink like sassafras tea or hot spiced apple cider. During the summer I hold a daily vacation Bible school for the neighborhood kids. Then we have a big picnic for the parents and kids at the neighborhood park. It's helped us grow too."

"Excellent. If some of you would like to do the same thing but feel you don't know enough about the Bible yet, find someone who is knowledgeable to help you, then you organize the people and invite that person in to do the teaching. You will soon know enough to take over. Ann?"

"We have Saturday night sings once a month, as many of you know. We invite about two-thirds Christian people and another third unbelieving neighbors so they can rub shoulders with believers. We sing Psalms and hymns and spiritual songs, and encourage folks to sing specials and bring their instruments too. Our own kids look forward to these meetings all month. People don't go to neighborhood things much anymore. We have fancy sandwiches and cookies or some finger-type dessert and something to drink. It definitely breaks down the walls that unbelievers build around themselves. Of course the idea is to be friendly to these people when they come and make them feel at ease with us. And also to show them that good clean fellowship between Christians is enjoyable. We don't have to find fun at the disco."

"These sings are really a blessing. Harold and I have been to several of them.

"This gives us an idea of what we can do to reach the lost. If each of us were to win ten souls to Christ a year and then discipled those people by praying with them, teaching them the Scripture, involving them in the local church, then encouraging them to win ten other people and disciple them, think what would happen! Even if we won one person to Christ a year and discipled that one to win one a year, we'd be making some headway.

"Remember, we're winning the enemies of God over to His side. Colossians 1:21 and 22 says:

> And you, that were sometime alienated and enemies in your mind by wicked works, yet now hath he reconciled.
>
> In the body of his flesh through death, to present you holy and unblamable and unreprovable in his sight:

"There are a lot of people out there who don't want to be alienated from God; they just don't know the way into the kingdom of Light. No one has bothered to tell them. This is one of the lies of the enemy: 'If you talk about religion, you'll offend someone. It's too personal and too controversial.' Humbug!

"Ask the Heavenly Father to loose the spirit of adoption upon the unsaved. Ask Him to draw them to His Son. If they're relatives, claim them under Acts 16:32. Ask the Holy Spirit to convict them. Then let your conversation be as becometh the gospel of Christ. Yes, Wanda?"

"We must pray for our husbands, our pastors, our Christian leaders and our government leaders. If a man (or woman) is totally confident that he will never be turned aside from following the Lord, he's a sitting duck in a pond of pride. Satan is eager to take such a man out of the battle by seducing him into heresy, fornication, the love of money, a love for power, or some other sin. Pray continually that God will put a hedge of thorns, an encampment of angels, and a wall of fire around them.

"Proverbs 12:4 says:

> A virtuous woman is a crown to her husband: but she that maketh ashamed is as rottenness in his bones.

Wanda continued, "Both Strong's and Young's concordances describe *virtuous* as force, strength, and valour like that of an army. Strong's represents *crown* as coming from a root word meaning to encircle for attack or protection. Like a crown, we should surround our husbands with our prayers and our presence."

"Excellent advice. Yes, Sheila?"

"We need to stay under the cover and protection of authority. We need to guard ourselves and seek the protective guard of our husbands to keep ourselves from the 'garden syndrome,' where Satan deceived the woman and then used her to lure the man into sin."

"An excellent point. So far we've been talking mostly about what we can do in the real physical realm. Now let's discuss what we can do in the spiritual realm, which is just as real.

"We should not attempt any endeavor which is not preceded by prayer and even fasting. If we are marching out to change the world and God wants us to stay home and change diapers, we will only build wood, hay and stubble. Know what God wants *you* to do. At different stages of our lives, we have different responsibilities. Our husbands have different needs in their lives too. If we are well-tuned to God's will and the will of our husbands, we shall be able to build gold, silver and precious stones upon the foundation we have in Christ.

"One thing we can do in this battle is to ask the Father to send angels to cut off the demonic messengers who supply the orders and the power from Satan to the Conspiracy, the New Age folks, and everyone who is part of Satan's Antichrist program. We can bind the princes over the Illuminati. We can bind the strongmen over the Illuminati. We can do the same for every organization or person that God lays on our hearts. We can bind up spirits of Mind Control over our congressmen, judges, the president, and his cabinet. We can bind up spirits of War throughout the world.

"We can also ask the Father to send ministering spirits to enter this warfare. Elisha was surrounded by Syrian soldiers during the night. His servant panicked; 'Alas, my master! how shall we do?' Elisha assured the servant that they that be with us are more than they that be with them. The prophet then prayed that the Lord would open the eyes of the young man. He was able to see the mountain full of horses and chariots of fire round about Elisha. The whole story is in II Kings 6.

"Missionaries in China, during the time of the Japanese invasion, tell of natives who saw huge shining warriors standing guard upon the missionaries' roof. Psalm 34:7 tells us:

> The angel of the Lord encampeth round about them that fear him and delivereth them.

"In Daniel 10, during the reign of Cyrus, king of Persia, Daniel saw a vision of a spiritual being. This spiritual being said to Daniel, (verse 12):

> Fear not, Daniel: for from the first day that thou didst set thine heart to understand, and to chasten thyself before thy God, thy words were heard, and I am come for thy words.
>
> But the prince of the kingdom of Persia withstood me one and twenty days: but, lo, Michael, one of the chief princes, came to help me; and I remained there with the kings of Persia.

"Now jump with me down to the end of verse 20:

> . . . And now I will return to fight with the prince of Persia: and when I am gone forth, lo, the prince of Grecia shall come.
>
> But I will shew thee that which is noted in the scripture of truth: and there is none that holdeth with me in these things, but Michael your prince.

"Turn now to Daniel 12. This explains a bit more about Michael's position. Verse l reads:

> And at that time shall Michael stand up, the great prince which standeth for the children of thy people:

"There is a hierarchy both in the kingdom of darkness and in the kingdom of Light. As believers seated positionally with Jesus Christ in heavenly places, we can take authority in His name over the spirit beings which rebelled against God.

"I want you also to realize that this is a warfare, and you will also have to continually bind up a spirit of Backlash. The demons do not appreciate your participation, and they will do everything they can to discourage you. We're in God's hands. I guess it's just a matter of whether you want to hide in the closet or dash out into the orchard with a broom to let everyone know whose side you're on.

"We do have the Lord's promise in Luke 10:19. Read that for us please, Sandy."

> Behold, I give unto you power to tread on serpents and scorpions, and over all the power of the enemy: and nothing shall by any means hurt you.

"Another important warfare Scripture is in II Corinthians 10:3-5. Wanda, read that for us, please."

> For though we walk in the flesh, we do not war after the flesh:
>
> (For the weapons of our warfare are not carnal, but mighty through God to the pulling down of strong holds:)
>
> Casting down imaginations, and every high thing that exalteth itself against the knowledge of God, and bringing into captivity every thought to the obedience of Christ;

"We don't have time today to go through each of these Scriptures, but read them over and ask the Holy Spirit to show you how to use them in binding and casting down the demonic powers which work through the men (and women) who are trying to push us into a one-world government, a one-world church, and the worship of Antichrist.

"Look at Psalm 149:6-9:

> Let the high praises of God be in their mouth, and a two-edged sword in their hand;
>
> To execute vengeance upon the heathen, and punishments upon the people;
>
> To bind their kings with chains, and their nobles with fetters of iron;
>
> To execute upon them the judgment written: this honour have all his saints. Praise ye the Lord.

"Bible scholars refer to this as a prophetic Psalm, but you'll notice the connection of praise to warfare in this passage, and you'll notice it throughout Scripture now that I've called your attention to it.

"In II Chronicles 20, a great multitude was coming to attack Judah. Jehoshaphat, the king, feared and set himself to seek the

Lord, and proclaimed a fast throughout all Judah. And Judah gathered themselves together to ask help of the Lord. They came from everywhere to seek the Lord. Read Jehoshaphat's whole prayer. I'm just going to read verse 12:.

> O our God, wilt thou not judge them? for we have no might against this great company that cometh against us; neither know we what to do: but our eyes are upon thee.

"Now there's a man after my own heart. He totally leans on God. And God answered him too; He likes leaners. He spoke through a prophet and told the folks that they shouldn't be dismayed, for the battle wasn't theirs, it was the Lord's. He told them to go out against them the next day, but they wouldn't even need to fight. So they had a praise session and got up early the next morning.

"Now Jehoshaphat appointed singers unto the Lord to go out before the army. Look at verse 22:

> And when they began to sing and to praise, the Lord set ambushments against the children of Ammon, Moab, and mount Seir which were come against Judah; and they were smitten.

"The enemy killed each other and when Jehoshaphat and all the trusting, praising people came upon their enemy, there wasn't anyone left alive to fight. It took three days for Judah to gather up all the spoil. They went rejoicing and praising all the way back home too.

"Praise is an important tool in the spiritual warfare. Do not underestimate this weapon. When we praise God, we focus our attention upon Him. When we don't, we tend to focus our attention on other things. That's why it is so important to be in fellowship with other believers on a regular basis. That's why people who get lax about coming to church usually get lax about their relationship with the Lord, too.

"Look at Psalm 107. The pattern throughout the Psalm is that men are in a terrible mess so they cry unto the Lord and He delivers them. Then we find this verse. The first time it's verse 8:

> Oh that men would praise the Lord for his goodness, and for his wonderful works to the children of men.

"But alas they do not praise God and so He has to allow them to repeat their mistake again and again and again. We find that same verse repeated in 15, 21 and 31. When people do not focus their attention upon God through praise, they tend to forget God.

"The lesson for us is to focus our attention upon God in praise so He doesn't have to get our attention through trouble. Don't just praise Him in the church meetings; sing and praise Him in your home too. Teach your children to praise. Why should they croon some ditty that the world's kids are singing that puts a focus on Satan, when they belong to the King of Kings? Incidentally, if they listen to TV and the radio all day, where will their focus be?

"Turn to Matthew 12:25. Jesus had cast a devil out of a blind and dumb man. The Pharisees said that he cast out the devils by Beelzebub the prince of the devils. Betty will you read verses 25-30, please?"

> And Jesus knew their thoughts, and said unto them, Every kingdom divided against itself is brought to desolation; and every city or house divided against itself shall not stand:
>
> And if Satan cast out Satan, he is divided against himself; how shall then his kingdom stand?
>
> And if I by Beelzebub cast out devils, by whom do your children cast them out? therefore they shall be your judges.
>
> But if I cast out devils by the Spirit of God, then the kingdom of God is come unto you.
>
> Or else how can one enter into a strong man's house, and spoil his goods, except he first bind the strong man? and then he will spoil his house.
>
> He that is not with me is against me; and he that gathereth not with me scattereth abroad.

"Pat Brook's new book, *A Call to War with Prayer Power,* is an excellent book on this subject. There's no use in my trying to communicate to you what she has already written so well here. You can borrow my copy, and there are several others here who have copies.

"There are a number of Christian organizations which you can join that will send you informative literature about what is going on in the government. Your membership in these groups gives them lobbying power to speak on your behalf. Just be sure they are really doing what they say they are.

"I trust this lesson has given you some food for thought. Don't be dismayed; God is still on the throne. Praise Him as Jehoshaphat and the people of Judah did. He will give us the victory. However, it is not a time for apathy and indifference. We can fast and pray voluntarily now or involuntarily later. If God would have spared Sodom and Gomorrah for ten people, perhaps he will hear the cries and prayers of women who have determined in their hearts that they will take a firm stand for righteousness in these evil days

"If you're not sure that you are in the kingdom of light, you can make that choice for certain today. There is no kingdom of twilight. You're in one kingdom or the other—light or darkness. God doesn't claim the people who sit on the fence. In Matthew 12:30 Jesus said, 'He that is not with me is against me.' Again in Revelation 3:15 and 16 He says:

> I know thy works, that thou art neither cold nor hot: I would thou wert cold or hot.
>
> So then because thou art lukewarm, and neither cold nor hot, I will spue thee out of my mouth.

"However, what He really wants is to come into our hearts and kindle a fire there. In verse 20 of Revelation 3 He says:

> Behold, I stand at the door and knock: if any man hear my voice, and open the door, I will come in to him, and will sup with him, and he with me.

"First, repent of your sins. Surrender to the Saviour, Jesus Christ. When we talk about having salvation or being saved, we're talking about being saved from sin. If you do not surrender totally to Jesus Christ, how can He possibly deliver you from your sin. Ask the Lord Jesus Christ to forgive you of all your sins; then ask Him to come into your heart and live His life through you. I John 5:13 gives us the assurance that when we put our trust in the Lord, He will give us eternal life:

> These things have I written unto you that believe on the name of the Son of God; that ye may know that ye have eternal life. and that ye may believe on the name of the Son of God.

"Let us spend a few minutes in prayer before we go home. You are dismissed now. When you finish praying, leave quietly so you don't disturb anyone. I'll put the bibliography on the back pew. Don't forget to pick up a copy."

The ladies knelt in the pews, and some went forward to kneel at the altar. As I turned to kneel, I saw Shirley walk out the door. She didn't pick up a bibliography because Aunt Emily hadn't made it back there with them yet. "Lord, help her," I prayed. "I fear she's making a wrong decision."

When I finished praying and sat back on the pew, I saw Dori collecting a stack of books from Emily. Her face looked so different—free, I would call it. She gave Emily a hug and left, picking up a bibliography on her way out.

I picked up my own bibliography and stood by the open door. Shirley had waited for Dori in the parking lot. I heard Dori exclaim clearly, "I don't care if I have to give up my rights, I'm not going to position myself in the kingdom of darkness for all the so-called rights in the world. The feminists are in the wrong camp and I'm not going to be in there with them anymore. When the whole thing is all over, I'm sure I'll be glad I made this decision. God's banner over me is love; I'll follow His leadership."

Shirley didn't answer her; she just got into her car and left.

As Emily and I drove home, I shared with her what Dori had said.

"She expressed the same thing to me when she came up to borrow a stack of books. She's made an about-face. However, I think Shirley has hardened her heart to the Lord. I fear for her. The look on her face was one of rejection and rebellion. That's one of the results of teaching the truth; there are some who will reject it. God sent several of His prophets to preach to Israel or Judah and told them from the outset that the people would not receive the truth. It breaks your heart, though, when you see someone aligning themselves with the enemies of God. I'll continue to pray for her. She may come running back home when her taskmaster beats her badly enough."

"Aunt Emily, I have mixed emotions. I hate to leave tonight. I've had such a good time; I've learned so many good things. I'm not going back with just baskets of food for thought; I'm bringing back a whole bread truck. On the other hand, I am eager to get back and start putting all these good concepts into practice. I'm eager to start rehearsing what I've learned to my ladies' class."

Harold was repairing the front fence when we pulled in. He waved and smiled as usual. "No wonder he's so pleasant; Emily brings constant cheer into his life as she ministers God's love to him," I thought to myself.

"I'm going to take a little nap, June. You go ahead and make your outline and get your things packed. Harold will carry your suitcase out for you after supper. We'll hate to see you go; we've enjoyed your company and you've been a big help with the work."

I spread out my notes as usual across Ruth's bed and sat beside them to put together my outline.

1. The spirit of Antichrist and Satan are liars who promote 'The Lie.'
2. Those who love and make a lie will be outside the gates of heaven.
3. The basic premise of 'The Lie' is "Ye shall be as gods" and its corollary, "ye shall not surely die"—both from Satan in the garden of Eden.
4. Many people are content to be deceived because if they follow the truth they must repent and they love their sin too much for that.
5. The kingdom of darkness and the kingdom of light are opposite in their goals, their philosophy, and their religion.
6. We are soldiers in this conflict under our Captain, Jesus Christ.
   a. We have to set aside entanglements. II Tim. 2:3,4.
   b. We aren't fighting flesh and blood, but the demonic powers working through the people we encounter. Eph 6.
7. From our position in the heavenlies, we can see Satan's forces conspiring against us.
   a. The Illuminati.
   b. The New Age Movement.
   c. The Feminist Movement.
8. God is polarizing mankind to separate the sheep from the goats.
   a. We're being tried by the powers of darkness and forced to make bigger and more costly choices to declare our loyalty to Jesus Christ.
   b. The Antichrist will appear only when it is God's time for him to do so.
   c. When that time comes, we need to be ready.
9. The feminist movement is closely aligned with socialism, humanism and the New Age Movement.

5. The kingdom of darkness and the kingdom of light are opposite in their goals, their philosophy, and their religion.
6. We are soldiers in this conflict under our Captain, Jesus Christ.
   a. We have to set aside entanglements. II Tim. 2:3,4.
   b. We aren't fighting flesh and blood, but the demonic powers working through the people we encounter. Eph 6.
7. From our position in the heavenlies, we can see Satan's forces conspiring against us.
   a. The Illuminati.
   b. The New Age Movement.
   c. The Feminist Movement.
8. God is polarizing mankind to separate the sheep from the goats.
   a. We're being tried by the powers of darkness and forced to make bigger and more costly choices to declare our loyalty to Jesus Christ.
   b. The Antichrist will appear only when it is God's time for him to do so.
   c. When that time comes, we need to be ready.
9. The feminist movement is closely aligned with socialism, humanism and the New Age Movement.
10. Women, following Betty Friedan's advice, have left the feminine mystique for the feminine mistake and are reaping a crop of weeds from the bad seeds they have sown.
11. Only by being made complete in Christ will women find fulfillment whether they are fulltime homemakers or whether they are involved in an outside career
12. Our discontent has come because humanism has come into the Church.
13. The Conspiracy is particularly attacking our ministry as wives and mothers.
    a. High taxes are pushing wives out of the home to work.
    b. Secular humanistic education in the government schools is being used to undermine the family.
    c. Pornography is devastating to marriages.
    d. We have become tolerant of immorality.
14. What can we do to occupy until Jesus comes?
    a. God's people can repent.
    b. We can pray for our nation.
    c. We can fight the Constitutional Convention.

and thrones and dominions. Keep me close to Yourself and Your Word so I don't become a casualty in this battle. Live Your life through me so my life will convict the people around me of sin. Show me what to do in the natural realm to fight immorality and the legislation that is undermining our families and our freedoms. Father, I praise You right now for Who You are and what You've done for me. Teach me to be grateful. Help me to praise You throughout each day. I want to focus my attention on You. Make me a crown to my husband with my prayers and my presence. In Jesus' Name. Amen.

Perhaps you'd like to pray something similar.

Well, aren't you glad you came along? I hope you learned a lot; I surely did. That's the end, or perhaps I should say, the beginning.

# *Fulfilled*

*My ministry is in this home*
*I'm keeper here; I need not roam.*
*My hands are busy washing pots.*
*I'm ironing clothes and scrubbing spots.*

*My service to the ones I love*
*Flows from the heart of God above.*
*Through me, His vessel in this house,*
*He loves my kids, He loves my spouse.*

*My love is glue that holds us tight.*
*The nest's secure both day and night.*
*I'm always here to dry a tear.*
*To rub a back or calm a fear.*

*My "house band" makes an iron band*
*Around our hearts, our house, our land.*
*Secure, surrounded with his care.*
*We frolick in the love we share.*

*And in this circle I'm the heart.*
*I pump the blood to every part.*
*God's love flows out from me to each.*
*Then rebounds back from every reach.*

*Let others go their dreams to build.*
*My place is here; I am fulfilled.*
*I'm loved and praised; my heart is set.*
*By giving, all my needs are met.*

# NATURAL GRAIN AND HONEY RECIPES

## GET UP AND GO GRANOLA

Preheat oven to **350°**

In a very large bowl, combine the following:
9 cups rolled oats
3 cups unsweetened raw shredded coconut
2 cups hulled raw sunflower seeds
2 cups raw wheat germ (always keep refrigerated)

Mix well and add:
1 cup corn oil
1 cup honey (1 1/2 if you like it sweeter)
4 teaspoons pure vanilla flavoring
2-3 teaspoons pure almond flavoring

Stir well until dry and moist ingredients are well blended. Pour half of mixture into a shallow baking pan (like a roast pan) and spread out evenly.

Bake 10 minutes and stir well away from sides and bottom. Bake another 5 minutes and stir again.

Watch carefully from this point. It will take another 5-10 minutes. It's best when baked to a dark tan color. If it's too dark, it will be a bit bitter. If too light, it will taste raw.

Immediately turn into a cookie sheet to cool while you bake the second batch.

Store the finished product in closed containers such as coffee cans in the freezer or refrigerator.

## COME AGAIN CORNBREAD

Preheat oven to **350°**

For a **9"x13"** pan:
Sift into a mixing bowl the following:
2 cups whole wheat pastry flour
2 cups yellow corn meal
2 tablespoons baking powder

Add:
2 eggs
2/3 cup corn oil
2 cups milk
1/2 cup honey

For an 8x8" pan:
Sift into a mixing bowl the following:
1 cup whole wheat pastry flour
1 cup yellow corn meal
1 tablespoon baking powder

Add:
1 egg
1/3 cup corn oil
1 cup milk
1/4 cup honey

Stir together thoroughly and bake 20-30 minutes in a well greased baking dish (Use margarine or butter wrappers that you save in the refrigerator.)

When done the top will crack slightly, it will spring back when touched lightly and will not stick to an inserted toothpick.

Cut in large squares.

The tastiest way to eat this sweet style corn bread is to slice your piece horizontally in half, smother with butter and honey (like an open-face sandwich) and eat it with a fork.

## OH BOY OATMEAL COOKIES

Preheat oven to **350°**

Mix together until creamy:
1 1/2 cups corn oil
2 1/2 cups honey
2 eggs
2 teaspoons pure vanilla
1/8 teaspoon almond extract

Sift together into wet ingredients:
2 1/2 cups whole wheat pastry flour
1 teaspoon salt (optional)
2 teaspoons cinnamon
2 teaspoons baking powder

Stir, and then add:
7 cups rolled oats

Mix thoroughly.

Optional: add 2 cups raisins and/or 1/2 to 1 cup sunflower seeds or chopped nuts.

Drop by teaspoonfuls on cookie sheets and bake for 10-15 minutes.

Watch carefully. Tops should be light tan and bottoms light brown. They'll be moist and quite soft, but will "set up" when they cool. Remove carefully with a spatula to a flat plate or clean table top to cool.

Can be baked in large batches and stored in the freezer.

## ZUCCHINI BREAD

Preheat oven to **325°**

Beat together until foamy:
3 eggs

Add and mix well:
1 cup of corn oil
2 cups honey
2 cups peeled and grated zucchini
1 teaspoon vanilla

Sift together and add:
4 cups whole wheat pastry flour
3 teaspoons baking powder
2 teaspoons cinnamon

Mix well, and then:

Stir in 1/2 cup nuts and 1/2 cup carob chips

Bake in well greased, preferably glass, pan for 45 min. to 1 hour. When it feels springy and an inserted toothpick comes out clean, it's done.

Cool on a cake rack and loosen carefully with a knife before removing from pans.

## WHEAT TREAT MUFFINS

Preheat oven to **375°**

Sift together into a large bowl:
2 cups whole wheat pastry flour
2 Tablespoons baking powder
1/2 cup soy flour (or Ezekiel bread flour)

Add:
1 cup wheat germ (always refrigerate)
1 cup bran (oat bran is best)

Stir, and add:
2 1/4 cups milk
4 eggs
1/2 cup honey
4 Tablespoons corn oil

Stir until moistened.

Fold in:
1/2 cup hulled raw sunflower seeds or nuts
1 cup raisins, apple pieces or blueberries.

(For lighter texture, separate eggs, whip whites until stiff and fold into finished batter.)

Bake in well greased muffin tins (or spray with Pam) for 15-25 minutes.

Tops should spring back when touched lightly and an inserted toothpick should come out clean when done.

## ZUCCHINI DROP COOKIES

Preheat oven to **375°**.

Mix together in large bowl:
- 2 cups grated zucchini
- 4 teaspoons baking soda
- 1 1/2 cups honey
- 3 tablespoons maple syrup
- 1 teaspoon black walnut flavoring
- 1 cup corn oil
- 2 eggs

Put in sifter and sift into wet ingredients:
- 3 1/2 cups whole wheat flour
- 1 cup soy flour
- 2 teaspoons cinnamon
- 1/2 teaspoon cloves

Stir and Add:
- 1 cup chopped nuts and 1 cup raisins

Drop by teaspoons on greased cookie sheet and bake 12-15 minutes.

## CARROT CAKE

Preheat oven to **300°**

Stir together:
- 1 1/2 cups vegetable oil
- 1 1/2 cups honey
- 3 cups shredded carrots or zucchini
- 1 teaspoon pure vanilla

Add four eggs, one at a time, mixing well after each one.

Sift together and add:
- 2 1/4 cups whole wheat flour
- 1 teaspoon cinnamon
- 5 teaspoons baking powder

Mix well.
Add 1/2 cup pecan pieces

Pour into a greased 9 1/2" x 13" glass baking dish and bake for 55 minutes. cake will be moist but springy to the touch and an inserted toothpick will come out clean when the cake is done.

**Frosting:**

Combine in a double boiler top:
- 2 egg whites
- 1/2 cup honey

Place over boiling water and beat with electric hand mixer (an egg beater will do if you have the endurance. It will take 5-10 minutes; but it's worth it)

Beat until the frosting stands in stiff peaks.

Add a teaspoon of pure vanilla and another teaspoon of pure lemon extract if you like it.

Continue beating until frosting is white again.
Spread immediately making wave like peaks.
Sprinkle with walnut pieces.

## BERRY GOOD CHEESE CAKE

Boil 1 cup water.
Put in blender:
1 Tablespoon unflavored gelatin (Walnut Acres sells beef gelatin)
1/2 cup honey
Blend well, adding:
1 cup boiling water
Two 8 ounce packages cream cheese
1 banana
1 teaspoon pure vanilla
Pour into prepared graham cracker crust
Refrigerate.

## BERRY SAUCE

Thaw 1 quart frozen strawberries, blueberries or 1 pint raspberry puree, or use fresh berries of any kind.

Place 1 Tablespoon of gelatin in a small pan with berries until softened.

Add 1/2 cup honey and heat until dissolved.

Cool thoroughly and pour evenly over cheese cake. (Make sure cheese cake is firmly set)

Refrigerate until ready to serve.

An option is to thicken the berries with corn starch rather than use the gelatin, especially if you're taking this treat to a picnic where the heat will melt the gelatin. You can also combine the cheese cake and the sauce in the blender, skip the graham cracker crust, and pour into fancy tall stemmed glassware. Top with a dollop of whip cream and/or a slice or two of berry. For a party, pour the combined cheese cake and sauce in a shallow sheet cake pan until set. Slice into squares and use as a topping on shortbread cookies like Lorna Doones. These are fancy fare at wedding receptions. A little artistic decoration of white cheese cake saved aside and applied with a cake decorator will add the final touch to the bright pink of the combination. Be creative!

## ALMOND/SUNFLOWER HAIR RAISERS

This is a candy or a cracker/sandwich spread.

They're chock full of nutrients that feed the hair and scalp. Do not test on billiard balls.

Pulverize well one cup at a time in the blender:

2 cups almonds
2 cups raw hulled sunflower seeds

Stir well and add honey until it is the consistency of peanut butter.

Form balls and roll in ground pecans, coconut, peanuts, or walnuts.

Or, roll into 10" logs and roll in nuts, refrigerate until firm. Slice into 1/2 inch candies.

For a sandwich/cracker spread, thin the mix with a small amount of water until it is soft enough to spread on bread without tearing it.

If you can find some natural food coloring, it will make it more attractive.

For elegant sandwiches to serve at parties or wedding receptions, use three pieces of bread with this spread between.

Cut the crusts off neatly and cut sandwiches diagonally in halves, quarters, and then eighths.

Serve on end in a fancy design on a serving tray. The plain sandwiches are also nourishing and sustaining for the lunch pail.

## GELATIN DESSERTS AND SALADS

(Basic recipe)

Combine in a medium sauce pan:
2 Tablespoons unflavored gelatin
2 cups unsweetened real fruit juice (Not fruit drink).

Allow gelatin to soften then heat until dissolved.

Add 2 cups of cold juice

Add unsweetened fruit and refrigerate.

### CHERRY BERRY "B"

Applying above recipe, use Juicy Juice punch flavor and add pitted sweet cherries, blueberries, and bananas.

### SALAD ORANGE DELIGHT

Applying above recipe, use Juicy Juice tropical flavor or orange juice and add one 20 oz. can of crushed pineapple in its own juice. (Measure the juice from the pineapple first then add the remainder of the cold juice to it to equal 2 cups.

To make it a salad, add finely shredded carrots. Fresh or canned orange segments are good as well.

### WALDORF SALAD

Applying the above recipe, use tropical flavored Juicy Juice, diced apples, chopped walnuts or pecans, and chopped celery.

## SUMMER SALAD

Applying the above recipe, use tropical flavored Juicy Juice, pineapple in its own juice, shredded cabbage, and cottage cheese

Other fruits that are good in gelatin desserts are natural applesauce, kiwi, pears, peaches, seeded or seedless grapes, If the combination is not sweet enough, add 1/3 to 1/2 cup honey to the saucepan the next time you make it.

Whip cream, stiffly beaten and sweetened with 1/4 cup honey can also be folded into a dessert gelatin when it is partially set, then returned to the refrigerator.

No matter which of these recipes you create, ENJOY!!!

# BIBLIOGRAPHY AND FOOTNOTES

The following books will give you a broader understanding of the various facets presented in *The Ministry of a Wife*. A very few are secular books whose authors may not share a Biblical outlook on life. They are listed here because what they say may offer you some help. There are so-called Christian books on the market which I would not recommend because what they say is not biblical. When you read any book, filter it through the Bible. Take the fish and leave the bones. You may find some bones in this list, but on the whole, the reader will benefit from reading each of them.

The number to the left of an author's name corresponds to a footnote in the text indicating that I have quoted from that work with permission from the author and/or publisher.

## MARRIAGE AND FAMILY


Christianson, Larry. *The Renewed Mind.*
Minneapolis, Minn.: Bethany House Publishers, 1974.

Deutsch, Ronald M. *The Key to Feminine Response in Marriage.*
New York: Random House, 1968.

Elliott, Elizabeth. *Love Has a Price Tag.*
Ann Arbor, MI: Vine Books, 1982.

Elliott, Elizabeth. *Let Me Be a Woman.*
Wheaton, IL.: Tyndale House, 1976.

Elliott, Elizabeth. *The Mark of a Man.*
Old Tappan, New Jersey: Fleming H. Revell, 1981.

Institute in Basic Youth Conflicts (Seminars held by Bill Gothard in major cities across the country)
IBYC Information Office, Box One, Oak Brook, Illinois 60522-3001.

Garton, Jean Staker. *Who Broke the Baby.*
6820 Auto Club Road.
Minneapolis, Minn. 55438: Bethany Fellowship Inc.,1979.

18 Glickman, S.Craig. *A Song for Lovers.*
Downers Grove: InterVarsity Christian Fellowship of the USA, 1976. Quotations used by permission of InterVarsity Press, P.O. Box 1400, Downers Grove, IL 60515

Handford, Elizabeth Rice. *Me? Obey Him?*
Murfreesboro, Tennessee.: Sword of the Lord, 1972.

LaHaye, Beverly. *I Am a Woman by God's Design.*
Old Tappan, New Jersey: Fleming H. Revell Company. 1980.

LaHaye, Beverly, *The Spirit Controlled Woman*
Irvine, CA: Harvest House, 1976.

LaHaye, Beverly. *Who But a Woman.*
Nashville, Camden, New York: Thomas Nelson Publishers, 1984.

LaHaye Tim and Beverly. *The Act of Marriage.*
Grand Rapids: Zondervan Press, 1976.

10 LaHaye, Tim and Phillips, Bob. *Anger is a Choice.*
Grand Rapids, MI.: Zondervan Publishing House, 1982.

9 LaHaye, Tim. *How to Win Over Depression.*
Grand Rapids, MI: Zondervan Publishing House. 1974.

12 Lloyd-Jones, D. Martyn. *Spiritual Depression: It;s Causes and Cures.*
Grand Rapids, MI: Wm. B. Eerdmans Publishing Company, 1965.

MacDonald, Gordon. *Magnificent Marriage.*
Wheaton, Illinois: Living Books, Tyndale House Publishers, Inc. 1980.

MacDonald, Gail and Gordon. *If Those Who Reach Could Touch.*
Old Tappan, NJ: Fleming Revell, 1985.

Ortlund, Ann. *Disciples of a Beautiful Woman.*
Waco, Texas: Word Books, 1986.

6 Pentecost, Dorothy H. "Winning an Unsaved Husband," *Good News Broadcaster.*
Lincoln, Nebraska: The Good News Broadcasting Association, Inc., 1970.

19 Pride, Mary. *The Way Home.*
Westchester, IL.: Crossway Books, A Division of Good News Publishers, 1985.

## DELIVERANCE

Brooks, Pat. *Out in the Name of Jesus.*
91 Lytle Road, Fletcher, NC.28732: New Puritan Library, 1985.

Brooks, Pat. *Using Your Spiritual Authority.*
580 Pittsburg St. Springdale, PA. 15144: Whitaker House,

Brooks, Pat. *Healing of the Mind.*
Altmonte Springs, Florida: Creation House, 1987.

Hammond, Frank and Ida Mae. *Pigs in the Parlor--A Practical Guide to Deliverance.*
Kirkwood, MO.(137 W. Jefferson Ave. 63122):Impact Books, Inc. 1973

8 Ness, Alex W. *Transference of Spirits.*
P.O. Box 89, Pefferlaw, Ontario LOE 1NO, Agapre Publications Inc., 1978.

Penn-Lewis, Jessie. *War on the Saints (Unabridged)*
Thomas E. Lowe, Ltd., Suite 1500, 2 Penn Plaza, NY 10001.

Worley, Win.
*Battling the Hosts of Hell—Diary of an Exorcist.* 1976, 1980
*Conquering the Hosts of Hell—An Open Triumph.* 1977.
*Demolishing the Hosts of Hell—Every Christian's Job.* 1978.
*Annihilating the Hosts of Hell—The Battle Royal. Books 1 and 2.* 1981.
*Eradicating the Host of Hell—Uprooting the Hidden Enemy.* 1983
*Smashing the Hosts of Hell—The Believer's Privilege.* 1983.
HBC, Box 626, Lansing, Illinois 60438
(The reader will find further recommendations for books concerning deliverance and the world conspiracy in the appendix of each of the above books by Win Worley)

11 *Warfare Prayers.*
HBC, Box 626, Lansing IL. 60438.

## SOCIAL AND POLITICAL

Allen, Gary. *None Dare Call It Conspiracy.*
P.O. Box 3380 Kailua-Kona, Hawaai 96740: Concord Books, 1972

Brooks, Pat. *The Return of the Puritans.*
Fletcher NC (91 Lytle Road 28732): New Puritan Library, Inc. 1987.

Bobgan, Martin and Deidre. *Psycho Heresy.*
Santa Barbara, CA 93110: East Gate Publishers, 1987.

Brooks, Pat. *A Call to War With Prayer Power.*
Fletcher NC (91 Lytle Road 28732): New Puritan Library, Inc., 1985.

Call, Max. *Hand of Death.*
LaFayette , LA: Prescott Press, Inc., 1985

Chastain, Jane. *I'd Speak Out on the Issues If I Only Knew What* to Say.
Ventura, CA, Regal Books, 1984.

Courtney, Phoebe. *Beware a "Con Con"!* (TAX FAX No 219)
The Independent American, P.O. Box 636, Littleton, Colorado 80160. 2 for $1.00.

Cumbey, Constance. *The Hidden Dangers of the Rainbow.*
Shreveport, Louisiana: Huntington House, Inc. 1983.

Epperson, A. Ralph. *The Unseen Hand.*
Tucson, Arizona: Publius Press, 1985.

Hunt, Dave. *America, the Sorcerer's New Apprentice.*
Eugene, Oregon: Harvest House Publishers, 1988.

13 Hunt, Dave. *Peace Prosperity and the Coming Holocaust.*
Eugene, Oregon: Harvest House Publishers, 1983.

Hunt, Dave and McMahon, T.A. *The Seduction of Christianity.*
Eugene, Oregon: Harvest House Publishers, 1985.

Jepsen, Dee. *Women Beyond Equal Rights.*
Waco, Texas: Word Books, 1984.

Kirk, Jerry. *The Mind Polluters.*
P.O. Box 141000 , Elm Hill Pike, Nashville, TN: Nelson, 1985

14 LaHaye, Beverly. *"Do These Women Speak for You?"* (Tract)
Concerned Women for America (CWA)
370 L'Enfant Promenade, S.W., Suite 800 Washington, D.C. 20024.

LaHaye, Tim. *Battle for the Mind.*
Old Tappan, N.J. Fleming Revell, 1980

15 Morris, Barbara M. *Change Agents in the Schools.*
Upland, CA.: The Barbara Morris Report P.O. Box 756, 91786, 1979. (Was unable to obtain an answer to my request for permission to quote.)

Skousen, W. Cleon. *The Naked Capitalist.*
Salt Lake City, Utah: The Reviewer (2197 Berkeley Street 84109), 1970.

Stratford, Lauren. *Satan's Underground.*
Eugene, Oregon: Harvest House Publishers, 1988.

Stormer, John.
*None Dare Call It Treason.*
*Death of a Nation.*
P.O. Box 32, Florissant, MO: Liberty Bell Press, 1983

Tranter, John W. *Images.*
Wetumpka, AL.: TWO Communications, Inc., 1986. (TWO Ministries, Inc. P.O. Box 834 Wetumpka, AL 36092)

Whitehead, John W. *The Stealing of America.*
Westchester, IL, Crossway Books (A division of Good News Publishers) 1983.

## BIBLE AND WORD HELPS

17 Emery, HG. and Brewster, K.G. *The New Century Dictionary.*
New York, NY: P.F. Collier and Son Corp. 1927.

16 Mawson, C.O. Sylvester and Whiting, Katherine Aldrich (editors). *Roget's Pocket Thesaurus.*
630 Fifth Ave. New York 20, NY: Pocket Books Inc. 1963.

7 Pfeiffer, Charles F.; Vos, Howard F.; Rea, John. *Wycliffe Bible Encyclopedia, Volume I and II.*
Chicago: Moody Press, 1975.

Smith, Hannah Whitall. *The Christian's Secret of a Happy Life.*
Old Tappan, NJ: Spire Books, 1942.

Smith, Malcolm. *How I Learned to Meditate.*
Plainfield, New Jersey: Logos International, 1977.
Smith, Malcolm. *The Humble Slave. (Cassette tape)*
Logos Tapes, 3103 Highway 35, Hazlet, New Jersey, 07730.

1 Strong, James. *The Exhaustive Concordance of the Bible.*
Nashville, TN: Abingdon-Cokesbury Press.

4 *The Amplified New Testament.*
Grand Rapids, MI: Zondervan Publishing House. 1958.

2 Wigram. *The Analytical Greek Lexicon of the New Testament.*

Woodrow, Ralph. *Babylon Mystery Religion*
Riverside, California (P.O. Box 124 92502) Ralph Woodrow Evangelistic Association, Inc. 1966.

3 Wuest, Kenneth S. *Wuest's Expanded Translation of the Greek New Testament.*
Grand Rapids, MI: Wm. B. Eerdman"s Publishing Company, 1959.

5 Vine, W.E. *Vine's Expository Dictionary of New Testament Words.*
Iowa Falls, Iowa: Riverside Book and Bible,

## NUTRITION

Davis, Adelle.
*Let's Cook It Right*, 1988.
*Let's Eat Right to Keep Fit*, 1988.
*Let's Stay Healthy*, 1983
New York, NY: New American Library.

Davis, Adelle. *Let's Get Well.*
New York, NY: Harcourt Brace (paper NAL), 1965.

Davis, Adelle. *Let's Have Healthy Children.*
Bergenfield,NJ: New American Library, 1988.

Josephson, Elmer A. *God's Key to Health and Happiness.*
Old Tappan, NJ: Fleming H. Revell Co., 1976

Kinderlehrer, Jane. *Confessions of a Sneaky Organic Cook.* 1971
Rodale Press, Inc., Emmaus, PA. 18049

Kline, Monte L. and Strube, W.P. Jr. *Eat, Drink and Be Ready for Tomorrow You Will Live.*
Ashland, OR: World Wide

McMillan, S.I., M.D. *None of These Diseases.*
Old Tappan, New Jersey: Fleming H. Revell Company, 1972.